The Great Image

The Great Image

THE LIFE STORY
of VAIROCHANA
THE TRANSLATOR

Compiled by YUDRA NYINGPO
AND OTHER DISCIPLES

Translated by ANI JINBA PALMO

Foreword by DILGO KHYENTSE

SHAMBHALA *Boulder 2004*

Shambhala Publications, Inc.
4720 Walnut Street
Boulder, Colorado 80301
www.shambhala.com

Printed in the United States of America

♾ This edition is printed on acid-free paper that meets
the American National Standards Institute Z39.48 Standard.
♻ Shambhala Publications makes every effort to print on recycled
paper. For more information please visit www.shambhala.com.
Distributed in the United States by Penguin Random House LLC
and in Canada by Random House of Canada Ltd

Library of Congress Cataloging-in-Publication Data
The great image: the life story of Vairochana the translator /
translated by Ani Jinba Palmo; compiled by Yudra Nyingpo and other
disciples.—1st ed.
p. cm
Includes bibliographical references and index.
ISBN 1-59030-069-6 (pbk. : alk. paper)
1. Vairocana, 8th cent. 2. Rñin-ma-pa lamas—China—Tibet—Biography.
3. Rdzogs-chen (Rñin-ma-pa)—India—Biography. I. Palmo, Ani Jinba.
II. Yudra Nyingpo.
BQ994.A437G74 2004
294.3'923'092—dc22
2004010462

CONTENTS

 # FOREWORD

DILGO KHYENTSE RINPOCHE

As the illustrious Lochen Ngok, a great translator from the New Schools of Later Translations of Tibet, said:

> Vairotsana's knowledge is equal to the sky,
> Ka and Chok are like the sun and the moon, and
> Rinchen Zangpo is like a star at dawn.
> Before them I am like a butterfly.

Worthy of this praise, the great translator Vairotsana, crown ornament of all the Indian and Tibetan scholars, who was equal in realization and accomplishment to the second buddha from Oddiyana, extended the life force of the Buddhist teachings and living beings in Tibet in one lifetime. Understanding that his wondrous biography, the *Great Image*, is indispensable for spreading the light of the Dharma all over the world these days, the faithful Ani Jinba, born in Holland, translated this into English and checked it with many learned ones. Having seen the need for this publication, the old Dilgo Khyentse wrote this foreword. May it be virtuous.

Baudhanath, Nepal, 1989

INTRODUCTION

Putting the Story in Historical Context

THINLEY NORBU RINPOCHE

ACCORDING TO THE Hinayana tradition, a previous incarnation of our Buddha Shakyamuni took the vow to attain enlightenment from his teacher, Shakya Thubpa Chenpo, many eons ago. According to the Mahayana tradition, one thousand princes took the bodhisattva vows from the enlightened Essence of Jewels at the time of King Tsipkyi Mukyo. Among these princes was a minister named Pollen of the Ocean, praised by buddhas and bodhisattvas as being as rare as a white lotus. Praying five hundred great prayers for the enlightenment of all beings, especially the beings of the *kaliyuga*, he later emanated as Buddha Shakyamuni. Within beings' phenomena of time and space, Buddha Shakyamuni was born in this world, where he accomplished the twelve deeds according to general Buddhism. These included turning the wheel of Dharma with the Four Truths according to the Hinayana, the two truths according to the Mahayana, and the sole truth according to the absolute teaching. He showed the noble path by which the high realms could be achieved and the state of enlightenment ultimately attained. Just before Buddha entered *parinirvana*, his disciples requested, "Buddha, you already spoke about the vehicles of the three guardians. Why did you not reveal the Absolute Vehicle of the spontaneously accomplished indivisibility of cause and result, which is without the need of searching elsewhere for buddhahood?" The Buddha replied, "I turned the wheel of the Causal Vehicle for those who wished for it. The

Vajrayana method, which is the shortest path to enlightenment, will come in the future." After the Buddha entered parinirvana, his Hinayana teachings were maintained and spread by the Seven Patriarchs and his Mahayana teachings were held and spread by the Six Ornaments and the Two Supreme Ones. Also, from his miraculous wisdom mandala, the Buddha revealed various outer and inner tantric teachings, such as the *Assembly of Secrets*, to King Indrabhuti and his retinue in accordance with their keen faculties. As the Buddha predicted, many *vidyadharas* and *siddhas*, such as the Eight Vidyadharas and Eighty-four Mahasiddhas, came at various times to various places, including the eight charnel grounds and Oddiyana, where he revealed the Vajrayana teachings. Eventually, as he himself had foretold, his teaching flourished toward the north in the snow mountain rosary of Tibet. During the reign of Lha Thothori Nyenshel, when the three holy images that came from the sky appeared with the prediction that their meaning would be revealed in future, the dawn of Buddha's teaching began. During the reign of King Songtsen Gampo, who was an emanation of Avalokiteshvara, the tradition of formulating profound Dharma terms in the Tibetan language was started by Thonmi Sambhota, and the laws of the ten holy virtues and sixteen worldly virtues were established, like the light that appears just before the sun is rising from behind the eastern mountains. During the reign of King Trisong Deutsen, who was an emanation of Manjushri, the sun of the Buddha's teaching had risen and was shining in the ten directions. King Trisong Deutsen was seventeen years old when he found the historical records of his ancestors and discovered that the Buddha's teachings had appeared once before in Tibet. Eager for the Buddha's teachings to flourish, he invited Shantarakshita and Padmasambhava to build Samye, the Sublime Palace of Inconceivable Self-Accomplishment. Upon completion of this monastery, King Trisong Deutsen gathered many sacred languages, including Sanskrit and Tibetan, for the purpose of translating all of the Buddha's teachings so that they would thrive throughout Tibet. But when Shantarakshita and Padmasambhava started to teach the Sanskrit version of taking refuge in the Triple Gem, the children did not pronounce it correctly and the king was disappointed.

Padmasambhava comforted the king with the prophesy of the birth of Genjak Tangta, an emanation of Ananda, the closest disciple of Buddha. King Trisong Deutsen and his retinue went to search for this emanation and found an exotic child singing a song in the midst of a group of herdsmen. The king asked him, "Do you know Drenza Karkyi?" (the child's mother). The child answered, "Yes, of course, I know her, but she has gone to fetch eyes." By this he meant that his mother had gone to find oil for their lamp, but his actual profound meaning was that everything could be seen through light. Then the king asked the child, "Do you know Pagor Hedo?" (the child's father). He answered, "Yes, of course, I know him, but he went in search of gossip." By this he meant that his father had gone to find wine, which causes tongues to wag, but his actual profound meaning was that for those who drink in an ordinary way, wine permeates the channels and then affects the karmic airs so that, whether positively or negatively, much talking occurs due to the movement of the mind. For practitioners who drink with the phenomena of offering, the body is the mandala of wisdom deities rejoicing from the *amrita* of the offering. When the mandala of the speech *chakra* opens, many hymns of realization arise, which are the sounds of Dharma. The king was very impressed with the child's surprising answers and again asked him, "Then tell me your family name." The boy replied, "I have no certain caste, because I am from the lineage of buddhas. I have no name, because I am Vairochana [Buddha]. I have no country, because my country is *dharmadhatu*. I was not born, because I am Ananda. I have no self, because I am self-manifesting *vajra*. I have no benefit for beings, but I dispel darkness in the country of Tibet."

The first answer that he has no family refers to stainless *dharmakaya*. His having no name shows *rupakaya*, and specifically, among the aspects of rupakaya, Nampar Nangdze, who is the inconceivably perfect *sambhogakaya* form of the wisdom-body family of the buddhas. This inconceivability has no name because it is beyond ordinary perception. *Nampar* means "in any form of the buddhas," including their innumerable pure lands, and *nangdze* means "the activity of manifesting." Then, the rupakaya of nirmanakaya manifests as Vairochana's pure land, Gangchen tsho yi shingkham. In general, *gangchen* means "great snow" and *tsho* means "ocean"; in this case, these are much vaster than streams and rivers. In fact, no massive, substantial snow or ocean can compare with the vastness of the inconceivable qualities of these pure lands. So this pure-land name refers to the emanation of the nirmanakaya land, which is all of existence including the subdued of this world, namely, sentient beings, and their subduers, the emanation forms of the nirmanakaya and their teachings. That he has no country shows the vastness of dharmadhatu, which cannot even be compared to the sky and in which all buddhas abide. The fourth answer, that he has no birth, shows that even though there is no reality of birth within his nondualistic mind, through unobscured compassion the form of Ananda appeared as a nirmanakaya. That he has no self shows that since there is no self, there is no penetrable object or subject, so there is always uncompounded, self-occurring vajra body, speech, and mind. That he has no purpose shows the nonduality of his wisdom because, according to his phenomena, there are no sentient beings to benefit. However, it also shows the unobstructed compassion that is the nature of the buddhas and that benefits all beings, including Tibetans, according to their dualistic phenomena. The king was extremely joyful upon hearing the child's words. Thus, through Padmasambhava's prophecy and the child's own answers to the king, Genjak Tangta was recognized and taken to the king's palace at Samye, where he remained as the king's servant until he was fifteen years old. He then went to India to learn Sanskrit and many other languages and to meet many sublime saints, including Shri Singha. He studied and received all the Buddhist teachings until he was fifty-seven years old. He had many hardships and came close to death. Upon his return to Tibet he, along with many other scholars and translators including Padmasambhava and Vimalamitra, translated and gave teachings on the speech of the buddhas and the *shastras* of sublime beings from Hinayana and Mahayana up to and including the Dzogchen teachings. Exiled to Tsawarong, Vairotsana spread the Dharma and put all the citizens of Tsawarong on the path of enlightenment. He also went to China to meet various scholars. When he returned from exile, everybody was happy, worshipping and prostrating to him, his main disciple Yudra Nyingpo, and Vimalamitra, and honoring him with praise:

> A great translator such as you, Vairotsana,
> Has definitely never come before and definitely will not
>   come again in the future.
> Your knowledge goes from the Tripitaka up to the Great
>   Perfection.
> A supreme scholar such as you, Vairotsana,
> Has definitely never come before and definitely will not
>   come again in the future.
> In the future, whoever just understands colloquial Indian
>   language

Will think they are great translators, but they will not even
  come close
To a part of a little bit of the knowledge of Vairotsana.
Even though Vairotsana is called a translator, he is actually
  a sublime scholar.
You Tibetans must know how much you owe to him for
  Dharma.
In the future, if reverse shastras occur,
Judge them by Vairotsana's translations.
The light of his teachings, you Tibetans,
Can purify the darkness of ignorance.

During Trisong Deutsen's reign, many scholars and translators gathered, establishing assemblies of red-robed monks and white-clothed yogis and yoginis. They also taught and translated all the sutras and shastras. The empowerments of many precious *sadhanas* were given by Padmasambhava, including *Ocean of Dharma That Embodies All Teachings*. Many sacred places, such as Samye Chimphu, were filled by people doing retreat with wisdom deity sadhanas, including Padmasambhava's twenty-five disciples and many others who attained rainbow body. The Buddha's activity flourished perfectly, pervading like the light of the midday sun. This is a rare occurrence in this world, since even though the Buddha's teachings spread to other countries, they were not the complete Mahayana and Vajrayana teachings as they were in Tibet. At one time, by the grace of such scholars and saints as Vairotsana, Tibet was the center of Dharma in the world. Even though there have been political disasters in these degenerate times, many wondrous, sublime histories and teachings of the buddhas and bodhisattvas can be still heard in the world nowadays, sparkling from one country to another, which have Dharma phenomena because of Tibetans; and much will still be heard that originates from the Nyingmapas. So, whoever has an actual human being's noble, refined mind has to think of the kindness of the Nyingma tradition and its teachings, honoring them in order to benefit countless beings. We must consider how to follow sublime beings such as Vairotsana, who is the emanation of the wisdom body of the Buddha Vairochana. Without relying on Vairotsana and his original translations, the Buddha's speech and the shastras of sublime beings would not have been complete in Tibet. Even when we just translate banal things from one language to another, it is difficult to achieve the actual meaning. If we translate even a single page of the Buddhist canon, due to our stupidity we build enormous passions higher than Mount Meru, instead of following Vairotsana's dustless sky mind. If we consider how fortunate we are to hear the Buddha's own words and the shastras of sublime beings through the grace of Vairotsana's translations of the Sutrayana and Mantrayana teachings, how can we not be awed and how can we not honor him? The great Ngok Lotsawa Loden Sherab, whose emanation was predicted in the *Mula Tantra,* which is the same as the *Manjushri Root Tantra,* praised Vairotsana and other sublime scholars and translators:

> Vairotsana's knowledge is as pervasive as the sky.
> Kawa Paltsek and Chokro Lui Gyaltsen are like the sun and moon.
> Rinchen Zangpo is like a dawn star.
> Before them, I am like a butterfly.

Even the king of the vidyadharas, Padmasambhava, praised Vairotsana by saying, "Vairotsana is the same as me."

This life story, called the *Great Image,* has been translated into English by Ani Jinba, who, with devotion, studied with many great Tibetan teachers for many years. She has received many teachings to benefit all beings, including those who have faith in the sublime nirmanakaya Vairotsana by reading his life story in order to attain the enlightenment body of Vairotsana, who is the embodiment of abiding in immeasurable sambhogakaya's pure land. At her request, I wrote this brief introduction. Particularly, when one reads any books about Dharma, including the histories of sublime beings, I must beg readers first to recognize the characteristics of the two different kinds of magic. Black magic is the suffering of samsara that tortures beings who are grasping at unreal phenomena such as time, place, and the similarity or dissimilarity of the nature of beings and their ideas, while thinking they are real. These beings circle between rejection and acceptance and continuously suffer because there is no certainty that phenomena exist. This black magic should be abandoned because it always lures us, pretending to be true, even though it is not, created by deluded habit as it is. White magic, on the other hand, is the manifestation of wisdom qualities of all sublime beings, which is the non-grasping freedom of the display of unobstructedness, without any thought of anything within time and space or of the similarity or dissimilarity of the nature of beings and their ideas, and without rejection or acceptance, manifesting continuously in exaltation because no certainty or uncertainty exists within nondualistic wisdom. White magic always brings us the inspiration of joy, always creates love and faith, and always brings about compassion and wisdom, which are the sources of enlightenment, not pretending to be either real or unreal, which is the uncreated manifestation of self-accomplishment.

So whenever we have the time and space, we should read biographies of sublime beings and ponder their qualities in order to receive their blessings and go beyond time and space as they have done. There are many biographies of sublime beings from Tibet; among them, one of the most precious is the life history the *Great Image* of Vairotsana. Since the wisdom of dharmakaya lacks characteristics, being indivisible from this unceasing dharmakaya, the wisdom manifestations of rupakaya radiate in various forms. As it is said in the *Guhyagarbha Tantra*:

The wisdom body has no front or back;
The wisdom face sees clearly in all directions.

I pray that all sentient beings, including all those who have made the great connection with this book, may attain the state of *gyalwa namnang kuntu shal,* which means "the face that is everywhere," the aspect of manifestation that is the origin of all victorious wisdom forms.

New York, 1989

INTRODUCTION

The Significance of This Biography

DZONGSAR KHYENTSE RINPOCHE

OUT OF HIS limitless compassion, the Buddha has sent forth many emanations—kings, ministers, normal people, prostitutes, even animals. Due to individual karma and pure perception, beings could meet them. Others were not able to recognize these emanations because they lacked the karma and merit. Instead, they would become envious and angry and so rob or kill the normal people, have intercourse with the prostitutes, worship the kings and ministers, and use the animals for their own benefit.

Though Tibet was a country of barbarians, the Buddha sent many emanations, such as King Trisong Deutsen, Padmasambhava, and Shantarakshita, who established the doctrine in Tibet. People like Thonmi Sambhota went through countless difficulties to create the letters of the alphabet.

In that dark land, many translators, headed by the great Vairotsana, translated countless Dharma texts. Contemporary translators are quite inferior. These days translators are only motivated by the desire for fame or titles. They do not know Tibetan very well, rely on dictionaries, and jot things down without really knowing anything about practice or context. Vairotsana, on the other hand, never translated anything before he received many teachings and had practiced and realized them. He was also a great inventor of words, unlike contemporary translators who try to invent new words. For example, if *tong pa nyi* is translated as emptiness, it falls into the extreme of void. But when Vairotsana translated the word *shunyata*, he considered it from many angles and came up with *tong pa–nyi*, which expresses a lot of potential, the complete opposite of the word "empty."

I would like to suggest that you not read this biography as an ordinary novel. Reading novels about love and anger only creates attachment or hatred accordingly. Reading complicated books will just cause dullness. Many philosophical texts have already been translated into English, so I feel that it is now very beneficial to make biographies available. You see, worldly life is based on mimicking. Whoever mimics best is the most successful, even among Dharma practitioners. Anyone who wants to be a genuine human being has to mimic someone; for example, all the great lamas of the past mimicked the buddhas and bodhisattvas. People sometimes say, "I don't know what the Dharma is or how to practice it," while holding a difficult book on Madhyamaka. They are like travelers without a guide. If they would read biographies, they would know how the great beings of the past lived, how they found their guru and treated and served him. By reading their biographies you can learn how tolerant you should be. You would no longer expect the highest teachings at your first meeting with a guru or expect great experiences as soon as you received teachings. Nor should you keep changing gurus or expect good dreams. Seeing how the great beings of the past acted will help one's practice very much. Biographies, like this one, can have a very positive influence on your life, so you should keep an open mind about it. You may find that there is a lot of repetition, but in one's daily life things are repeated all the time. You should be tolerant when reading these repetitions; it is Tibetan style to repeat things.

Just by reading such biographies one will gain understanding about how to live and practice. But mere understanding is not enough; you need to put what you have learned into action. So I would like to explain some Dharma. As this is not an ordinary biography, the view, meditation, and action are explained in detail. So, if you do not know the main points of the Dharma, it will be difficult to understand this biography. If you have some understanding of the Dharma, you will understand how to practice Buddhism, Mantrayana, and especially Dzogchen.

There are many general Dzogchen teachings, but it is very hard to find a real Dzogchen practitioner, a Dzogchenpa. There is a difference between those two. The Buddha said: "Don't depend on a person, depend on the teachings." Of course, one has to depend on the teachings, but it is important for beginners to have an example of how to practice and approach the teachings. It is said that the Buddha taught more than 84,000 different methods to cure the defilements of sentient beings. He is the supreme doctor to cure sentient beings' diseases of conflicting emotions. Ordinary doctors only give medicine for one particular disease, but the Buddha has countless different ways to subdue the different defilements of countless different beings. Some beings have more anger, some more desire, and some more ignorance. Some methods teach to give up the defilements, some that the defilements have no essence, some how to use the defilements on the path, and others that desire is useless and should be abandoned. These are methods to subdue those who think mostly about themselves and don't have the ability to benefit others in an elaborate way. The Buddha himself cut his hair, wore robes, carried a begging bowl, and through his twelve acts subdued beings, teaching them how to live, to give up desire, practice celibacy, and so on. In harmony with the social mores of 2,500 years ago, he lived in a particular way and taught specific methods. For those who do not think only about themselves, who have a broader mind, are more responsible, have more capacity to benefit others, who have the guts to listen to the ultimate teachings, the Buddha did not teach them to shave their heads, wear robes, and so forth. They could wear fancy clothes and have long hair. Since for them desire was hollow, it was useless to abandon it. For them, the Buddha manifested in sambhogakaya form. Such people might have strong desire, but they can accept everything; whatever teaching is given to them fits in their brain. Such beings are like rare jewels. For one and the same conflicting emotion the Buddha taught countless different methods in countless different forms and places, using completely different styles and words.

Subduing one's mind is of foremost importance; as the Buddha said: "Tame your own mind, that is my doctrine." Many different methods exist for taming the mind. Some people say that there is a mind, some that there is no mind; some say that objects and mind are different, others that objects and mind are inseparable. Whatever the case, taming one's own mind is still the most important point. All worldly happiness and suffering is experience; nothing solid exists that is not dependent on one's own experience. For example, if one thinks that behind the mountain there is a lake, it depends on one's experience; you can call that "the expression of one's personal experience." There is impure experience, such as hells, hungry ghosts, animal realms, birth, death, illness, and old age, as well as pure experience, such as the *kaya*s and wisdoms. Yogis practicing the path have experiences that buddhas and sentient beings do not have. What buddhas see is one thing, what sentient beings see is another, and what yogis see is something else again. However, it is all mind.

In the snowy land of Tibet many great beings and learned ones established many Dharma institutes, argued about the doctrine, wrote commentaries, established monasteries, colleges, and innumerable methods to subdue the mind. Some would say that mind has to be destroyed, some that it has to be transformed, and some that it has to be analyzed. Likewise, there are countless extraordinary methods. Among these extraordinary methods Dzogchen is one of the best, as it combines appearances and emptiness, as well as awareness and emptiness. Indivisible awareness and emptiness is the *trekcho* practice, and indivisible appearances and emptiness is the *thogal* practice. This combination makes the Dzogchen path unique. Though it contains many high words and so forth, the Dzogchen teachings are just another way to tame the mind.

Many places are mentioned in this biography, such as Akanishta and other buddha-fields, about which the ordinary reader will understand little, if anything. In this worldly realm you have to know where things come from; even if you are buying a pen, you should know where it was made, and so on. People are in the habit of asking where things come from, where they were made, etc. Similarly, it is important to understand the history of everything; by doing so you can inspire people by providing information about people and things. For example, if you provide good information about somebody, people will accept that person, and so on. In general, each religion has its own history. It is important to know who gave the teachings and where they originated. The ordinary history of the Buddha explains that he performed twelve acts, such as being conceived in his mother's womb, taking birth in Lumbini, and so on, until he passed into nirvana. All three vehicles are in agreement that the Buddha taught three sets of teachings. But when it comes to the extraordinary history, people often ask, "Where did this Vajrayana teaching come from? There are no facts about where it was taught and to whom. Where did it originate? The history books don't say where it was taught!" So they do not believe in it and think Vajrayana is not a Buddhist teaching. Some say the Vajrayana teachings, especially those of Dzogchen, are Bonpo, and some say they are Hashang.

So, in brief, the outer history is that of Shakyamuni and the inner history is that of Samantabhadra, which is beyond time and so lacks dates and such. Usually, people like to hear about what came first and what came last; but to describe Samantabhadra in this way is impossible. Samantabhadra is not subject to limits of time, place, or physical conditions. Samantabhadra is not a colored being with two eyes, etc. Samantabhadra is the unity of awareness and emptiness, the unity of appearances and emptiness, the nature of mind, natural clarity with unceasing compassion—that is Samantabhadra from the very beginning. His retinue is not separate from him; it is the five buddhas teaching Dharma to those of highest capacity. The five buddhas do not teach accepting or abandoning anything good or bad, such as samsara is bad and nirvana is good. As the term *samsara* does not even exist, neither is there any relief from samsara or attainment of enlightenment. That is the actual truth. The five buddhas explain the real nature of things without words or phrases, beyond explaining or explanation; but due to our defilements, we do not accept this fact. On the other hand, yogis with pure vision will recognize the five buddhas, not as five-colored forms but as the pure nature without any defilement. As Samantabhadra is not something made by the mind, he cannot teach anything mind-made, such as time. Nor is where he teaches conditioned, such as a place you can reach by train, like Bodhgaya or Sarnath. It is not limited by any distance, boundary, or center, and the wheel of Dharma never ceases turning. This is the secret history of the doctrine.

So, while reading this biography, you should use Vairotsana as an example of how to act, practice, and contemplate and try to become like him.

Prapoutel, France, 1990

INTRODUCTION

A Summary of the Text

ALA ZENKAR RINPOCHE

RECENTLY, THE GREAT Dharma Senge found six different copies of the *Great Image*. Comparing these different editions, he edited together a definitive version, which he had carved on woodblocks and printed. This text describes the life of the supreme Vairotsana, his place of birth, the names of his parents, and his name as a child. He himself had five names during his life. When he was eight years old, he met King Trisong Deutsen, studied languages, and acted as his outer and inner minister for seven years. At the age of fifteen, he went to India to search for the pith instructions. The *Great Image* describes the actual journey and the sixteen hardships he went through.

The first chapter describes the appearance of the effortless doctrine coming from Akanishta. This doctrine was taught through four kayas: the *svabhavikakaya* doctrine was taught through clarifying self-pointing-out, the dharmakaya doctrine was taught by direct self-liberation, the sambhogakaya doctrine was taught through self-essence, and the secret kaya was taught through the method of great bliss.

The second chapter describes the doctrine being taught in gradual stages to those without the good fortune of understanding and realization. Particularly in the realms of the World of Endurance, the Buddha Shakyamuni and others tamed beings in whatever way was effective. In the celestial realms the doctrine was first taught through the vehicle of characteristics and secondly through the Secret Mantra Vehicle. The Secret Mantra consists of the outer tantric doctrine of the Muni and the inner magnetizing vehicle, comprised of the Maha Yoga tantras, the Anu Yoga transmissions, and the Ati Yoga teachings. The Maha Yoga tantras first appeared when King Ja received transmission through seven dreams. When the books and an image of Vajrapani descended on the roof of his house, King Ja started practicing the first chapter of the Vajrasattva tantra. After practicing for six months, he had a vision of Vajrasattva, who gave him a staff and a Dharma wheel and empowered him. After that he fully understood the texts and then classified them into eighteen tantras.

The second chapter deals with the Anu Yoga transmissions. The five noble beings went to the top of Mount Malaya and fervently prayed to all the buddhas, who discussed their request and decided to send Vajrapani. So Vajrapani went to Mount Malaya and taught the *Scripture of the Embodiment of the Realization of All Buddhas*. Then, in Oddiyana he gave the glorious Yangdag tantras and instructions to the nirmanakaya Prahevajra.

The third chapter describes how the special Ati Yoga doctrine came to the celestial and human realms. The Secret Mantra teachings appeared because the six necessary conditions were present. In the Heaven of the Thirty-three, the god's son Sem Lhagchen (Adhichitta in Sanskrit) had a very special dream. He prayed to the buddhas, who invoked Vajrasattva. Vajrasattva then emanated Vajrapani from his heart, gave Sem Lhagchen a precious wheel, and called him Sattvavajra. After receiving the mind essence of the five buddhas, Vajrapani gave the empowerment of direct anointment to Adhicitta, along with the empowerments and instructions of *Ten Miraculous Scriptures*, *Threefold Spontaneous Accomplishment*, *Great Sphere*, *Unchanging Firmness*, *Immediacy of Awareness*, *Nondual Mingling*, *Vajra Statement*, and many other empowerments and tantras. All these were given in an instant, and Adhicitta was empowered as a regent. That concludes the third chapter, about the doctrine coming to the three celestial realms.

The fourth chapter describes the Ati doctrine coming to the human realm. In the Dhanakosha district, King Dhahena Talo's daughter Parani, who was a nun, saw a swan that was an emanation of Vajrapani, which touched her three times with its beak. When the time had come, a five-pronged vajra issued from her heart, which transformed into a small child. This was Prahevajra. Prahevajra was empowered by Vajrapani, who gave him the complete empowerment of direct anointment and all the other empowerments, tantras, instructions, etc., so that Prahevajra became the lamp of the doctrine. He received and realized the complete root and explanatory tantras, the *Twenty Thousand Sections of the Ninefold Expanse*, the branch tantras of the five buddhas, and all the tantras of the Lord of Secrets. He directly attained enlightenment through Ati Yoga and then gave the Dzogchen tantras.

Prahevajra transmitted all this to the son of Brahmin Palden Dekyong, Manjushrimitra, who was also called Sarasiddhi and Samvarasara. He attained accomplishment in Yamantaka and wrote the *Instructions on Bodhichitta Written in Pure Gold on Stone*. The mind lineage of the buddhas includes everyone up to Prahevajra. This concludes the fourth chapter.

The fifth chapter describes the general lineage from Prahevajra's grandfather King Dhahena Talo, his son Thuwo Raja, Princess Parani, Naga King Nanda, Yakshini Changchubma, the prostitute Barani, the Kashmiri abbot Rabnang, the abbot Maharaja from Oddiyana, Princess Gomadevi, Atsantra Aloke, the earlier Kukkuraja, the sage Bhashita, the prostitute Dagnyima, Nagarjuna, the later Kukkuraja, the later Manjushrimitra, Devaraja, Buddhagupta, Shri Singha, the nun Kungamo, and Master Vimalamitra.

The special lineage described in this chapter goes as follows: Prahevajra, Manjushrimitra, and Shri Singha to Vairotsana. Then there is a lineage of seven through Prahevajra, Manjushrimitra, Dhahena Talo, and so forth down to Shri Singha, who passed it on to Vairo. The special lineage was the Distinguishing Brahmin's Cycle, the Resolving King's Cycle and the Instruction Cycle Directly Pointing Out Self-Liberation. Of these three, the instruction cycle belongs to the mind lineage of the buddhas. Prahe gave these instructions to Manjushrimitra and bestowed the empowerment of direct anointment on him. Then he gave him the five root tantras, such as *Perfection of Wisdom, Universal Light*, the twenty-five branch tantras including *Ninefold Expanse*, the entrustment of the precious treasure revealing Prahevajra's mind essence, the seven streams of empowerment including the empowerment of direct anointment, and the secret initiation, and empowered him to protect the doctrine through the three *mamo*s.

Giving this to Devaputra, it was transmitted through Naga King Nanda, Yakshini Changchubma, the monk Kukkuraja, and Shri Singha. This is the symbolic lineage through the awareness of the vidyadharas. This completes the fifth chapter.

The sixth chapter describes the effortless doctrine coming to Tibet.

During the reign of Lha Thothori Nyentsen [also known as Nyenshel], the doctrine began; during the reign of Songtsen Gampo, it was established; and during the reign of Trisong Deutsen, it developed. The first transmission was by Padmasambhava, the second by Shantigarbha, the third by Buddhaguhya, the fourth by Humkara, and the fifth by Vairotsana, who taught the doctrine beyond cause and effect.

Vairotsana was born in Tsang Nyemo. His father was called Pagor Hedo and his mother Drenza Karkyi. His birth name was Genjak Tangta. At the age of eight, the king took him to Samye where he studied with the two masters, Padmasambhava and Shantarakshita. He was ordained as a monk and learned many languages. He used five different names for his translations. For Sutrayana translations he used the name Yeshe De, for Mantrayana translations Vairotsana, for Bon translations Genjak Tangta, for astrology translations Indravairo, and for medicinal translations Chobar. He served as outer and inner minister for three years and as the king's personal attendant for three years. At the age of fifteen, he promised to go to India, a commitment that no one else could make, which was his first trial. His second trial was the preparation for the journey. His third trial was being blocked by the snow and nearly dying. Escaping the nonhuman obstacles was his fourth trial. His fifth trial was escaping robbers, his sixth trial was escaping wild animals, and his seventh trial was crossing a narrow path with nowhere to go. His eighth trial was escaping the bamboo swords of the border guards by performing a miracle. His ninth trial was escaping wolves and other wild animals that came to eat his horse's corpse and wanted to eat him as well. His tenth trial was escape from Magadha in India. His eleventh trial was his escape from the snakes at Krisha, and his twelfth trial was escaping King Bhibhira's prison sentence. His thirteenth trial was escaping from a poisonous sulfur lake in Magadha. His fourteenth trial was escaping the beatings from Mon tribesmen in Avadhuti. His fifteenth trial was escaping the masks and snakes in Arya Palo and his sixteenth trial was to get rid of the poison that women gave him in Edhakesha. When he arrived in central India, he heard that the most learned and realized master was Shri Singha. The instruction teachings were to be kept very secret, but his attempts to get them through various skillful means were successful, and he received them all from Shri Singha. He then learnt speed walking to move quickly. This concludes the eighth chapter, describing Shri Singha giving the entire doctrine to Vairotsana.

The ninth chapter describes how, through speed walking, Vairo returned to Tibet and on the way met the proud king called Rahula Bhibhi. He tamed this king through his instructions. The tenth chapter describes his arrival in Tibet.

The eleventh chapter describes him teaching the common and special instructions while remaining in Tibet for about five years. During that time, the Indian Dharma king decided to send people to slander him, resulting in the king of Tibet being forced to get rid of Vairo. Trying to avoid this fate, however, the king pretended to kill Vairo by throwing a beggar in the river. Later, the king was actually forced to banish him. Vairo sang many songs about his hardships and predicted that Tibet would be ruined and that the queen would go to hell. He begged them to let him stay, but due to past karma he was forced to go to Tsawarong. The king and ministers escorted him by horse; they asked his advice about the future so he gave many predictions. This concludes the eleventh chapter about being banished to Tsawarong.

The twelfth chapter describes how the people from Gyalmo Tsawarong threw him into a frog hole for three days and then into a louse pit for seven days. Vairo told them that in his last life there he was a prince called Purna who had killed many frogs and lice and that this was the karmic result of that. The queen of Tsawarong and her attendants and subjects then offered confession and did many prostrations. Next he met Prince Yudra, who became his main student. Vairo trained the prince in the nine precepts and thirteen courages and then gave him all the teachings. When Vairo was reciting the *Great Space Tantra* from the louse pit, though he heard it only once, Yudra memorized it. Some editions mention that Yudra told the people of Tsawarong to take Vairotsana out of the pit; other editions mention that Vairo paid for Yudra, who was the son of King Rinchen and Queen Tsogyal, bribing them to give Yudra to him. So there are three different stories. Taming the gods and demons, Vairo miraculously had a stupa built in one day, which appeared like a stupa from the outside and was a temple inside. During the daytime, he gave teachings on the Causal Vehicle, in the evening he taught the inner Secret Mantra, and at night he gave Yudra and some others the instruction teachings. Yudra's realization became equal to that of Vairotsana. During that time, King Trisong Deutsen invited Vimalamitra from India to Tibet. Vairo told Yudra to go to Tibet, prove that his teachings were superior, and spread the instruction teachings in Tibet. This concludes the twelfth chapter.

The thirteenth chapter describes Vairo going to China and receiving teachings from Chinese masters and yogis such as Kusula Bhitigarbha, Dharmabodhi, Vajra Sukha Deva, Pandita Barma, Tsenda Ritropa, Mahabodhi, Shri Ani, Hashang Bhibi, Surya Ghirti, Satipa, and so forth— altogether nineteen great yogis and yoginis. Then he went back to Tsawarong.

All the instructions he received from the Chinese masters he gave to Yudra in Tsawarong. Yudra gave them to Nyag Jnana Kumara, who gave them to Sangye Yeshe, who gave them to Sogpo Palkyi Yeshe. Then Yudra went to Tibet and met Vimalamitra in Samye. Everyone was extremely devoted and respectful.

On his way back to Tsawarong Yudra met Pam Sangye Gonpo, who had heard stories about Vairo; having become very devoted, he went to see Vairotsana. Then Yudra met Gya Lodro Shonnu and gave him all his instructions. He then went to lower Do Kham, met Bes Dorje Gyaltsen, and gave him many tantras and instructions. Then he went to Tsawarong where he met Vairo. Telling him everything, he praised him in eleven verses; Vairo was very happy. At that time, the Tibetans discussed and decided to invite Vairo back to Tibet. Three people were sent to invite him back, and he promised to come.

Then Vairo prepared to return to Tibet, and Queen Dru and the others saw him off with a very elaborate farewell. On the way he met Pam Mipham Gonpo, a very old man. Vairo instructed him by putting him in the right posture with a stick and a meditation belt and small sticks to keep his eyes open. Upon receiving the teachings, he attained immediate realization and embraced Vairotsana. At that time Mune Tsenpo passed away. Vairo and Yudra arrived during the funeral in the presence of a large gathering of people. Invited to sit in the center of the assembly, Vimalamitra and Yudra sat on either side [of Vairotsana] and did the elaborate funeral ceremonies. Then they started an institute and turned the wheel of Dharma in an elaborate way. Everyone did confession to Vairotsana, and he accepted and forgave them. He again told them about all his hardships in India to obtain the instruction teachings. At that time Shantarakshita, Vimalamitra, and a gathering of 108 translators would meet at the Translation Hall and translate the sutras and tantras. All the texts that they translated miraculously manifested from the divine realms, *naga* realms, and sacred dakini places as well as from Oddiyana, Nalanda, and so forth through the two masters. These texts still exist today because of the kindness of these great masters. Vairotsana also translated mixed texts of medicine and astrology as well as many thousands of tantra classes and instructions. From twenty-six hundred tantras he translated sixty-two million instructions. He then transformed into the form of Vairochana and dissolved into the space of *dharmata*. Again he came back and stayed in Samye Chimphu for one year. Then he went back to Tsawarong once more, where he was invited to Kham. In Kham he stayed in the Rong Chamchen Hermitage. At that time Vimalamitra and other *panditas* went to visit him, and they translated the Sadhana Sections. The first lineage is the teachings that Vairo secretly gave to Trisong Deutsen, that is, the Five Earlier Translations of the Mind Class and the *Ocean Expanse Instructions*, which he received in India. The middle lineage is the teachings that Yudra gave to Nyag Jnana Kumara and Ma Rinchen Chok. The last lineage is the teachings that Yudra gave to Pam Mipham Gonpo, Gya Lodro Shonnu, and Bes Dorje Gyaltsen. He again went to Samye Hepori for a brief stay, at which time the king offered a large feast offering. Vairo told Pam Mipham Gonpo to benefit beings for five hundred years and Yudra to benefit beings for three hundred years. He said that among his students 170 would attain the rainbow body. Then he dissolved into a blue dot with a white syllable A in the center and dissolved into space. He then variously appeared as Vairochana, a vajra, light, Ananda, Shakyamuni, a sacred text, and so forth.

When Vairotsana was about to finally pass away into the pure lands, Yudra asked him about his future emanations. He said he would appear as Atisha from Zahor, as Drawa Ngonshe, as Dorje Lingpa, as Rechung Dorje Trakpa, as Jonang, as the one called Yak, as Zangkar Lotsawa, as the siddha Kharnak, as Kunkyong Lingpa, as Phagmo Drupa, as Myogom Repa, and as many other emanations. Litsa Tsultrim Dron arrived and attained the same realization. Then Yudra and Jingyon's son and others asked Vairo to relate his biography, and Yudra wrote it down. This biography is a real treasury of the buddhas, the ultimate history, and the image that truly represents Vairotsana. It is the index of the effortless doctrine.

In answer to the request for the essence of the teachings, Vairo gave many instructions, saying not to get involved in samsaric activities, not to ignore those to be tamed, not to search for the buddha outside, and that if they had faith and devotion, they were inseparable from him. After that he flew into the sky, his right hand playing a damaru, and dissolved into space. That concludes the thirteenth chapter.

I am very grateful that Ani Jinba Palmo from Holland, a student of Dilgo Khyentse Rinpoche and other great masters, who knows quite a few languages, who studied and practiced the Kagyu and Nyingma teachings, and who keeps the outer Vinaya accordingly, translated this life story of the great translator Vairotsana. I am confident that this translation will directly and indirectly benefit innumerable readers.

New York, 1998

TRANSLATOR'S PREFACE

THE GREAT IMAGE: The Life Story of Vairotsana is the biography of the great Tibetan translator Vairotsana as recorded by his foremost disciples. There are two versions of this text, which is commonly known as the *Drabag* (*'Dra 'bag*), or *Replica*. One version was concealed as a treasure and revealed by Jomo Menmo, and the other one was orally transmitted. This is the canonical version, which was edited by Dharma Senge, the compiler of this biography. It not only contains the details and events of Vairotsana's life, but also the history of the Ati Yoga doctrine in general and the historical background of the Buddhist doctrine in detail, including how it appeared in the celestial and human realms through the mind lineage of the conquerors, the symbol lineage of the vidyadharas, and the hearing lineage of individuals.

I began this translation of the *Great Image* in 1982 while working for the Ethnological Museum in Leiden, the Netherlands. I was hired to translate some of the manuscripts from their Tibetan collection, but was unable to make a choice. Taklung Tsetrul Pema Wangyal Rinpoche suggested this text, though I had no idea what I was getting into. During the next three years, while I was in retreat in France, Tulku Pema Wangyal kindly guided me through the first draft of this work and was extremely helpful in explaining the general doctrines of Nyingma and Dzogchen.

It was not until the late eighties that I took up the project again and worked on the second and third drafts with the help of my first editor,

Michal Abrams. Engaged in other translation projects, I again left this work for more than ten years, but thanks to the constant encouragement of the great translator Erik Pema Kunzang and the inspiring support of another great translator, Matthieu Ricard, I made another attempt to go through it. This time I was able to complete it with the editorial assistance of Michael Tweed.

The text I used for this translation is the xylographic Lhasa edition of the *'Dra 'bag chen mo*, which is no other than the engraved Kahma version edited by Dharma Senge. Later, I obtained a clearer copy published by Khochen Tulku in Dehra Dun. In the late nineties I obtained a copy of the Sichuan edition printed with Ala Zenkar Rinpoche's help, which was very useful for making the divisions within the chapters. It also has far fewer misspellings. I used various copies of the Chronicles to clear up doubts about the various misspellings and old Tibetan words that nobody was able to understand, as explained in the notes. For the endnotes I have widely relied on the texts mentioned in the bibliography.

The name of the Tibetan translator is often spelled *Vairochana*. Even though Shambhala Publications has insisted on using this spelling on the cover, I have used the spelling *Vairotsana* throughout. In addition to distinguishing between the Buddha Vairochana and the Tibetan translator, this spelling also follows that used by Thinley Norbu Rinpoche in his introduction.

In the past, Tibetan scholars like Vairotsana, Kawa Paltsek, and Chokro Lui Gyaltsen could translate the Sanskrit Buddhist texts with great accuracy because they had fully realized the essence of enlightened mind. But in the present conditions, despite our total absence of inner realization, we are obliged to translate Tibetan literature for the sake of preserving and propagating it for future generations. Though lacking the confidence to claim to have understood the profound words of Vairotsana, I feel extremely fortunate to have had the opportunity to try to translate this wonderful text. This is just an initial attempt to make his biography available to readers so that they may develop faith in such a great being and feel inspired to follow such a way of life.

May well-informed readers exercise restraint in the knowledge that the translator takes full responsibility for errors that inevitably exist, and may those endowed with wisdom eyes be able to make a more accurate translation in the future. I pray to the buddhas, lineage masters, and Dharma protectors to forgive my inability to translate with accuracy, as well as any mistakes of omission or addition and any improper disclosure of secret teachings committed in preparing this book.

By the virtue of this work, may the Buddhist doctrine spread in the ten directions; may the lives of the lineage holders be stable and long; and may all sentient beings, including all that come into contact with this text in any way, attain happiness and enlightenment.

The Great Image

Vairotsana with Yudra Nyingpo (second from right) and other disciples.

THE
HOMAGE

HOMAGE TO THE BHAGAVAN,
THE GLORIOUS SAMANTABHADRA,[1]
SPONTANEOUSLY PRESENT GREAT BLISS
BEYOND ACTION.

PREFACE

How the Effortless Ati Doctrine Was Taught

SAMANTABHADRA ABIDES within the state of perfect and complete buddhahood, wisdom beyond clarification or obscuration, within the indivisible expanse of great bliss. Skilled in great compassion, from within the state of the three kinds of knowledge,[1] for the sake of sentient beings he taught the eight vehicles of cause and result[2] in general and the effortless Ati Yoga[3] doctrine in particular. Ati Yoga is the realization of all the buddhas of the three times. It is the essence of all doctrines, the summit of all vehicles, the king of all tantras, the main point of all scriptures. It is the root of all instructions, much more secret than secret; it is the innermost marvel.

The historical background of how the effortless Ati Yoga doctrine was taught and how it appeared consists of two sections: the history of this precious doctrine in Akanishta[4] and its history within the celestial and human realms.

1 ❖

How This Precious Doctrine Occurred in Akanishta

A T FIRST, in the great pure land of the all-encompassing nature, the spontaneously present dharmadhatu[1] palace, the spontaneously accomplished conquerors of the five kayas and the like remained in the state of great evenness beyond coming or going, their minds beyond clarification or obscuration, completely perfecting the specific state of all the tathagatas[2] and knowing all phenomena to be enlightened from the very beginning. At that time the mother of all the victorious ones, dharmadhatu Samantabhadri,[3] urged them to make the svabhavikakaya[4] and dharmakaya[5] of all the buddhas appear as pure lands and teachers. Appearing as the pure lands of all the buddhas, all the places where the teaching is given, and the teachers of the four kayas, primordial awareness manifested all phenomena beyond clarification or obscuration. Knowing mind to be primordially awakened in the great evenness, defined and completely perfect, they remained clear and distinct in the dharmadhatu nature without limit or center, their minds in great bliss without coming or going, beyond clarification or obscuration. Without saying anything, this was the great speech showing all phenomena as enlightened from the beginning, untainted by obscurations. As they remained thus, the mother

Samantabhadri beseeched the victorious ones so that the doctrine might appear:

> For those who have the fortune to understand and realize
>   the mind of the victorious ones,
> Please introduce the dharmakaya, awakened from the very
>   beginning, the state of great bliss!
> For those without the fortune to understand and realize it,
> Please teach the vehicles of the progressive path!

Because of her aspiration, the Secret Mantra[6] appeared in Akanishta and the like, and in particular, the marvelous essence of the doctrine, the Ati,[7] appeared for those with the good fortune to understand and realize it.

The history of this appearance has four sections: the doctrines of the svabhavikakaya, dharmakaya, sambhogakaya,[8] and *guhyakaya*.[9]

The History of the Svabhavikakaya Doctrine

First, as to the origin of the svabhavikakaya doctrine: Its pure land is the all-pervasive, spontaneous, great pure land, the vast space of the dharma-dhatu, the extent of which is beyond measure, without limit or center. The unconditioned dharmadhatu palace of awareness located there is beautifully adorned with the self-existing spontaneously present ornament of unobstructed great wisdom without limit, center, outside, or inside. In this naturally perfect dharmadhatu palace abides the self-existing svabhavikakaya teacher, the spontaneously accomplished buddha of the five kayas. His body mandala is utterly perfect within the mandala of knowledge. His mind is in a state of effortless great bliss, naturally distinct and completely perfect, without coming or going, clarification or obscuration. He dwells together with his circle of disciples, the spontaneously accomplished vidyadhara[10] regents of the buddhas of the three times; there is no distinction between them and him. The time is inconceivable and beyond limit. The doctrine is not taught through words and symbols; it is expounded through the form of the teacher by the self-radiant nature of the dharmakaya, without clarifying or obscuring the mandala of knowledge. The disciples attain the realization of the teacher without clarifying or obscuring the cognitive mandala, so the minds of teacher and disciple become equal and beyond good or bad.

The one who compiled this is the glorious Samantabhadra, who gathered the meaning of the Ati Yoga teachings within the expanse of his awareness, beyond clarification or obscuration.

The History of the Dharmakaya Doctrine

Secondly, as to the origin of the dharmakaya doctrine: Its pure land is the realm of the great all-encompassing nature, pervading all of space. In this intrinsic nature beyond measure, without limit, center, or bias, abides the celestial palace of radiant wisdom, the ultimate Akanishta, without inside or outside, inseparable from the innate nature. In that place the teacher, the dharmakaya Samantabhadra, abides in the dharmadhatu state, unborn, unceasing, beyond clarification or obscuration, his mind in great bliss, without coming, going, clarifying, or obscuring. His circle of disciples consists of those who naturally gather as the dharmakaya retinue, completely and precisely perfecting all of samsara[11] and nirvana.[12] In particular, he dwells together with his circle of disciples, which consists of the buddhas of the three times appearing in sambhogakaya form, all the inconceivable, spontaneously accomplished vidyadhara regents of the five kayas who abide in his company beyond meeting and parting; there is no distinction between them and him. This is the time of equality of the four times, when past, present, and future are inseparable. At the time of great evenness the doctrine is not taught through symbols or words, but the teacher, the dharmakaya Samantabhadra, introduces it through the blessings of the nonarising, unborn, and unceasing and without clarifying or obscuring the dharmadhatu. The disciples attain the teacher's realization free from arising, ceasing, clarifying, or obscuring the dharmadhatu, and the minds of the teacher and his disciples become equal.

At that time the compiler is the glorious Vajrasattva.[13] From the three aspects of development and completion,[14] in particular, he gathers the meaning of Ati within the expanse of his awareness beyond meeting and parting.

The History of the Sambhogakaya Doctrine

Thirdly, as to the origin of the sambhogakaya doctrine: Its pure land is the Sukhavati[15] paradise, equal to the extent of space, where the whole of samsara and nirvana are enjoyed as the innate nature of great bliss. Its location is the dharmadhatu palace of Akanishta, a celestial palace made of various jewels, which is inner luminosity when looking from outside and outer luminosity when looking from within. In that celestial palace, which perfects all mandalas and is beautifully adorned with various precious ornaments, the teacher remains in sambhogakaya form, realizing all phenomena without exception, perfecting them as great bliss and enjoying them free of duality. His body has the major and minor marks[16] and is beautifully adorned with various jewel ornaments. The five general buddha families and the conqueror, the glorious Vajrasattva, abide within the realization of great bliss.

This is the time of meditative insight, when the doctrine is transmitted through symbols. The face of the teacher in sambhogakaya form, without front or back, is directly present in each of the ten directions. His mind is beyond meditating or entering meditation, and his realization is transmitted through symbols, without clarifying or obscuring his great bliss mind. The circle of disciples attains the teacher's realization as before, and they become spontaneously accomplished vidyadharas of the five kayas and buddhas.

The svabhavikakaya and dharmakaya doctrines are taught through mind transmission of the three aspects of development and completion. The three outer sections of Secret Mantra conforming to the sambhogakaya are also taught, and at that time the compiler is Vajradhara, the Lord of Secrets.[17] Among the three outer sections of Secret Mantra[18] and particularly the three aspects of development and completion, he collects all the Ati teachings within the expanse of his awareness.

The History of the Guhyakaya Doctrine

Fourthly, about the origin of the guhyakaya doctrine: Its pure land is the Lotus buddha-field, the dharmadhatu space of the secret consort. In that completely pure sphere, its place is the womb of the secret consort that gives birth to all the victorious ones through unconditioned great bliss.

There the guhyakaya of the teacher, the great bliss sambhogakaya, appears as the teacher of the secret empowerment.[19] At that time his circle of disciples consists of those who are indivisible from him, as well as those who are together with him: the sambhogakaya buddhas and the spontaneously accomplished vidyadhara regents of the five kayas—a host of victorious ones that dwell in his company.

This is the time of conferring the profound secret empowerment, which accomplishes the path, when the doctrine is the profound secret empowerment given through the guhyakaya of the teacher. He gives empowerments of the co-emergent wisdom of unconditioned great bliss of emptiness, inherent wisdom, and thorough pointing out.

The circle of disciples attains the teacher's realization, the inborn wisdom of unconditioned great bliss emptiness, so that the minds of teacher and disciples become equal, and they all attain enlightenment.

The compiler of these teachings is the great guhyakaya: the Lord of Secrets appearing as the guhyakaya, who gathers the doctrine of the profound empowerment, the meaning of the unconditioned great bliss of emptiness, within the expanse of his awareness.

Thus, this amazing and marvelous Ati Yoga doctrine, which is the intent of all the buddhas of the three times, the essence of all teachings and the summit of all vehicles, appeared in the past in Akanishta and the like as the doctrine of the four kayas of the conquerors. The victorious ones and the compilers gathered it within the expanse of their awareness, beyond clarification or obscuration, and remained discussing the wondrous Secret Mantra teachings of the Mahayana.

 This was the first chapter of the Great Image, *the history of the appearance of this precious doctrine in Akanishta.*

2 ❖

The History of the Appearance of This Precious Doctrine in the Celestial and Human Realms

THE SECOND chapter concerns the request to teach the vehicles of the progressive path to those who lack the good fortune of understanding and realization.

In all the infinite, inconceivable, and indescribable worlds appear infinite, inconceivable, and indescribable emanations of the buddhas, such as the Six Munis[1] and others. Through infinite and inconceivable doctrines such as the Tripitaka,[2] they benefit in whatever form is effective with whatever is appropriate. Particularly, in this Saha[3] world system, the Six Munis, such as the Buddha Shakyamuni[4] and others, appear and benefit beings as required.

The second topic, the origin of the doctrine in the realm of the gods and humans, consists of the history of the philosophical teachings based on the cause[5] and the history of the Secret Mantra teachings based on the result.[6]

The History of the Causal Philosophical Teachings

First, concerning the philosophical teachings based on the cause: In the three-thousandfold Saha world, specifically in Varanasi,[7] Bodhgaya,[8] Vulture Peak Mountain,[9] and elsewhere in the Jambu continent,[10] the Buddha Shakyamuni, the nirmanakaya teacher, benefited beings by means of the twelve acts, such as his migration from Tushita.[11]

His circle of disciples consisted of those who were not different from him, those who were together with him, and those who were separate from him. The first were Avalokiteshvara, Manjushri, Vajrapani,[12] and others, who appeared as the retinue of the previous buddhas, acting for the doctrine. The second were the four types of direct disciples, who actually saw and heard the Buddha while he was physically present. The third were those who entered the Buddha's doctrine after he passed away, practiced many of his teachings, and accepted what he said.

In general, it was the time of establishing the torch of the doctrine and, in particular, the time when a human life span was one hundred years and the Buddha Shakyamuni taught the doctrine of the Tripitaka verbally. Turning the wheel of the Dharma with his first teachings on the Four Noble Truths,[13] he taught the *pitaka* according to the *shravakas*,[14] such as the *Four Collections of Statements* on the Vinaya.[15] Turning the wheel of the Dharma with his middle teachings on the absence of characteristics, he taught the aspects of the *paramitas*,[16] as well as part of the Abhidharma sutras.[17] Turning the wheel of the Dharma with his final teachings on the ultimate meaning, he taught the sutras on absolute truth with equal sections of the three pitakas. At that time, the compilers were Ananda[18] and others; they collected the teachings into the Tripitaka with words and syllables.

To his exceptional disciples Shakyamuni taught some Secret Mantra. It is said that he taught Kriya Tantra[19] at the Nairanjana River and the Singhala Forest, the Upa Tantra[20] of *Eminent Courage* at Sandal Grove, and Yoga Tantra[21] at Blazing Mountain and other places.

The inner Secret Mantra was taught by Shakyamuni himself in sambhogakaya form at Sitavana,[22] Changlochen,[23] and other places. He taught the Yoga Tantra of the Secret Mantra in the gods' realm. At the Excellent Dharma Celestial Palace, he taught Kriya Tantra to Vairochana and the other principal buddhas, to the three main bodhisattvas, and to Indra, the

ruler of the gods.[24] In the Mansion of Complete Victory on the summit of
Mount Meru[25] in the gods' realm, he taught Yoga Tantra to his eight chief
spiritual sons.[26]

The History of the Resultant Teachings of the Secret Mantra

The history of the resultant teachings of the Secret Mantra consists of the
Muni's vehicle of the outer tantras and the inner vehicle of transformation through skillful means. The former, the outer tantras, were taught in
the gods' realm and the human realm as explained above. The latter, the
inner vehicle of transformation through skillful means was foretold by
the Victorious One, the nirmanakaya Shakyamuni, at the time of his
passing into nirvana. He predicted the coming of the Secret Mantra doctrine thus:

> Twenty-eight years
> After I have ceased to appear in this world,
> The sublime essence of the teaching,
> Acclaimed throughout the three celestial realms,
> Will be taught in the southeast of the Jambu continent
> To one known as King Ja,[27]
> A noble and fortunate human being,
> Preceded by auspicious omens.
> On the peak called Fearsome Mountain,
> Vajrapani will teach it
> To the king of Lanka,
> And to his companions of lesser rank.

When the Bhagavan had fully passed into nirvana, the doctrine of the
three aspects of development and completion appeared.

Concerning the teachings of the Maha Yoga[28] tantras: Twenty-eight years
after the nirmanakaya had passed away, King Ja received seven indications
in his dreams. After he was authorized, Vajrapani taught him.

To the southeast of Mount Malaya[29] is the secret Asura Cave where
King Ja's palace was located. Mount Malaya is the sacred place where all
the buddhas taught the Secret Mantra. This mountain is extremely auspi-

cious and stunning in appearance. Some people have the pure karma to see it as being made of different precious materials, some see it as a steep high mountain with very sheer cliffs, and some see it as blazing meteoric iron, completely unreachable. On its slope is a sandalwood tree, at the root of which dwells the king of wild beasts, the lion. At the side is a white lion-shaped cliff where the king of birds, the vulture, has its nest. At its base is a sandalwood forest that is the home of the tiger. On the peak is an eight-spoked wheel where Vajrapani has his palace: That is where the fortunate ones gather and expound the secret doctrine; unsuitable people cannot reach it.

To the southeast of that mountain is the secret Asura Cave. The entrance of the cave is shaped like a half-moon, and inside is an eight-faceted jewel with the auspicious signs, adorned with both sun and moon. On the side of the mountain, the *kalantaka*[30] bird has made its nest. That is where King Ja received these seven indications in his dreams: the dissolution of the attributes of body, speech, and mind; the descent of precious books; the discussion of the Dharma; his being proclaimed by all as a saint; the making of large offerings; the shower of gems; and the prediction that he would attain enlightenment.

He first dreamt that all the buddhas had gathered on the summit of Mount Malaya. From the forms of the buddhas and Vajrapani multicolored light rays radiated that burnt and purified the whole universe. Gathering back in the form of blazing sunlight marked with the syllable OM, this light illumined the darkness and dissolved into the crown of King Ja's head. Then light rays radiated from the buddhas' speech, proclaiming the Mahayana teachings with the roar of a thousand thunders over the three-thousandfold world. Gathering back in the form of blazing moonlight marked with the syllable A, it dissolved into the soles of King Ja's feet and throat center. Then wisdom light spread out from the buddhas' hearts, illuminating all phenomenal existence. Gathering back in the form of a blazing vajra, it dissolved into King Ja's heart center. Then he ate all apparent existence as food, and the whole phenomenal world moved around inside his stomach. That was his first dream.

Again sleeping for a while, he dreamt that precious gold-colored clouds like sunlight and moonlight rose in the sky, and from between them, out of a great jewel casket, golden books written in powdered lapis lazuli appeared like falling meteors, completely covering the roof of his house. That was his second dream.

Another time he dreamt that all the buddhas came; some were riding on the sun and moon, and some were holding thousand-spoked wheels as a sign of turning the wheel of the Dharma, guiding the three levels of existence. The roof of King Ja's house resounded with their discourses on Mahayana tantra. That was his third dream.

During another period the king dreamt that all the buddhas and vidyadharas praised and proclaimed him as holy. In the sky they called out:

> King Ja, destined and worthy one,
> You have been predicted in the past.
> You, meritorious noble one,
> Have incarnated according to the predictions
> And now have actually appeared here.
> Through our miraculous blessings
> We bestow upon you the holy essence of the
>   doctrine,
> The supreme of all vehicles, the Secret Mantra,
> In order to enable you to utilize samsara.

Such was his fourth dream.

During another period he dreamt that vidyadharas, bodhisattvas, a large crowd of gods, and a big group of *yakshas*[31] made infinite offerings and circumambulations to the precious volumes (that had fallen from the sky) and praised them in verse. This was his fifth dream.

During another period he dreamt that various jewels covered the sky like clouds and a loud magical thunder resounded. The jewels began to move like thousandfold lightning illuminating all of apparent existence, and as a shower of jewels covered the phenomenal world, he picked some jewel flowers and adorned himself and others. That was his sixth dream.

During another period he dreamt that jewel lamps removed all darkness, nectar medicine purified the chronic diseases of beings, the sound of the vajra yoga of all beings was proclaimed throughout the universe, and all the buddhas predicted:

> King Ja, fortunate meritorious one,
> You will directly attain clear realization
> Of the essence of the doctrine, the meaning of the Secret
>   Mantra,

And be equal to the Buddha himself.
In the Sukhavati paradise
You will become fully enlightened.

Then all the buddhas of past, present, and future said:

You should look at the three holy treasures,
The secrets of the great Vajradhara,[32]
Which are perfectly written in volumes,
And proclaim them by gradually transmitting them
To divine and human vidyadharas.

That was his seventh dream. When he awoke the next morning, he
gathered his retinue and told them his dreams:

Last night I dreamt that the palace of Vajrapani
Was on top of Mount Malaya.
From Vajrapani's body radiated light that burnt everything;
His speech sounded like thunder over the three-
    thousandfold world;
And his heart emitted light that illuminated all of apparent
    existence.
The sunlight from his body dissolved into the crown of
    my head,
The moonlight from his speech dissolved into the soles of
    my feet,
A blazing vajra dissolved into my heart,
And the three seed syllables dissolved into my three
    centers.

I dreamt that I ate the phenomenal world as food,
That jewels covered the sky like clouds, and
In their blazing sunlight, from a maroon jewel box,
Golden books written in powdered lapis lazuli ink
Descended like falling stars.

I dreamt that buddhas and bodhisattvas
Came riding in the sky on the sun and moon.

With golden wheels in their hands
They guided the three existences,
Debating on the Secret Mantra.

I dreamt that all the buddhas and vidyadharas
Proclaimed me as the holiest of all.

I dreamt that the buddhas, bodhisattvas, vidyadharas,
Dakinis, gods, yakshas, and so forth,
All did prostrations and circumambulations
To those great books,
Made offerings, and praised them.

I dreamt that jewels covered the sky like clouds,
Flashing like lightning with the magical sound of
     thunder.

I dreamt that it rained precious stones
And I picked jewel flowers.

I dreamt that from the light rays of the buddhas' speech
It was predicted that I would attain enlightenment.

As he related these dreams everyone was amazed. When they looked
on the roof, there were many golden volumes of the Secret Mantra tantras
written in powdered lapis lazuli and a statue of Vajrapani eighteen inches
high. The king prayed:

In return for previously acquired karma from past lives,
The holy essence of the Dharma
Has never been forsaken in this place.
Supreme deity, your amazing wondrous form
Is known as the perfect holy guide.
Supreme deity, I have a karmic connection with you;
May I hold you as a support for my devotion, EMAHO!

The king looked at the volumes, but he couldn't understand the words
and wept from sorrow. Then it occurred to him that there might be other

educated persons who understood them, so he invited some learned panditas.[33] The panditas thought things would go well if they all knew the books, but they were afraid of being embarrassed should they not understand them; therefore, they were unwilling to come. "Bring the books here," they said. All the volumes were loaded on an elephant and brought to them, but none of the panditas understood them. They gave them back to the king, who wept with despair. He thought about it for a while and decided that it was because he had not purified his obscurations or perfected his merit.

When he prayed to the volumes of *Vajrasattva's Body Tantra*, his obscurations were purified and he attained a minor accomplishment. As he looked at the books, he understood both the chapter on *Vajrasattva's Magical Heart Sadhana* and the chapter known as "The Vision of Vajrasattva." With the support of the Vajrapani statue he practiced the *Heart Sadhana*. After six months he had a vision of Vajrasattva, who asked him, "What siddhi[34] do you want?" He answered, "I wish to understand these books." Vajrasattva handed him a staff and a Dharma wheel, gave him permission to confer empowerment, briefly explained the meaning, and disappeared. Then the king looked at the books and understood every syllable without exception, which made him very happy.

In this way, Vajrasattva taught the vehicle that had been taught by the sambhogakaya in Akanishta to King Ja in the human realm. It was divided into eighteen great tantras and gradually transmitted.

Concerning the Anu Yoga scriptures: Twenty-eight years after the Buddha passed away, from the summit of Mount Malaya the five eminent beings[35] contemplated all the tathagatas of the ten directions:

> Alas! Alas! Alas!
> Now that the light of the Buddha has disappeared,
> Who will dispel the world's darkness?
>
> Without his authentic presence,
> Won't the genuine doctrine be misunderstood
> By those who wish to practice it?
>
> Who will make sure that the vows are correct?
> Revealing the teachings to benefit

Beings who haven't found certainty,
May the doctrine become established!

Now that the eyes that discriminate right and wrong
    are closed,
When wrong views are accomplished
By disrespecting the teachings,
Won't the power of evil increase?

As the clouds of a corrupted doctrine thicken
And the sun and moon of the doctrine of two truths
    decline,
Won't those beings in search of the path
Wander in darkness?

Now that the Buddha has passed into nirvana,
Who will subdue the demons, ogres, heretics,
Yakshas, evil spirits, nonhumans, and
Malignant and vicious ones?

It would be unacceptable
If the nectar of this stainless doctrine declined;
Who will have the skill
To kindle and illuminate it?

It would be impossible to be without
The trainings of the precious true doctrine;
Which sublime being
Will uphold the principles?

Now that the Buddha has passed away,
Who is the predicted one
Among his many noble disciples?

Maintaining different interests
Within the skylike doctrine,
Won't selecting and disputing
About "what is" and "what is not" increase?

The one authentic lineage
Will be divided into contradictory views.
Won't the succession of two different lineages
Be corrupted and contrived?

Won't different unskilled beings
Who regard things without value as precious,
Influenced by emotional passion,
Substitute poison for the doctrine?

Without the Buddha, the Dharma king,
Who was present until now,
When unscrupulous ones cause harm,
Won't mischief spread?

As long as the doctrine endures,
How will it remain as one?
In the future what will become of
What came in the past and what comes at present?

During the last period of the Buddha's doctrine,
How true will it be?

How will the disciples that hold the trainings
Behave in the final period?

Now that the Buddha has passed into nirvana,
Where did he go and whom is he teaching?

In which pure land does he reside?
What doctrine does he preach?

Who will be the refuge and protector
For the helpless of this world?

Now that the magical understanding and counsel
    are lost,
Where should we seek reasoning and advice?

Now that we cannot find the true meaning,
What certainty can we maintain?

Now that our reliable object of worship is not present,
What will become of his relics?

Who will we worship in the future?
Now that the Buddha has passed away,
Will there be a successor?
Alas! Alas! Alas!

After the five eminent beings spoke thus to the only refuge of the beings of the three worlds, instructed by the ocean of victorious ones, all the
lords of compassion gathered in the Changlochen Palace, the dwelling of
the Lord of Secrets, and exhorted him thus:

Listen to us, Lord of Secrets, we pray!
Have you cast off the armor of your past resolve?
Do you not see the sufferings of this world?
Have pity and descend to earth;
Dispel the torments of this world!

Adapting to the different types,
Subdue all those vicious ones.
Through skillful instructions,
Transform their perceptions
According to their karma and conduct,
Explaining the teachings
So that they can attain the ultimate state!

At this fervent request, the *daka*,[36] the vajra-holding king, skillful in
subduing those who are difficult to train, the oceanlike supreme conqueror of this world, vajra-holder of the secret signs, rejoiced. Rising from
his seat, he displayed a great miracle to everyone and said:

You are the principal ones
Who have turned away from this world,
Prophesied as the fortunate ones.

You have excellent karma and capacities
And have been predicted by the conquerors.
Fortunate ones, you have great merit;
You have emanated according to the predictions.

Since you have manifested here now,
In order to reveal the essence of samsara,
Through the blessings of miracles
You should liberate fortunate ones
And teach the true essence of the doctrine
According to the predictions.

This mountain called Fearsome One,
The dwelling of the great protectors,
Is the source of the Mahayana secrets
For those who have attained the essence of wisdom.

Without beginning and without end,
It was praised by the sublime ones.
Without beginning and without end,
Infinite victorious ones
Have shown the mirrorlike mandala of the mind
In this great sacred place of the sublime protectors.

Likewise, without beginning and without end,
Responding whenever I am invoked,
I unfold my miraculous display.

Thus the Lord of Secrets promised. At that time King Who Subdues
Yakshas said:

As this mountain called Fearsome One,
Which, among the four continents, is situated in the Jambu
    continent,
The world of humans,
Is a place to subdue the yakshas.
Emanation who dwells in the state of compassion,
Go to the practice places of the doctrine-holders!

Then the earth shook, and miraculously everything was purified and appeared blissful. The fortunate ones from the past, the noble ones of lesser rank, appeared as the well-known human *kshatriyas*,[37] just like Prince Indra. At this the five eminent beings developed doubt, and cheerfully they asked these courageous questions:

> EMAHO! How wondrous and marvelous!
> Great being, who are you?
> Where do you come from and how did you emerge?
> Where did you appear and why?
> What do you teach and for what purpose?

The great miracle replied:

> I am not moved by anything;
> I am the unshakable vajra being.
> When my compassion is aroused,
> I am the unique friend of the three worlds of existence.

> My country is the great void;
> My family is Vajra Ratna;
> My father is the infinite supreme method;
> My mother is inexpressible knowledge.

> In beginningless time I lost my wish-fulfilling gem,
> Not knowing that I even had it
> Nor realizing that I had lost that nectar jewel.

> At that time everyone was afflicted by poverty
> And incurable disease;
> Wandering in dense darkness,
> Even the path for crossing was lost.
> Though tormented, they could not realize it.

> At that time my supreme spiritual friend,
> A loving protector, instructed me:
> "EMAHO! Don't you realize

That you have lost the precious gem
Through which everything seen
Becomes very significant?
Didn't you know that you had it?
How is it to be kept, and why?"
So said my supreme companion.

I answered: "I didn't know that I had it,
Nor did I realize that I had lost
Such an important thing.
Spiritual friend, show me a way to find it!"

That holy one guided me:
"If you want to find it quickly,
You should make an effort to search.
The holy guide points it out,
But though you may search for it along various paths
All over the earth and in darkness,
As it emerges from your own nature,
You won't find it elsewhere.
Finding that gem again,
The home of the holy ones
That was found before and will be found again,
Is the realization of those who find it."

Upon hearing this,
In order to find such a thing,
I received instructions from this teacher;
I investigated with true intelligence
And mounted the horse of the Mahayana.

Coming from the juncture of darkness and brightness,
I crossed dangerous paths along the four rivers,
Searched along various ways,
And entered the path of the holy ones.
Going through the stages and emancipations of the path,
I reached the city of nirvana.

Investigating the precious gem,
One discovers it in the home of the dharmadhatu
Without obtaining or acquiring.
This is finding what can't be found
Upon losing what can't be lost.

Since it is beyond having or not having,
It is beyond losing or finding.
Not originating elsewhere, it is self-existing.
As there is no notion of finding it,
Losing it is just a manner of speaking.

The time of having it, losing it, and finding it
Is beginningless time.
At the time when illusions appear
From what is not the innate nature,
I come to this realm of both darkness and
     brightness.

I am the skillful boatman
Who promised to liberate the three worlds
From the endless river of samsara.
Those who want liberation, come to this path!

I am the skillful eye doctor
Who promised to remove the cataracts
From the infinite blind ones in this world.
Those who want to see, come to this path!

I am the skillful doctor
Who promised to cure the chronic illness
Of the sick in the three cities.
Those who want to be well, come to this path!

I am the skillful guide
Who promised to lead without error
The beings who lost the path and went astray.
Come to this path that shows the right way!

I am the compassionate observer
Who promised to protect everyone
From the fear of hostile armies.
Those who want to be free of fear, come to this path!

I am the great vajra fortress
That promised to be a bastion for beings
Against samsaric wars and armies.
Those who need a fortress, come to this path!

I am the skillful merchant
Who promised to give great treasures
To those who can't satisfy their craving.
Those who want treasures, come to this path!

I am the skillful lamp
That promised to illuminate the darkness
For those who grope in dense obscurity.
Those who want clarity, come to this path!

I am the wish-fulfilling gem
With the promise to grant wishes
For those who have wishes in mind.
Those who want spontaneous accomplishment, come
    to this path!

I am the key to the teachings
With the vow to open
The boxes filled with secret teachings.
Whoever wants liberation, come to this path!

I am the great commentary
With the vow to truly elucidate
The volumes of profound teachings.
Whoever wants to know them, come to this path!

Those fortunate ones that enter
This great path of liberation

Should strive so that the shining precious gem
Definitely appears.
Upon recognizing this mirrorlike mind,
In actuality one is a buddha in human form.

Having clearly explained
The supreme sacred treasures,
Vajradhara's secrets of ultimate truth,
They will become known by gradually transmitting
    them
To celestial and human vidyadharas.

Removing all gloomy anguish
Of gods and humans in all universes,
The mandala of the mind will manifest,
So why should you be worried and confused?

If you are sad that the Buddha passed into nirvana,
Recognize that he possesses a skylike body
Beyond passing and not passing,
Unchanging, like space!

This speech from the emanation made the former noble beings extremely happy. Greatly rejoicing, they bowed down very respectfully, and in front of him they prayed:

As lightning reveals the atmosphere
On a dark cloudy night,
From the space of suchness
Without beginning or end,
You, accomplished one,
Known as the Lord of Secrets,
Appear as the pure path,
Upholding the esoteric teachings of the sublime ones.

You are praised for elucidating the teachings,
And known as the Great Commentary.
Shining as the sun of the three secret treasures

In the mandala of the mind,
Because you clarify all cognitive obscurations,
You are known as the Bright Sun.

Subjugating whoever is difficult to subdue
And conquering the most vicious of demons,
You frighten even a crowd of terrifying ones
And are known as the Devil of Devils.

When your eyes perceive the forms of all phenomena
As the luminous nature of mind,
The essence of suchness,
You are known as the Mirror of Phenomena.

Unmatched in soothing pain
Through the medicinal mandala that destroys poison,
You are known as the King of Doctors,
The enemy of all illness.

When you rejoice,
You are known as the One Who Dispels Longing.
When you grant wishes,
You are known as the Wish-Fulfilling Gem.

Conforming with the holy ones,
Which sacred emanations will appear
For us vidyadharas?
How will the sacred light spread?
How will the secret transmission occur?

Please expound upon the esoteric lineage!
Please give a talk on the vajra space!
Please express your realization in three words!

In answer to their prayer, the Lord of Secrets said:

You who were predicted in the past,
Bodhisattvas in the bodies of beings,

With your yearning questions,
Be free of your illusory thoughts and listen!

The mandala of mind as it is
Never declines, like the sky.
Its nature has always been luminous;
Whatever obscures it is removed by it.

Whenever it is examined with the two types
    of logic,
The subject itself will serve as valid cognition.
It is the root of right and wrong,
But it is not changed by them.

No sun or moon can make
The luminous nature of mind more brilliant.
The Buddha did not pass into nirvana,
Nor will the Dharma decline.

In order to benefit lazy ones,
Emanations act as if they pass away,
But not until space is destroyed
Will they pass into nirvana.

Whoever is evil and corrupt
Will be skillfully trained through egoless voidness.
Through the display of self-existing wisdom,
The profound and luminous ocean
Of the unconditioned doctrine
Will shine and spread light everywhere.

The highest training in mind essence,
The supreme training of all,
Will be upheld by bodhisattvas
Accomplished in the highest levels
Who will appear in future in the bodies of beings.

The limitless sentient beings
Who dwell in the heart of awakening from the very
   beginning
Will definitely transform into suchness,
Reaching the state of nonlearning, as predicted.

The naive debate
Over whether mind exists or not.
But from the beginning, the wise never argued over it;
They do not talk about existence or non-existence.

Because my esoteric Secret Mantra
Is the most secret of all Secret Mantra,
By trying to guess the meaning and understanding some-
   thing else,
A secret word can be misinterpreted.

When the ignorant and stupid
Alter this secret transmission of the holy ones,
It is like adding poison to nectar:
It is ruined, and both will be spoiled.

When the bright mirror that illuminates everything
Shows things exactly as they are,
Like the sky, there is no bias,
And even attacks are but sudden clouds.

As long as supreme enlightenment exists
The doctrine will remain,
Appearing without beginning or end,
Without before or after.

Describing its nonexistence from the beginning,
In the end it will also be indescribable.
The nature as it is will not change
From the first lineage-holder to the last.

Having seen the nature as it is,
Abiding in the realm of all-pervading evenness,
The luminous mandala of mind
Is perceived as suchness.

For the sake of the naive, a miraculous display
Called Unknown
Appeared in the universe called Array of Flowers,
But this appearance only seemed to manifest.

Likewise, the emanations of buddhas
Appearing in the pure lands
Are magical illusions that don't actually manifest,
Though others perceive their appearance.

Through the compassion of the unshakable supreme
     vajra mind,
Blessed emanations,
Self-occurring and self-subsiding,
Appear and disappear in the infinite universes.

In the expanse of unborn original wakefulness,
The primordial *sugatagarbha*[38]
That is obscured by sudden karmic thoughts
Is the total refuge and protector of beings.

The intent of the conquerors in three words,
The magical supreme idea and advice
That is always of great importance,
Appears in the sphere of higher intellect.

Resting the mind in the essence
That dwells in the natural state as it is:
That itself is the certainty
Of the mind blessings of all the conquerors.

Since the quality of all phenomena is like space,
How can relics come from the remains

Of the wisdom bodies of the conquerors,
Which have no material substance?

In order to benefit beings,
Through compassion they seem to leave
Illusory relics the size of mustard seeds,
Which emanate from nothingness.

Wanting real relics
Is like extracting butter from sand;
Not until sesame seeds can be harvested from
      planting rice
Can real relics exist.

Vajrasattva, the protector of beings, said that
He who profoundly explains that apparent forms
Are by nature the three vajras of body, speech and mind
Is the sacred teacher to rely upon.

The infinite victorious ones
Come from sentient beings in samsara;
When the flow of samsaric beings is cut,
The flow of buddhas is also cut.

For example, a rainbow in the sky
Doesn't first come from somewhere else
And in the end go anywhere else;
It spontaneously appears and disappears.

Emanations are self-occurring and self-subsiding,
In themselves unmistaken.
Not separated by passing away, they do not differ,
Yet when they don't pass away, they are not one.
As they are beyond past and future,
How can there be separation and no separation?

So what are you sad about?
Your confused longing is an illusion!

How wondrous this is!
From now on, how can you fall into delusion?

Teaching thus, the Lord of Secrets gazed like a lion. Those deluded due to yearning were delighted, and their sadness completely cleared up. As the Lord of Secrets remained in the unaltered state, the mandala of his face became totally luminous.

This is how he taught the *Scripture of the Embodiment of Realization*[39] and other teachings to the five eminent beings on the summit of Mount Malaya. At Dhanakosha[40] in the western land of Oddiyana[41] the Lord of Secrets Vajrapani taught the *Tantra of the Essence of Secrets*[42] with its pith instructions and explained in detail the transmissions of the tantras of Kila, Mamo, and others to the nirmanakaya Prahe.[43]

 This was the second chapter from the history of the Great Image, *about the transmission of the vehicles based on cause and effect in the human realm.*

3

The History of How the Effortless Vehicle Appeared in the Three Celestial Realms

T HE HISTORY of the origin of the Ati Yoga doctrine relates how the mind lineage of the conquerors,[1] the awareness lineage of the vidyadharas,[2] and the hearing lineage of individuals[3] became known in the realms of gods and humans.

First, the Mind Lineage Through the Conquerors

First, concerning the mind lineage through the conquerors, the origin of the doctrine of the conquerors' four kayas in Akanishta is as explained earlier. As the svabhavikakaya, the Buddha taught through the self-luminous pointing-out instruction; as the dharmakaya, the Buddha taught direct self-liberation through blessings; as the sambhogakaya, he taught through the intrinsic nature; and as the guhyakaya, he taught through the method of great bliss. As the Lord of Secrets, the Buddha empowered the nirmanakaya Prahevajra[4] as doctrine-holder of these teachings. As Prahevajra taught this doctrine of the four kayas, it became known in the realm of the gods and humans.

Here follows the history of the origin of the doctrine in the celestial and human realms and how the nirmanakaya Prahevajra taught it in beautiful poetry.

First, at the time of the sixfold omen predicting the appearance of the Secret Mantra, the effortless Ati Vehicle came about.

> When emotions gain strength and devotion weakens,
> When, due to karma, life spans become shorter
> And only the literal meaning of the teachings is taught,
> When the two doctrines[5] are adulterated by unwholesome
>   beliefs,
> When remedies are ineffective and diligence in practice
>   is feeble:
> That is the time when the notion of awareness will appear.

Thus, it describes the time when emotions become more intense, when the power of faith and devotion has grown weak, when the karmic life span is shorter, when only the literal sense of the Buddha's words is regarded as the meaning, when the doctrine has degenerated with unwholesome beliefs, when remedies are ineffective and perseverance is weak. That is the time when Ati will appear, revealing the distinguishing, resolving, and self-liberation in actuality.

It was at this time that, in the Heaven of the Thirty-three[6] the god named Deva Bhadrapala had 501 sons, of which the eldest was called Ananda Garbha.[7] He was more intelligent and physically gifted than his brothers. Whereas the other young gods liked to play music and games, sing, dance, bathe, and compose poetry in their pleasure gardens, Ananda Garbha preferred to stay alone in a meditation hut and practice the vajra recitation; so he became known as Devaputra Adhichitta, the god's son of superior mind.

In the first month of the year of the female water ox, this young god had four symbolic dreams. In the first he dreamt that all the buddhas were emanating light rays in the ten directions, and the luminous forms of the Six Munis encircled him and dissolved into the crown of his head. In his second dream he swallowed Brahma, Vishnu, and Pashupati.[8] In his third dream both the sun and the moon rose in the sky and then appeared in his hands, filling the whole universe with light. In his fourth dream a rain of nectar fell from a jewel-colored cloud in the sky, and all at once there burst forth crops, forests, precious plants, flowers, and fruits. The next morning he went to tell this to the king of the gods, who uttered this praise:

> EMAHO!
> Now is the time for the genuine essence to appear!
> The perfectly enlightened one of the three times
> Could manifest an emanation to dispel the world's darkness
> And subdue the end of time.
> What a wonder, this heart son, the splendor of the Jambu
>   continent!

Having spoken these words, the king of the gods explained the dreams' significance: "The first dream means that you will realize the wisdom mind of all the buddhas of the three times and will be their representative. The second one means that you will subjugate all demons, and eradicating the three poisons without rejecting them, you will attain true and complete enlightenment. The third one means you will dispel the darkness in the minds of disciples through the vehicle beyond cause and effect and become the lamp of the doctrine. The fourth one means that the self-existing nectar of the pith instructions will wash away the disturbing emotions forever so that the effortless fruition will be spontaneously present." Saying this, the king of the gods was delighted, and looking into the four directions, he invoked all the victorious ones:

> All you lords of speech
> Have taught the entire vehicle of endeavor.
> Why don't you teach the Effortless Vehicle?
> Is your compassion vanishing or something?
> When there are destined disciples,
> You should teach spontaneous accomplishment!

As he prayed in this way, all the buddhas of the ten directions gathered in the sky like clouds and unanimously invoked Vajrasattva in these words:

You are the compassionate nature
Of all the buddhas of the three times:
Manifest as the actions of all buddhas!

You are the wisdom nature
Of all the lords of speech:
Illuminate everything as their bodhichitta!

You are endowed with the essential form
Of all tathagatas without exception:
Appear as a wondrous display of body!

Please show the destined ones
The essential gate to the miraculous jewel
That completes the meaning in a single word!

Thus, they entreated Bhagavan Vajrasattva by praising his body, speech, mind, qualities, and activities. They also requested him to teach the Effortless Vehicle according to the understanding of the disciples:

You who possess the jewel of miraculous means,
Open the gate according to what beings desire
And introduce them to the effortless state!

Upon hearing these words, Bhagavan Vajrasattva emanated Vajrapani from his heart center, and placing a wheel of naturally glowing jewels in Vajrapani's hands, Vajrasattva made this request:

Wisdom beyond duality, hidden reality,
Primordial buddha, free of effort and action,
Reveal this straight path of the Great Middle Way
To the gathered assembly!

Requested thus, Sattvavajra[9] promised to teach with these words:

Vajrasattva, Great Space,
That which is beyond the scope of words,

> Is very hard for me to express.
> But for those who have not realized it I shall use words
> To point out the meaning. So that they may realize it,
> I shall use whatever means are needed to liberate them.

Having made this pledge to teach, in order not to contradict the view of the buddhas of the three times, Vajrapani posed these questions, to clear his doubts about ground and fruition, to all the buddhas of the three times abiding as the identity of the five families.[10]

In Vajraloka, the eastern buddha-field, as the Tathagata Vajraguhya was giving Secret Mantrayana teachings about the natural state to the circle of disciples that was inseparable from him, Sattvavajra asked:

> How can arising and ceasing occur
> In the nature of mind, which is like a vajra?

The perfect and complete Tathagata Vajraguhya replied:

> The unchanging vajra nature of the mind
> Neither arises nor ceases.
> Arising and ceasing occur for the thinking mind.

Then in Ratnaloka, the southern buddha-field, as the Tathagata Ratnapada, seated on a naturally bright shining throne, was giving Secret Mantrayana teachings on the natural state to his circle of disciples, Sattvavajra asked him:

> Since the nature of enlightened mind
> Is not dependent on cause, condition, or effort,
> How can qualities arise as a result?

In response to his question, the Tathagata Ratnapada spoke in these words:

> Just like the *dagskaka* ornament,
> The fulfillment of cause and effect is complete in the
>   ground.

Everything is the supreme self-existing essence.
When it is realized through the secret method,
The result is like the rays of the sun.

Then in Padmakuta, the western buddha-field, as the Bhagavan
Padmaprabha, seated on a stainless lotus, was giving Secret Mantrayana
teachings about the natural state to his circle of disciples, Sattvavajra
asked:

If the nature of mind is pure like a lotus,
How can stains, the nature of form, be purified?

The Bhagavan Padmaprabha answered:

The lotus stays in the swamp
But is not stained by the mud of the swamp.
The nature of enlightened mind
Is not stained by samsara.
Samsara is created by the thinking mind.

Then in Vishuddhasiddha, the northern buddha-field, as the Tathagata
Siddhyaloka, seated on a naturally shining throne, was giving Secret
Mantrayana teachings on the natural state to his circle of disciples, Sattva-
vajra asked him:

If the nature of mind is beyond effort,
How can one act for the benefit of others?

In response to his question the Tathagata Siddhyaloka spoke these
words:

When the self-existing vajra wisdom is realized,
Buddha activity arises spontaneously.

Then in Viyoganta, the central buddha-field, as soon as Vajrapani arrived in the presence of the Tathagata Vairochana, the Buddha welcomed
him and said:

You should make the retinue gathered here
Realize the secret wisdom,
The heart essence of all the victorious ones!

Upon hearing this, Vajrapani got up from his seat and requested the Tathagata Vairochana:

You, lion of speech,
Please introduce the secret wisdom!

Vairochana answered:

Sattvavajra, listen!
The nature of secret wisdom
Is that buddhas and sentient beings are the same,
Pervading everything, like space.
There is no difference between ignorance and wisdom:
Whether realized or not, the path is the same.

The essence of secret wisdom
Is self-cognizant luminosity, utterly pure,
Where thoughts dwell as original wakefulness.
This natural precious treasury, intrinsic to the ground,
Is self-existing, uncultivated, and primordially pure.

Though intangible, the form of secret wisdom
Manifests in various ways.
Being continuously aware of
This unperceived, inherently present magic: that is
    the view.

Thus he spoke.

Having distilled the essence of all the buddhas' wisdom, every aspect of Ati Yoga, the marvelous essence of the doctrine, the spontaneous, effortless realization beyond cause and effect, Vajrapani went to the Heaven of the Thirty-three to see Devaputra Adhichitta. In the central chamber on the top floor of the All-Victorious Palace, which had a life-pillar topped by a nine-pronged vajra, Adhichitta arranged a dazzling jewel-encrusted throne on top of the nine-pronged vajra and spread out a canopy of various gems. Vajrapani sat on the throne and transmitted the complete empowerment of direct anointment[11] to Adhichitta. He also bestowed on him the pith instructions of the *Ten Miraculous Transmissions*.

Having conferred the empowerment of *Threefold Spontaneous Accomplishment*, he gave him the instructions on *Encountering Body, Speech, and Mind*. Having conferred the empowerment of the *Great Sphere*, he gave the pith instructions on *Unchanging Mind Essence*. Having conferred the empowerment of *Unchanging Firmness*, he gave the pith instructions on *Insight in Experience*. Having conferred the empowerment of *Immediacy of Awareness*, he gave the pith instructions on *Identifying Original Wakefulness*. Having conferred the empowerment of *Nondual Mingling*, he gave the pith instructions on Mahamudra.[12] Having conferred the empowerment of *Vajra Statement*, he gave the pith instructions on *Regent Training*. He also gave many other initiations, pith instructions, and tantras, transmitting them in their entirety in a single instant. Vajrapani empowered him as his representative and pronounced these words:

> May this miraculous essence of the teachings
> Become renowned in the three celestial realms
> And be propagated in the center of the Jambu continent
> By the reincarnated heart-son.

Thus, he caused the doctrine to spread throughout the three celestial realms.

 This was the third chapter of the Great Image, *about the Effortless Vehicle becoming known in the three celestial realms.*

4 ❈

The History of the Appearance
of the Effortless Atí Doctrine
in the Human Realm

To the west of India lies Oddiyana, the land of the dakinis. There, in the region of Dhanakosha, was a lake called Kutra, on the banks of which was a cave called the Place of the Vajra. There lived a king called Dhahena Talo, who came from a highly educated family. He had a son called the elder Rajahasti and a daughter called Parani, who was highly talented, virtuous of heart, and had immense bodhichitta. Free of faults and deceit, she had been ordained as a nun and kept her vows with utmost purity. She had given up male company and lived with a following of five hundred nuns.

During the year of the female wood ox, at dawn on the eighth day of the second summer month, she dreamt that all the tathagatas sent forth light that transformed into a sun and moon. She dreamt that the sun dissolved into her through the crown of her head, moving downward, and the moon dissolved into her through her feet, moving upward. Thinking about it in the morning, she went to bathe at the shore of Kutra Lake. Looking toward the east, she saw Vajrapani, who had taken the form of a golden swan and who had turned Adhichitta into the syllable HUNG. Along with four other emanated swans, they came down from the sky to wash themselves. After bathing, four of the swans flew away, and the swan that was a manifestation of the Lord of Secrets clung to the breast of the princess. Touching her breast three times with its beak, a brilliant syllable HUNG dissolved into her heart. Then the swan flew up and disappeared.

The princess was astonished; she told her father and attendants about the dream and the story of the swans. Her father was amazed and, overjoyed, said, "We can expect an emanation of the Buddha!" He took great care and had many ceremonies performed.

Within a year a nine-pronged vajra made of various jewels sprang from the princess's heart and everyone was struck with wonder. The vajra disintegrated by itself and became a child bearing the major and minor marks, holding a vajra in his right hand and a jewel staff in his left and reciting Vajrasattva, Great Space, and so on.[1] Everyone was delighted. They showed the child to a Brahmin versed in the art of reading signs. Utterly amazed, the Brahmin declared the child to be an incarnation who would hold the teachings of the highest vehicle.

The child was called Prahevajra, and from an early age he surpassed everyone in games and sports. When he had finished his education and was about to take over the kingdom, Vajrapani appeared to Prahevajra in person and gave him the complete empowerment of direct anointment and other empowerments. Summoning the three *putras*[2] from the upper and lower charnel grounds in the southwest, he empowered them and bound them under oath. In an instant he transmitted all the tantras, initiations, and pith instructions, including the *Twenty Thousand Sections of the Ninefold Expanse*,[3] to Prahe and empowered him as the Lamp of the Doctrine. He commanded the oath-bound[4] to assist yogis and guard the doctrine.

Right there, in an instant the nirmanakaya Prahevajra truly and completely awakened to the level of the effortless Great Perfection so that his realization became one with all the buddhas of the three times. In general, he fully comprehended all the teachings on cause and result without exception. In particular, he actually realized the intent of the inconceivable tantra sections and of the four kayas of the conquerors, including the root tantras of the effortless doctrine of the Great Perfection, the *Twenty Thousand Sections of the Ninefold Expanse* taught by Samantabhadra, the branch tantras taught by the five families of conquerors and the Lord of Secrets, and the exposition tantras and subsidiary tantras. The pith instructions of the words of the conquerors that directly show self-liberation, the empowerment of direct anointment, the stream of empowerments of the four kayas of the victorious ones, and all other teachings were perfected within his mind so that he remained proclaiming the doctrine of the effortless and self-existing Great Perfection to some special disciples.

At that time an emanation of the noble Manjushri, foremost in knowledge, was born as the son of the Brahmin Sukhapala and his wife, the Brahmini Kuhana. He was very qualified and intelligent and was called Brahmin Sarasiddhi, also known as Samvarasara. He became a monk skilled in the five sciences, expert in the teachings of cause and result, and was the most outstanding among five hundred panditas. During that time all the panditas heard that there was an incarnation, Prahevajra, who was proclaiming something superior to all teachings of cause and result, the marvelous essence of the doctrine, a teaching known as the effortless Ati Yoga transcending cause and effect.

Meanwhile the Brahmin Sarasiddhi received the following prophesy from Manjushri: "Go west to the Dhanakosha region in the land of Oddiyana. On the shore of Kutra Lake is a vast charnel ground called Golden Sanctuary of Expanding Delight. Nearby there is a cave called the Place of the Vajra, where the nirmanakaya Prahevajra is living. He is an emanation of Vajrasattva, assigned as the effortless torch of all the buddhas, and has the marvelous essence of the doctrine, called Ati Yoga, through which instant enlightenment can be attained without effort. Receive that and become the nirmanakaya's compiler!"

The other panditas found the news that there was something higher than the teachings on cause and effect irrational and made plans to refute it. Secretly wishing to show the greatness of the emanation, the Brahmin Sarasiddhi pretended to agree with their plans for a refutation. When the panditas discussed who should go, many of them complained that Oddiyana was so far away and so difficult to reach, so only seven of them, Sarasiddhi, the elder Rajahasti, and five others, were sent off.

These seven went to the Place of the Vajra Cave where they met the nirmanakaya Prahevajra. While exchanging views about the teachings, they tested him by describing the greatness of the vehicle of cause and result. But when discussing the causal teachings of the Tripitaka, they couldn't defeat Prahe. Even when discussing both outer and inner Secret Mantra teachings based on the result, the panditas couldn't withstand him. As they debated, with the panditas taking the position of the Causal Vehicle and the nirmanakaya Prahe taking the position of the Ati beyond cause and effect, no one could defeat Prahe. Samvarasara then feigned to consult the other panditas about requesting the nirmanakaya Prahe for the teachings beyond cause and effect or not. Some of the panditas were displeased and said, "We are too embarrassed!" Though the elder Rajahasti and some others wanted to request the teaching, they said, "We don't dare ask because of the disrespect we have shown him." Samvarasara and others then decided to apologize to the nirmanakaya Prahevajra. Some of them did prostrations and circumambulations, some cried and shed tears, and Manjushrimitra prostrated, burst into tears, and prepared to express his confession by cutting off his own tongue. The nirmanakaya Prahevajra knew this and with a melodious voice he sang:

> Unconfined equality, spontaneously present great bliss:
> While this is the awakened essence of all phenomena,
> Beings of the six realms, fettered by attachment, take hold
>   of objects
> And accept the extreme wrong views of eternalism and
>   nihilism.
> In dualistic fixation clinging to what is and what isn't
>   within the eight vehicles themselves,
> With bias and ambition they cling to basic space as having
>   sides.
> Dividing the state of evenness into parts and divisions,
> They ignore what they have and search for it elsewhere.
> They cast aside what is spontaneously present and willingly
>   make effort,
> Regarding enlightenment as something depending on time.
> Such limited views of longing do not realize equality.
> I pity these boastful and tiresome views!
> Instead, overcome the poison of one-sided clinging
> And join the easy path of unconfined equality!

Thus singing, he said: "Sarasiddhi, cutting off your tongue will not purify your obscurations! Write a teaching that transcends the law of cause and effect; that will atone for your transgression!"

The panditas who lacked the karma and good fortune then returned home. Manjushrimitra assimilated the entire doctrine, attaining instantaneous realization by merely being shown a gesture. Even though he was fully realized, to make the teachings perfect and complete, Prahe gave him the empowerment of direct anointment and all the other tantras and pith instructions without exception, including the *Twenty Thousand Sections of the Ninefold Expanse*. Then Prahe gave him the name Manjushrimitra.[5] Summarizing the instructions, Prahe sang in a melodious voice:

> The nature of mind is awakened from the beginning,
> And this mind, beyond arising and ceasing, is like space.
> Once you realize that all things neither arise nor cease,
> The training, then, is to let be without searching for this
>   nature.

At this, Manjushrimitra understood the nature of realization. Having perfected the essence of the doctrine, he described his own realization as follows:

> I am Manjushrimitra,
> Who has attained the accomplishment of Yamantaka.[6]
> I have realized the total equality of samsara and nirvana;
> Omniscient wisdom has arisen within me.

He composed the *Instructions on Bodhichitta Written in Pure Gold on Stone*[7] and became the compiler.

King Dhahena Talo, the elder Prince Rajahasti, Princess Parani, Naga King Takshaka, Yakshini Changchubma, Kukkuraja[8] the Elder, and others all met Prahevajra in person, received his teachings, and were part of his close circle of disciples. Up to and including the nirmanakaya Prahevajra, this is the lineage of transmission through the minds of the conquerors.

 This was the fourth chapter of the Great Image, *about the appearance of the doctrine in the human realm.*

5

The History of the Effortless Ati Doctrine Flourishing in India

The History of the General Lineage

King Helu Bhadhe and his wife, the Brahmini Effortful, had a son, King Dhahena Talo, who was a direct disciple of the nirmanakaya Prahe from whom he had received the transmission of mind essence. Dhahena Talo also requested Manjushrimitra for the complete transmission. This is when Manjushrimitra condensed the meaning for Dhahena Talo in a song:

> Enlightened mind is the five major elements:
> Not manifest and all pervasive, it is space.
> Wisdom earth produces buddhahood in the mind.
> Wisdom water washes away habitual tendencies.
> Wisdom fire burns up dualistic fixations;
> Wisdom wind carries you to the unshakable state.
> The nature of mind itself also appears as the five elements;
> When you clearly realize their source as being no different
>   from mind,

Rest in the uncontrived training of self-manifesting and
    self-subsiding.

Thus he sang. Then King Dhahena Talo perfectly understood what this
meant and expressed his own realization as follows:

I am Dhahena Talo,
Whose mind is like the expanse of space.
The expanse of space has neither center nor limit,
And enlightened mind has neither center nor limit.
To remain undistracted within that nature
Without limit or center is meditation.

Thus he sang. He realized the essential truth and gained mastery over
longevity.

King Dhahena Talo and his wife Queen Victorious Effort had a son, the
elder prince Rajahasti, who received the transmission of mind essence
from the nirmanakaya Prahevajra and who also requested it from his father, King Dhahena Talo. Dhahena Talo summarized the essential meaning for his son, the elder Rajahasti, in a song:

Enlightened mind is the buddhas of the three times:
From there the past buddhas came,
There the present buddhas abide,
And there the future buddhas will be awakened.
The intent of the buddhas of the three times is your own
    mind.

Thus he sang. The elder Prince Rajahasti understood perfectly what
this meant and expressed his own realization as follows:

I am the elder Prince Rajahasti;
Having realized enlightened mind to be nonarising self-
    knowing,
I hold the lineage of Samantabhadra and Vajrasattva.
Without progressing in the three stages I instantly reached
    buddhahood;
My mind is equal to the buddhas of the three times.

Thus he sang. Princess Parani had received transmission of the mind essence from the nirmanakaya Prahevajra and also requested it from her elder brother Rajahasti. The elder Rajahasti summarized the essential meaning for her in a song:

> As mind is without aggregates, it doesn't grow or decay;
> As mind is without birth or death, it can't be wounded or
>   killed;
> As everything is contained in mind, mind itself is dharmakaya:
> Realizing this is the wisdom of the buddhas.

Thus he sang. Princess Parani understood perfectly what this meant and expressed her own realization as follows:

> I am Princess Parani,
> For whom enlightened mind does not arise or cease.
> Once you realize that mind is free of arising and ceasing,
> You attain the view of the conquerors of the three times,
> Beyond meeting with or parting from the expanse of
>   realization.

Thus she sang.

Naga King Takshaka, an emanation of a bodhisattva who benefited the nagas,[1] perceived that the wondrous essence of the doctrine, the Great Perfection, had appeared in the human realm. He took birth as the son of the outcaste Apar Dharmu Jnana and his wife Sagara and was called Naga King or Nagaraja Sitrita. He met the nirmanakaya Prahevajra in person and heard his words. He received the maturing empowerment from the elder Prince Rajahasti and requested Princess Parani for the essence of the teachings. The princess summarized the essential meaning for Naga King thus:

> Don't block the six sense fields, enjoy them at ease and
>   with joy,
> So that whatever you enjoy enhances enlightenment.
> Confident in mastering this king of awareness,
> The training is to let the six senses remain free.

Thus she sang.

Naga King understood perfectly what this meant and expressed his own realization as follows:

> I am Naga King Nanda,
> For whom the unrejected emotions are the five great
>   wisdoms.
> Not giving up the three poisons, I perfect them as body,
>   speech, and mind.
> Not indulging in samsara, it is the great bliss path of
>   enlightenment.
> The realization of the buddhas of the three times has
>   arisen in me!

Thus he sang.

The daughter of King World Guard, Yakshini Changchubma, who was qualified, intelligent, and very devoted, requested Naga King Nanda for the essence of the teachings. He fully bestowed it and summarized the essential meaning in a song:

> Enlightened mind is the never-waning banner of victory.
> Unchanging throughout the three times, it is a swastika;
> It is the standard of triumph over the battle with samsara:
> To understand this is the king of realization.

Thus he sang. Yakshini Changchubma understood perfectly what this meant and expressed her own realization as follows:

> I am Yakshini Changchubma,
> Whose mind is awakened from the beginning,
> The great self-existing bhagavan.
> Samsara has always been utterly pure;
> Realizing the nature of mind I found the intent of the Buddha!

Thus she sang. A man of low caste called Rahuta and his wife, Joyful Dhari, had a daughter called Barani, who was a prostitute. She was very clever and intelligent and definitely the Mahayana type. She requested the essence of the teachings from Yakshini Changchubma, who gave it and summarized the essential meaning in a song:

Buddhas and sentient beings are inseparable from the
    beginning;
That is the essential point to understand.
Once you fully realize your nondual mind as dharmakaya,
There is nothing else to train in.

Thus she sang. The prostitute understood perfectly what this meant
and expressed her own realization as follows:

I, the prostitute Barani,
Have realized the king of views, enlightened mind.
As mind is neither male nor female, union does not intimi-
    date me.
Mind is without birth or death; it won't die through killing.
Since all phenomenal appearance is nectar, nothing is clean
    or unclean from the beginning.

Thus she sang. The son of the Kashmiri king Bhibhi Rahula and his
wife, Shila Kumara, the Kashmiri abbot called Rabnang, a pandita who
had reached the highest degree in learning, requested the essence of the
teachings from the prostitute Barani. She bestowed it in full and summarized the essential meaning in a song:

The result of enlightened mind does not depend on a cause.
The instruction of enlightened mind does not depend on
    the statements.
The awakening of enlightened mind does not depend on
    mind.
Nonapparent and causeless, enlightened mind is like space;
Devoid of color, it has no reference point.

Thus she sang. Rabnang understood perfectly what this meant and
expressed his own realization as follows:

I, the abbot Rabnang,
Have realized the self-existing, naturally calm great
    dharmakaya.

> All phenomenal existence occurs from the nature of this
>   great being.
> However it occurs, mind does not diminish or increase.

Thus he sang. In the country of Oddiyana, Shri Raja and his wife, Renowned, had a son called Maharaja, who was a scholar in Oddiyana. He was learned in the five sciences and became a great pandita in the Topknot area in Oddiyana. He was interested in the essential truth and requested it from the Kashmiri abbot Rabnang, who transmitted it in full and summarized the meaning in a song:

> The nature of mind is awakened from the very beginning;
> There is nothing else to do but get used to it.
> This training can't be understood through reason.
> Not to be distracted from the nature of mind, that is
>   meditation.

Thus he sang. The abbot of Oddiyana, Maharaja, understood perfectly what this meant and expressed his own realization as follows:

> I am Maharaja,
> Who meditated on mind and transcended the meditation
>   object.
> Watching the mind, there is nothing to see,
> But seeing that there is nothing to see is the real seeing.
> To be undistracted from this nature of non-seeing is
>   meditation.

Thus he sang. At that time there was a princess called Gomadevi, who was qualified and very inspired by the essential truth. She requested transmission of the essential meaning from the Oddiyana scholar Maharaja, who bestowed it in full and summarized the meaning in a song:

> The nature of the single sphere is indivisible from the
>   three times;
> In that nature of self-liberation, there is no path to be
>   traveled.

The nature of things is free from the limitations of words
and can't be engaged in;
Realizing the unlimited, there is no other object of
meditation.

Thus he sang. Princess Gomadevi understood perfectly what this
meant and expressed her own realization as follows:

I am Gomadevi,
For whom the five elements are the five families of
consorts
And the aggregates the five buddha families.
The constituents and sense bases are the male and female
bodhisattvas,
The all-ground is Samantabhadri,
And mind is Samantabhadra.
Nondual union of these buddhas with their consorts is the
accomplishment.

Thus she sang. It was then that the Rishi[2] Paratsa and his wife, En-
chanting Maiden, had a son called Atsantra Aloke, who became a master
in the teachings based on cause and effect. He was extremely inspired by
the essential truth and requested the essence of the teachings from
Princess Gomadevi. She bestowed it in full and summarized the meaning
in a song:

Hoping for *bhumis* and liberation postpones enlightenment;
Hoping to attain bliss is great suffering;
Hoping for nonthought is itself a thought:
When you realize this, give up seeking.

Thus she sang. Atsantra Aloke understood perfectly what this meant
and expressed his own realization as follows:

I, Atsantra Aloke,
Skilled in the means of liberation, have cut the flow
of arising;

Skilled in the means of union, have removed the limit
   of cessation;
Skilled in the means of activities, have achieved effort-
   lessness;
Skilled in the means of accomplishment, don't depend
   on others.
Skilled in the means of meditation, I rest in the uncontrived state.

Thus he sang. At that time Kukkuraja Gatu and his wife, Chandra
Rahu, had a son called Kukkuraja the Elder, who was a monk skilled in
the five sciences. He was especially learned in the Eighteen Maha Yoga
Tantras of the Secret Mantra and inspired by the essential truth. He requested transmission from Atsantra Aloke, who bestowed it in full and
summarized the meaning in a song:

Understanding through the dualism of mind and object is
   thought.
Realizing that these two are nondual is original wakefulness.
Comprehending freedom of origin and function is
   meditation.
Perceiving without clinging is the view of self-liberation.

Thus he sang. Then Kukkuraja resolved that his mind and all appearances were self-liberated; he understood the nature of the view and expressed his own realization as follows:

I am Kukkuraja,
Whose mind is Vajrasattva, free of birth and death.
Vajrasattva's form pervades everything;
Even the metaphor of the sky is inadequate.
To be undistracted in the realization of that nature is
   meditation.

Thus he sang. Rishi Bhashita, the son of Rishi Kumara and his wife,
Dhari, possessed the seven branches of the Vedas, and in order to perfect

the strength of original wakefulness he was interested in the essential truth. He requested the essence of the teachings from Kukkuraja, King of Dogs, who bestowed it in full and summarized the meaning in a song:

> Enlightened mind is without arising and ceasing,
> Appearing while having no self-nature.
> Enlightened mind cannot be cultivated;
> Yoga is to rest at ease in that free state.

Thus he sang. Rishi Bhashita then realized his mind without any effort; he understood the essential truth and expressed his own realization as follows:

> I, Rishi Bhashita,
> Have perfected the five elements within the expanse of
>   space.
> The summit of the vehicles is complete within Ati Yoga;
> The source of the buddhas of the three times is complete
>   within enlightened mind.
> Realizing enlightened mind is the awakening of the Great
>   Perfection;
> Free of seeking and trying, mind itself is the Buddha.
> This mind, without limit or center, is the great
>   immensity.
> This mind, beyond arising and ceasing, is total
>   accomplishment.
> There is no nature in which to train apart from this.

Thus he sang. Because all phenomena abide within the profound secret center of the consort, the prostitute Dagnyima[3] was inspired by the essential truth. She requested the essence of the teachings from Rishi Bhashita, who bestowed it in full and summarized the meaning in a song:

> When there is no mental activity,
> The greatest wisdom is realized.
> When there is no clinging to anything,
> That is the sign of having mastered meditation.

Thus he sang. Then the nun Dagnyima understood the essential truth and expressed her own realization as follows:

> I am the prostitute Dagnyima,
> For whom the five elements are the space of the five
>   buddha consorts.
> That itself is the expanse of Samantabhadri.
> I realize the ground of all, Samantabhadri,
> To be inseparable from the secret center.
> Enlightened mind is like the sun shining in the sky;
> Realizing mind essence is the greatest meditation.

Thus she sang. At that time the monk Nagarjuna, an expert in the five sciences who fully understood the meaning of the Tripitaka and knew a great deal about the Secret Mantra teachings based on the result, was in search of the meaning of the effortless Great Perfection. He met the nun Dagnyima and requested the essential truth. She bestowed it in full and summarized the meaning in a song:

> While reflecting, even realizing emptiness is deception.
> While clinging, even attachment to the deity fetters.
> While thinking, even understanding dharmakaya is
>   thought.
> While meditating, even cultivating nonthought is a
>   concept.

Thus she sang. Nagarjuna understood perfectly what this meant and expressed his own realization as follows:

> I, Nagarjuna,
> Am at ease because unborn dharmakaya is free of
>   aggregates.
> I am at ease because unspoken unceasing speech is free of
>   attributes.
> I am at ease because mindless wisdom mind is free of birth
>   and death.
> I have realized enlightened mind as great bliss.

Thus he sang. At that time Gyuhe Nagatama and his wife, Pure Mahina, had a son called Kukkuraja the Younger, who was very devoted and extremely intelligent. He became an abbot who knew all the teachings on cause and effect without exception and was interested in the essential truth. He requested the essence of the teachings from Nagarjuna, who bestowed it in full and summarized the meaning in a song:

> To be devoid of subject and object is emptiness.
> To be free of names and designations is realization.
> If there is no clinging to this, it is emptiness.
> Remaining in this state is the training in emptiness.

Thus he sang. Kukkuraja the Younger understood perfectly what this meant and expressed his own realization as follows:

> I, the abbot Dhahuna,
> Have realized the five aggregates and the five elements
> As male and female deities, the buddha families and their
>   consorts.
> Their nonduality is the all-ground of enlightened mind;
> The purity of all that appears and exists is the mandala of
>   the conquerors.

Thus he sang. Rishi Lahina and his wife, Highest Grace, had a son called Manjushrimitra the Younger, who was learned in the vehicles based on cause and effect and interested in the essential truth. He requested the essence of the teachings from Kukkuraja the Younger, who bestowed it in full and summarized the meaning in a song:

> Though it is called mind, it is beyond all concepts of names.
> Though illustrating mind with examples, it is beyond
>   analogy.
> It is nondual, inconceivable, and free of observed object.
> To be undistracted in the expanse of realization, without
>   reference point, is meditation.

Thus he sang. Manjushri understood perfectly what this meant and expressed his own realization as follows:

I, Manjushri Bhadra,
Continuing the training in the tantras of the two sciences,
Have accomplished my aim, cutting mind at its root.
At this very moment the fruition of perfect enlightenment
Is simply my own nature, totally beyond mind.

Thus he sang. Rishi Bhahi and his wife, Bhagula Royal Ocean, had a son called Devaraja, who was very qualified and highly intelligent. In search of the essential truth he met Manjushri Bhadra, from whom he requested the essence of the teachings. Manjushri Bhadra bestowed it in full and summarized the meaning in a song:

The extent of space is beyond center and extreme,
But even this example can't point out enlightened mind.
When you realize enlightened mind, which can't be
    defined,
Resting in that effortless state is meditation.

Thus he sang. Devaraja understood perfectly what this meant and expressed his own realization as follows:

I, Devaraja,
Have put this instruction on great bliss that derives from
    the scriptures
In the depth of my mind; it won't leave my mouth.
By realizing the perfectly free view of Ati Yoga,
I have attained the unchanging dharmakaya.

Thus he sang. At that time there was a monk called Buddhagupta, learned in the five sciences and expert in the meaning of Maha Yoga of the Secret Mantra, who was in search of the essential truth. He met Devaraja and requested the essence of the teachings from him. Devaraja bestowed it in full and summarized the meaning in a song:

The indivisibility of mind itself is the great eternity.
Since awareness manifests within mind, it is the supreme
    presence itself.
Since mind is free of samsara, it is the supreme nectar.

Since mind is beyond center and extreme, it is the great
    mandala.

Thus he sang. Then Buddhagupta understood perfectly what this meant
and expressed his own realization as follows:

I am Buddhagupta,
Whose mind is primordial great bliss.
Hidden from all the ignorant, it is totally secret.
To realize effortless enlightenment is the greatest training;
Beyond meditation and nonmeditation, it is the awakened
    state.

Thus he sang. At that time King Hetu and his wife, Nantaka, had a son
called Shri Singha Prabha, who had studied with five hundred panditas.
He was a great monk, learned in the five sciences and interested in the essential truth. He requested the essence of the teachings from Buddhagupta, who bestowed it in full and summarized the meaning in a song:

This nature of mind does not manifest
But is always present in apparent phenomena.
Once you discover the root of this unchanging mind,
Enlightenment is not accomplished elsewhere.

Thus he sang. Then Shri Singha understood perfectly what this meant
and expressed his own realization as follows:

I am Shri Singha,
Whose enlightened mind is beyond conceptual
    extremes.
Not perceived directly, it pervades all that appears and
    exists.
This self-cognizing wakefulness, free of limitations,
Can't really be pointed out, even by Vajrasattva.

Thus he sang. At that time Chamka and his wife, the prostitute Patu,
had a daughter who was a nun called Kungamo. She was learned in the
five sciences and felt inspired by the essential truth. Determined to find it,

she met Shri Singha and requested the essence of the teachings from him. He bestowed it in full and summarized the meaning in a song:

> Remain with the same attitude
> As someone who has abandoned an activity.
> When this is endowed with the strength of presence,
> It is definitely the buddha mind.

Thus he sang. Then nun Kungamo understood perfectly what this meant and expressed her own realization as follows:

> I am the nun Kungamo.
> Just as a great river
> Includes all smaller streams,
> The teachings of the nine gradual vehicles
> Are included within the Great Perfection.

Thus she sang. At that time, King Dhahena Chadu and his wife, Singha Shipitika, had a son called Vimalamitra, who was a monk skilled in the five sciences. He was inspired by the essential truth, met Shri Singha, and requested the essence of the teachings from him. Shri Singha gave him the complete transmission and summarized the meaning in a song:

> When not rejected the five poisons are the five great
>   wisdoms.
> When not renounced samsara is primordially pure.
> When you understand the fact that the Buddha is your own
>   mind,
> There is no enlightened mind other than that very
>   realization.

Thus he sang. Hearing this Vimalamitra understood the essential truth and expressed his own realization as follows:

> The innate nature, being inconceivable, is great space.
> The space of mind itself is free of all thought.
> Within the inconceivable enlightened mind
> The innate nature is not found through meditation.

Even without meditating it is primordially empty and
  never apart.
Meditating means abiding in the nature of nonthinking
  equality.

Thus he sang.

These stories relate the general history of the lineage masters.

Songs about the Meaning of Realization That Were Composed by the Lineage Masters

At midnight, after he attained complete realization, King Dhahena Talo, whose secret name was Powerful Treasure King, sang a vajra song of realization in the sandalwood forest:

> HUNG!
> The unchanging dharmakaya
> Is the unaltered all-ground, enlightened mind,
> Beyond the battle of dualistic thought.
> The nature of mind is like space;
> Resting without thought, undistracted and uncontrived,
> It is the dharmadhatu, which cannot be cultivated.
> I understand that there is not even an atom to meditate on.
> I, Dhahena Talo, whose pride is shattered,
> Have dissolved the idea that mind and phenomena are
>   separate.
> Destroying the self of my illusory aggregates,
> The light of Samantabhadra's mind has arisen in me.

Thus he spoke. Before midnight, after having attained complete realization, the elder Prince Rajahasti, whose secret name was Vajra Treasure Heir, sang a song at the sandalwood cottage:

> HUNG!
> The unaltered all-ground, the vast expanse as it is,
> The state of self-existing wakefulness equal to space,
> Is Samantabhadra, beyond word and sound;

It is the thought-free all-ground, enlightened mind.
The innate nature of enlightened mind is unchanging.
I understand that there is no meditation apart from this.
Since my illusory aggregates are thus destroyed,
The light of Samantabhadra's mind has arisen in me.

Thus he spoke. After having attained complete realization, Princess Parani, whose secret name was Vajra Elbow Treasure, sang this song at the night lily grove:

HUNG!
The all-ground, primordial nondual enlightened mind,
Unaffected by cause or condition, fearless,
Is the self-existing spontaneously present bhagavan,
The heart of Vajrasattva, beyond subject and object.
Not modified or adulterated, it is the wisdom of Vajrasattva.
I see no other realization but that.
As my illusory aggregates are thus smashed,
Samantabhadra's great mind treasure has been transmitted.

Thus she spoke. After attaining complete realization, Naga King, whose secret name was Secret Vajra Treasure, sang this song at the break of dawn on an island in the ocean:

HUNG!
The spacelike mind, beyond center and edge,
Is the dharmakaya, beyond speech and thought.
All apparent phenomena and living beings are primordially
    pure;
The highest path to liberation is nowhere else.
This is the realization of the tathagatas of the three times;
I have understood that there is nothing else to look for.
Now that my lowly physical body has been shattered,
I have reached the state that is not separate from the three
    kayas.

Thus he spoke. After attaining complete realization, Kukkuraja, King of Dogs, whose secret name was Supreme Vajra Mind Treasure, sang this song at the second stage of dawn on the island in the ocean:

HUNG!

The primordial spontaneous presence of Samantabhadra
Is enlightened mind, cognizant, thought-free, and un-
    constructed.
While resting awareness in unchanging and untainted
    evenness
Within the immutable nonconceptual dharmadhatu,
Without practicing or thinking about anything,
I understand that the training is merely to be
    undistracted
Within this unchanging all-ground, the great bliss
    dharmadhatu.
To be free of hope and fear is enlightenment.

Thus he spoke. At the last stage of dawn, after attaining complete realization, Nagarjuna, whose secret name was United River Treasure of the
Powerful Vajra, sang this song in the sacred place called Decorated Radiant Arm:

HUNG!

Striking the primordial great expanse of all phenomena
With the dagger of unchanging awareness,
Untainted by thought, without changing the expanse,
Not meditating on anything, pure as the sky,
Totally clear and unaltered: that is meditation.
I understand that there is no other training.
Supported by my physical body,
I reached the state that is inseparable from
    Samantabhadra.

Thus he spoke. After attaining complete realization, Kukkuraja the
Younger, whose secret name was Treasure of Full Attainment, sang this
song at the first break of dawn on the island in the ocean:

HUNG!

Enlightened mind is the five elements.
Uncontrived and naturally cognizant, it is pure like the sky.
Burning the dualistic fixation of beings, it is like fire.

Moving without focus, it appears like the wind.
Purifying the stains of subject and object, it is pure like
water.
Not disturbed by anything, it is like the earth.
The self-existing enlightened mind includes the great
elements.
I understand that other than this there is not even an atom
in which to train.
Once I released my ignorant thoughts,
I reached the state of great bliss without effort.

Thus he spoke. After attaining complete realization, Yakshini Chang-chubma, whose secret name was Flaming Goddess Treasure, sang this song at the second break of dawn on the island in the ocean:

HUNG!
Seeing enlightened mind, the dharmadhatu,
The watching mind appears totally clear,
Neither tainted nor altered by anything.
Having realized the nature of uncontrived enlightened
mind,
I am free of both watching and what is to be watched.
I understand that the training is nothing but that.
Once I liberated my clinging thoughts and tendencies,
I found the self-existing, spontaneously present view
without effort.

Thus she spoke. After attaining complete realization, the prostitute Dagnyima, whose secret name was Unobstructed Spontaneous Vajra Treasure, sang this song at the *nadrola* tree near Chila during the third stage of the red break of dawn:

HUNG!
The innate nature, enlightened mind, can't be shown.
Apart from mind, buddhahood can't be found.
The nature of mind is primordially awakened.
I understand that the wisdom of the buddhas is nothing but
The uncultivated self-existing heart of awakening,

Which is naturally evident without training in *samadhi*.
Spontaneously untying the knots of the aggregates, the
    thoughts,
The essential sun of nondual great bliss has risen.

Thus she spoke. After attaining complete realization, the later Manjushrimitra, whose secret name was Delighted Vajra Treasure, sang this
song in the evening, standing by the root of the banyan tree:

HUNG!
In the open innate nature, the all-ground,
The sun of wisdom has risen for me.
Once it shines, there is no rising or setting;
Enlightenment is not found anywhere else.
I understand that the wisdom of the buddhas
Is that itself, with nothing to contrive.
I have tasted the nectar of enlightened mind;
That taste is the vajra wisdom.

Thus he spoke. In the early morning, after attaining complete realization, Atsantra Aloke, whose secret name was Immutable Vajra Treasure,
sang this song at the root of the wish-fulfilling tree:

HUNG!
Enlightened mind is the unborn expanse of space,
Free of origin and cessation, naturally pure.
Once the sun of realizing nondual self-awareness dawns,
This is seen clearly, free of outside or inside, center or edge.
My realization is equal to the buddhas of the three times;
I understand that there is nothing apart from this.
Since this unconditioned state is swift, it is the unborn
    dharmakaya, the mind's nectar
That removes the chronic illness of samsara.

Thus he spoke. After midnight, when he had attained complete realization, the abbot Maharaja from Oddiyana, whose secret name was Vajra
Sadhu Siddhi Treasure, sang this song on the Jewel Island:

HUNG!
As mind itself is fully awakened,
There is no enlightenment other than mind.
Realizing that mind essence is primordially awakened,
I attained an unchanging vajra confidence.
I understand that the view of the buddhas of the three
    times
Is simply that.
In the great space of the innate nature
Soars the *garuda* of this yogi's awareness.

Thus he spoke. After attaining complete realization, Rishi Bhashita, whose secret name was Joyful Most Supreme Vajra Treasure, sang this song in the late evening at the Banyan Monastery:

HUNG!
All the planets and stars that move through the sky
Cannot disturb primordially pure space.
Whatever thoughts appear in enlightened mind,
They don't change the pure expanse of mind essence.
Now that the wisdom sun of this realization has risen,
I understand that my mind is the same as the buddhas'.
Realizing that, the great wind of awareness wisdom
Sweeps subtle thoughts into the nondual expanse.

Thus he spoke. After fully attaining perfect realization, Princess Gomadevi, whose secret name was Secret Vajra Treasure, sang this song:

HUNG!
The wisdom of the buddhas of the three times is the
    syllable A.
The nature of the syllable A is without substance from the
    beginning.
The source of all the tathagatas is the syllable A.
The main quality of the syllable A is primordially
    enlightened mind.
I understand that mind essence is nothing other than

Resting the unborn, nonconceptual, and self-existing
　　syllable A
In uncontrived and undistracted evenness.
Unborn enlightenment is awakened from the very
　　beginning.

Thus she spoke. After attaining complete realization, the Kashmiri Rabnang, whose secret name was Self-Existing Vajra Treasure, sang this song at the root of the sandalwood tree:

HUNG!
Enlightened mind is the primordial dharmakaya;
Without focus, pure as space, it is present everywhere.
All appearance without exception is total emptiness;
The nature of that emptiness is all appearance.
Once one has realized that appearance and emptiness are
　　inseparable,
The training is to be undistracted, never apart from
　　emptiness.
Through the nectar of the innate nature, enlightened mind,
The illness of the three worlds of samsara is cured and
　　purified.

Thus he spoke. In the evening, after attaining complete realization, Devaraja, whose secret name was Most Perfect Vajra Treasure, sang this song in the city called Glorious Qualities:

HUNG!
When one has realized apparent existence as dharmakaya,
　　enlightened mind,
The whole phenomenal world is Samantabhadra from the
　　beginning.
In this true nature there is nothing to be cultivated;
Totally pure perception is the nectar of body, speech, and
　　mind.
To rest undistracted in the realization of this nonarising
　　nature
Is beyond the limits of meditating and not meditating.

When one becomes accustomed to this unsurpassed intrinsic reality,
The unborn truth is realized, dawning as great wisdom
  within space.

Thus he spoke. After attaining complete realization, Buddhagupta,
whose secret name was Supreme Speech Siddha Vajra Treasure, sang this
song in a blissful sacred place:

HUNG!
The uncontrived nature of phenomena, enlightened mind,
Unaltered, is primordially Samantabhadra.
Having realized unchanging, self-existing, enlightened
  mind,
Through this self-occurring, unchanging, self-display,
I understand that while thoughts spontaneously occur and
  subside,
The training is not to rely on a remedy.
There is nothing that doesn't become nondual en-
  lightenment:
That is what is called awakening; it need not be sought.

Thus he spoke. After attaining complete realization, Shri Singha, whose
secret name was Sublime Vajra Heart Treasure, sang this song in his hermitage during the *ganachakra*:[4]

HUNG!
However it is conceived, it can't be cultivated.
However it is expressed, it can't be indulged in.
Within the expanse of great wisdom,
Luminosity without cause or conditions,
To rest undistracted in the evenness
Of nondual original wakefulness, free of concepts:
I understand that there is no realization other than this.
It is the most sublime yoga.

These are the songs spoken by the lineage masters. The general history of the
lineage masters ends here.

. . .

The special lineage consists of three successions: The first one is the treasury of Prahevajra, the middle one is that of Manjushrimitra, and the last one is that of Shri Singha. Vairotsana also has a lineage. There is also a lineage that descends from the nirmanakaya Prahevajra to Manjushrimitra, who transmitted it to seven of his disciples, such as King Dhahena Talo and so forth. Shri Singha received the transmission from all of these seven disciples and transmitted it to Vairotsana. There is no definite sequence in the lineage masters; each specific transmission of the lineage has its own manner of transmission. Among the teachings of these lineages, the most outstanding are the Distinguishing Brahmin's Cycle, the Resolving King's Cycle, and the Cycle of Instructions Directly Showing Self-liberation.[5] The explanation of the specific cycle of teachings from the mind lineage of the conquerors up to and including Prahevajra has been given earlier in this text.

The Lineage through the Awareness of the Vidyadharas

As to the lineage of transmission through the awareness of the vidyadharas: To the west of India lies the land of Oddiyana. There, in the region of Dhanakosha, was a lake called Kutra. On the bank of that lake was a charnel ground called Golden Sanctuary of Expanding Delight. Near there was a cave called the Place of the Vajra, a spontaneously accomplished dwelling that had miraculously occurred. It was there that the nirmanakaya called Prahevajra lived and proclaimed the self-existing effortless doctrine.

At that time there was a Brahmin called Sukhapala, who had a son called Brahmin Sarasiddhi. Sarasiddhi was a monk learned in the five sciences with a deep understanding of all the teachings based on cause and effect. He was an emanation of Manjushri. In a vision the noble Manjushri told him:

> If you, poor man, want to find your own treasure,
> Get the key from the reincarnated heart son
> At the Place of the Vajra Cave
> And enjoy your own treasure.

Thus he prophesied. Then Sarasiddhi became interested in the essential truth and with great joy and sincerity he set off, paying homage and praying to the nirmanakaya Prahevajra. When he arrived at the upper and lower cemeteries in the land of the dakinis, Tsamunshri, Tsamuntri, and Namdruma[6] spoke to him, saying:

> Can you ride on the course of a river?
> Are you happy wielding weapons to pierce the meaning?
> Do you observe the miraculous mirror?
> Shall I fetch the precious gem?

Thus, as the three of them showed indications and blessed him, he immediately arrived at the Place of the Vajra Cave. He made offerings of various precious things, and doing prostrations and circumambulations, he prayed and requested the essential truth.

First, from the cycle of the Mind Class,[7] Prahe bestowed the eight root tantras and the branch tantras with the detailed empowerments and pith instructions. From the cycle of the Space Class,[8] he gave the outer cycle of the Spoked Seal, the inner cycle of the Secret Seal, and the secret cycle of the Small Seal. From the entrustment cycle of the Instruction Class,[9] he gave the tantras and pith instructions of the Concentration of Mind cycle. He also conferred the complete transmission of infinite other Ati Yoga tantras and pith instructions.

Sarasiddhi, however, wasn't satisfied with this; with prostrations and circumambulations, he offered flowers of precious materials and requested:

> EMAHO! Matchless bodhisattva,
> You have bestowed the empowerments to install me as
>   regent.
> You have handed this poor man his own treasure.
> As you truly revealed it, I received it with devotion.
> If you confer the empowerments and the entrustment,
> Moistened with bodhi water by drinking the heart essence,
> The realization of the three kayas,
> Through the power of my fervent prayers, the sprout will
>   mature.

As mind follows pleasant and unpleasant things,
Would you like to tell this to other similar beings?

Thus he sang in a melodious voice. Then Prahevajra gave him the empowerment of direct anointment, and after clearly pointing out self-liberation, he gave him the outer name of Manjushrimitra. Internally, for initiation times, Prahevajra gave him the secret name Vajra Strength of Bliss and Clarity. Then he gave the five root tantras such as *Perfection of Wisdom*, which mainly explains the natural state; *Precious Embodiment of Light Tantra*; the twenty-five branch tantras, including the *Tantra of the Ninefold Expanse*; the entrustment of the precious treasure revealing the mind essence of the nirmanakaya Prahevajra; the eighteen minor sections of the victorious ones such as *Ninefold Expanse* and so forth; and the seven streams of empowerment including the empowerment of direct anointment. He then bestowed the secret empowerment and the empowerment to protect the effortless doctrine through the three mamos.[10] At that time Prahe put him in charge:

> Giving up words and summarizing the meaning,
> I entrust the blessings of Manjushri to my son.
> When you reveal the self-liberating pith instructions,
> Vajrasattva, Great Space,
> To other fortunate ones with the same nature,
> Sealing everything free of direction,
> Thought fabrication will be cut by the essence.
> Thus elucidate the five greatnesses and
> Hand over the great treasure. Guard this perfect gift!

Thus Prahe spoke, entrusting him with the three seals. It was then that Manjushrimitra was clearly introduced to self-liberation through the empowerment of direct anointment. After receiving the essence of self-existing nectar, he found the precious treasure of his own mind. Having perfected all the teachings in his mind, he expressed his realization and his gratitude for the nirmanakaya's kindness:

> Since beginningless time
> I have been without my own treasure, the wish-fulfilling
>   gem.

Now that my supreme teacher has shown it to me,
My poverty is over. I am happy! Thank you!

Thus he spoke. Near the Place of the Vajra Cave in the Dhanakosha region of Oddiyana was a forest with many fine trees, a naturally auspicious
place where many yakshas gathered. There, in a golden cave called Lifetree,
a sacred place where the Lord of Secrets, Vajrapani, and the nirmanakaya
Prahevajra had visited and where infinite dakinis gather, Manjushrimitra
gave the teachings to an eighty-year-old dakini, who then attained the ultimate state of effortless great bliss.

At that time, in the Heaven of the Thirty-three there was a divine king
who could heal by means of medicinal nectar. He had attained the
vidyadhara level of life-mastery and gained control over the enjoyment of
divine merit. Through his higher perception he knew that the effortless
Ati Yoga, the essential true nature, was in the human realm. He went to
the human realm and took birth in the Shakya family as the son of someone called Dharmashri. He became a human boy complete with all the divine characteristics, so they called him Prince Devaputra. When he went
to search for the essential true nature, the self-existing effortless Great
Perfection, looking with his divine eyes, he heard that Master Manjushrimitra, who had been matured by the nirmanakaya Prahe, was staying in the golden cave called Lifetree. He went there and met both the
nirmanakaya Prahevajra and Manjushrimitra. Prahe blessed him and predicted: "You have a connection with Manjushrimitra. Receive the essential truth from him."

At that time, Master Manjushrimitra had manifested as a young boy
with knotted hair, and Devaputra offered him many divine jewels. After
doing prostrations and circumambulations for three days, he requested:

In the Heaven of the Thirty-three,
I was healed with medicinal nectar
But didn't achieve the essential truth.
Accept me with the sunlight lasso of your kindness!

Thus he prayed. First, Manjushrimitra gave him many general teachings on the effortless Ati Yoga doctrine; but this didn't satisfy Devaputra,
who again pleaded, "I want something to directly attain effortless enlightenment right now!"

Then Manjushrimitra gave him the empowerment of direct anointment, clearly pointed out self-liberation, and entrusted him with his own
treasure, the true mind essence. He gave him the outer name Dharma King
and the inner name Powerful Vajra Treasure for initiation times. He conferred all the tantras, empowerments, and instructions and entrusted him
with the three seals:

> Through the pith instructions you requested,
> You fortunate stained one,
> Endeavor to wash yourself clean
> With the pure water of the uncontrived natural state.
> Rest your craving mind as it is, in its innate nature!

Then Dharma King of Nectar directly realized self-liberation and found
the treasure of his own mind. He received the true mind essence and attained the effortless state of great bliss. To express his gratitude, the divine
king offered his realization:

> I took pains to search for the effortless
> But didn't find that effortless state anywhere else;
> The effortful craving mind itself is free of effort.
> EMAHO! Thank you for this self-liberation!

Thus he offered his thanks. Then Dharma King of Nectar remained for
eighty-seven years in the Jewel Chest Pavilion, an extremely auspicious
place blessed by dakinis who naturally gather there; there he accomplished the effortless nature of great bliss.

Deep in the ocean, at a place adorned with wish-fulfilling gems, lived
the naga king known as Nanda, an emanation of a bodhisattva who acted
for the welfare of the nagas. Through his higher perception he saw that the
effortless Great Perfection, Ati Yoga, was in the human realm. He was very
pleased and took birth as the son of the low caste Yawadha Jnana and his
wife, Ocean Goddess. Due to karma from his former lives, he was born in
the form of a five-headed snake, so his parents were terrified. They
brought him to the charnel ground, where the putras predicted: "This is
an incarnation who cares for the essential truth. Due to a karmic connection you are his parents; therefore, you should raise him."

His parents believed this, so they took him back and raised him, calling him Nagaraja Samtra. He grew to be quite a tall child, matured extremely fast, and was very intelligent. Searching for the true essential nature, he met King Hasti, from whom he received the maturing empowerment and became a suitable recipient. Princess Parani gave him many teachings from the Mind Class, including the *Great Space Tantra*, but he was not yet satisfied. He knew that the nirmanakaya Prahevajra and Manjushrimitra were staying at the Place of the Vajra Cave, so he went there and met both the nirmanakaya Prahe and Manjushrimitra. They blessed him and showed him indications, "In the Jewel Chest Pavilion lives Dharma King of Nectar, with whom you have a connection. Go there and you will realize the essential truth." Thus they predicted.

When he went there, he met Dharma King of Nectar in the Jewel Chest Pavilion and did prostrations and circumambulations. Offering a radiant gem, he requested:

> I took birth as a wicked low caste person and
> Was brought to the charnel ground and adopted by putras.
> Though I have vicious animal karma,
> Caring for a body as a support for the essential truth,
> Through the karmic link with my parents,
> My fortune was not interrupted and I developed aggregates.
> Later, I was raised in auspicious virtue,
> But vicious karma matured me into an animal form.
> Though meritorious karma gave me infinite qualities,
> Lacking the essential meaning, I feel devastated without
>   the core.
> Please bestow the essential truth and hold me with the lasso
>   of your compassion!

Thus he prayed. First, Dharma King gave him many general tantras and pith instructions of the effortless Great Perfection. Then, Nanda prayed again and requested, "Please introduce me directly to the self-liberating essential truth without effort!" Dharma King introduced him with these words:

> Like putting lion's milk in a golden vessel,
> Entrusting the tantras to the noble one, the essence is
>   matured.

When you give up the evil mind, the essential truth,
Which is unseen by looking with the eyes, is realized.

Thus showing verbal indications, Dharma King bestowed the complete empowerment of direct anointment and clearly pointed out self-liberation. On the outer level he gave Nanda the name Blazing Glory of Virtue and on the inner level the secret name Powerful Essence of Qualities. Then the divine king gave Nanda the entire nectar stream of tantras, empowerments, and pith instructions, the supreme wheel of the victorious ones. Entrusting Nanda with the three seals, the divine king encouraged him:

Use the opportunity to reveal the self-liberating instructions
And explain the symbolic meanings through the impartial
    mudra.
This distinguished complex instruction
Is Vajrasattva, Great Space.

Thus he spoke. Then Naga King Blazing Glory directly realized self-liberation, received the quintessence of the true essential meaning, and spontaneously realized the transmission of the instructional teachings. Expressing his realization and gratitude to the divine king, he said:

The most supreme jewel of my mind
Was lost in a swamp of misery.
Though I never abandoned it, I lost it spontaneously.
Thank you for handing me the great treasure
And giving me the secret name Essence of Qualities.

Thus he offered his thanks. Then, on an island in the Ganges River, he meditated for a thousand Khasarpani[11] years on the essence of the self-existing nectar and accomplished it.

Yakshini Changchubma, from the northern side of Mount Meru, was the sister of Yaksha Vajrapani, who lived on the four pinnacles of Mount Meru. She had attained the vidyadhara level by means of Kriya and had become weary of her own powers. She knew that the genuine truth, the Ati Yoga, was in the human realm, and looking there with her clairvoyance, she took birth as the daughter of King World Guard in the human realm. Since this king had no sons, he lied and announced, "A son has been born!"

He appointed two nursemaids to take care of her on the top floor of a nine-storied building and said, "Though I love her very much, she must never be seen!" So, while being brought up, she was kept hidden. When she reached the age of twenty-four Bengali[12] years, she was dressed up in men's clothes to be installed as regent. Speaking in divine verse she predicted:

> I have prayed to abide in the essential nature,
> Yet I have to run the kingdom at the age of twelve.
> Put the son of Yaksha Renowned in charge
> So my prayers can be accomplished!

Then Yakshini called the son of her brother Renowned, who looked like Changchubma, and entrusted him with the kingdom. During his rule he was banished to Tibet because he used to wear strange clothes. And it is known that he improved Tibet.

By means of her perfect concentration, Yakshini Changchubma went to the Topknot area in Oddiyana to request Prahe and Manjushrimitra for the essential truth. When she met them they blessed her and predicted, "Naga King has your treasure; receive it from him." Her patron deity made the same prediction. Then she went to meet Naga King Nanda on the island in the Ganges River, made offerings of various jewels, and did many prostrations and circumambulations. Offering her body adorned with various jeweled ornaments, she requested in verse:

> Due to powerful emotions I obtained a Yakshini body.
> Inspired, through intense effort, I had a vision of the deity,
>   and
> Forced by the strength of my prayers, I came into the pres-
>   ence of my guru.
> Bestow the essential truth and hold me with the hook of
>   your compassion!
> Accept this beautiful body adorned with jewelry!

First, he gave her many general Ati Yoga tantras and pith instructions; finally, he taught her the instructions on the *Great Bliss Sphere* through the three transformations. He gave her the empowerment of direct anoint-ment, clearly pointed out self-liberation, explained it with instructions on the *Condition of Mindfulness,* and gave her the secret name Powerful Vajra Essence for initiations. With the three seals he placed her in charge of all the tantras and pith instructions and encouraged her with these words:

> Your devotion made you a special being.
> Because I gave you the treasure you desired as well as
>   a title,
> We became connected in the search for essential truth.
> Watch the taste of mind with treasure and title!
>
> When you are requested for the perfect transmission
>   endowed with the essence,
> If those to whom you give it realize original wakefulness,
> It is a symbol endowed with wisdom.
> Without cause and condition there is no accomplishment.

Thus he spoke. Then Yakshini directly realized self-liberation, increased the vital essence of self-existing great bliss, and unfolded the effortless essential nature. She expressed her realization and gratitude to her guru with these words:

> EMAHO! Everything is the unmistaken enlightened mind;
> I am tired of altering it through cause and effort.
> The aspired treasure and fame of mind is unmistaken.
> Thank you for showing the gestures and liberating my
>   being!

Thus she offered her thanks. Then, in the cottage called Ratnasiddhi, a blessed and auspicious place like a precious jewel, abundant with all needs and wishes, she meditated for fifty Oddiyana[13] years on the essence of mind and accomplished it.

The above stories were about the lineage through the awareness of the vidyadharas.

The Hearing Lineage through Individuals

Conch, the King of Dogs, had a son, the great monk called Kukkuraja, who was the great King Indrabhuti's court priest. He was an expert in the five sciences and especially learned in the Eighteen Maha Yoga Tantras. In a vision, his patron deity Vajrasattva told him:

> Yakshas are attached to the wealth of the rich;
> Sensuous girls rarely satisfy their lust.
> Therefore, bodhisattva of the three worlds,
> Give up preference for worldly phenomena and receive the
>   essence!

Thus speaking in verse, he predicted that Kukkuraja should receive the true essential nature. Kukkuraja knew that the nirmanakaya Prahevajra was staying at the Place of the Vajra Cave and went there to meet him. When he met both Prahevajra and Manjushrimitra, they blessed him, and Manjushrimitra predicted:

> As for the arrowhead ready to shoot from the bow,
> In the Ratnasiddhi Cottage
> The noble Yakshini Changchubma
> Has pierced the ultimate: Go and receive it!

Thus speaking, he directed Kukkuraja to Yakshini. Kukkuraja went to the Ratnasiddhi Cottage and met Yakshini Changchubma. He did prostrations and circumambulations, and tossing valuable flowers of gold and so forth, he requested:

> KYEHO! Accomplished Lady,
> Can I realize the great nature
> That is revealed by nondual wisdom?
> Yearning for it, I am here before you. Kindly accept me!

Yakshini Changchubma said:

> Within the omniscient state free of all bias,
> Substance and emptiness are inseparable.

Though it is a method for realization, it is unconfined.
Watch the awareness apprehending the absence of duality!

Thus she spoke. First, she gave him the Ati Yoga pith instructions and many general tantras; however, he wasn't satisfied, and making offerings and praying, he entreated her again. Finally, she gave him the complete empowerment of direct anointment, clearly pointed out self-liberation as enlightenment, and gave him the secret name Powerful Sublime Vajra Heart. She completed all the tantras, empowerments, and pith instructions and authorized him with *Stainless Secret Lamp*. Entrusting him with the three seals to guard the teachings, she encouraged him thus:

As to the pith instructions you requested:
Nonduality is not without duality;
Calling it the view is partial fixation.
Not transcending the freshness of natural awareness
Is unfabricated nonduality. Rest at ease in that state.

Then Kukkuraja directly realized self-liberation, the web of his sectarian thoughts collapsed, and he received the vital essence of carefree self-liberation. Expressing the nature of his realization and gratitude to his guru, he spoke:

EMAHO! Glorious hermit lady of great bliss,
Bhagavati, you who blessed me,
Engaging in acts that conform to my type,
You revealed the nature that exceeds great bliss. Thank you!

With these words he offered his thanks. Then he meditated for 105 Bengali years in Ratnasiddhi Cottage and attained accomplishment.

The son of King Hetu known as Shri Singha lived in the country of Singhala. He had studied with five hundred scholars, was an expert in the five sciences, and had received many teachings on the effortless Ati Yoga from Master Manjushrimitra and other saints. Kukkuraja had attained ultimate realization, and in the first half of his life he met King Devaraja, who was searching for the essential truth. He explained some instructions on Ati Yoga to the king; but due to his royal position, King Devaraja couldn't complete the teachings and did not receive the entrustment. In the latter part of his life Kukkuraja met Shri Singha. He saw that Shri Singha was destined and urged him with these words:

> KYEHO! Great practitioner,
> If you want to benefit yourself and others,
> Fetch the gem from the precious island
> So you can ease the poverty of numerous beings.

Thus he encouraged him. Delighted by these words, Shri Singha did prostrations, circumambulations, and requested:

> Great monk, lord of compassion,
> Without request you endeavor in the truth.
> Inspired, I long to serve you.
> Please help me realize the great bliss mind!

Then Kukkuraja manifested the Illuminating Blazing Gem mandala[14] in the middle Dhahena Hall and gave him the complete empowerment of direct anointment. He introduced and clearly pointed out self-liberation and gave Shri Singha the secret name Glorious Supreme Vajra Skill. He authorized him in the tantras and pith instructions like the lustrous essence of the sun, and having given him everything in full, he entrusted him with the three seals. Then the master said:

> As to the pith instructions you requested,
> Look at self-cognizance within. Carefree,
> Leave it as it is, unmistaken and unaltered.
> Not restricting the three doors, relax freely.
> Watch the adorned body!

Thus he spoke. At that, the glorious Shri Singha was directly introduced to self-liberation and attained the ultimate realization of the Ati nature. Fully comprehending the spacelike view, the carefree nature of evenness, he expressed his realization and gratitude to his guru with these words:

> Looking with hope, I became free of duality.
> Training in samadhi, the instructions were clarified.

Though involved in discrimination, I could relax freely.
Thank you for adorning me!

Thus he offered his thanks. Having attained ultimate realization, Shri Singha met all the great masters, such as the nirmanakaya Prahe and the others. His realization became one with theirs, and he requested them to perfect the effortless Ati Yoga doctrine in his mind. Within the realization of evenness, he remained in the Dhahena Talo Hall as master of the Dharma College.

These were stories about the pith instructions pointing out the direct realization of intrinsic freedom.

 This was the fifth chapter of the Great Image, *about the doctrine flourishing in India.*

6

The History of the Appearance of the Effortless Doctrine in Tibet

CONCERNING THE appearance of the effortless doctrine in Tibet: Its history is divided into three parts related to the lives of the kings that were connected with the holy Dharma.

During the life of the bodhisattva Lha Thothori Nyenshel,[1] Buddhism took root. During Songtsen Gampo's[2] life, the tradition was founded, and during Trisong Deutsen's[3] life, it flourished.

The Reign of Lha Thothori Nyenshel

First, during the reign of Lha Thothori Nyenshel, who was an emanation of the bodhisattva Samantabhadra, the sealed stupa,[4] the *Sutra Designed as a Jewel Chest*,[5] and the *Sutra of a Hundredfold Homage for Amendment of Breaches*[6] all appeared. The king called them the Awesome Secret and, as a virtuous practice, he venerated the stupa above his head. Through the Awesome Secret's blessings, though his body had matured, the king obtained the appearance of a sixteen-year-old boy; thus, this king had two bodies during one lifetime. This was the beginning of the Dharma in Tibet.

His son Prince Drong-nyen Deu stopped making offerings to the Awesome Secret and became very ill with leprosy. His son Tagri Nyenzigs made offerings, through which he recovered from blindness and saw the wild sheep on Tag Mountain. As he had been blind, two kings had defects. Up to this time the royal remains had disappeared into the sky.[7] From his son Namri Songtsen onward, royal tombs were established, which were the landmarks of descending to the kingdom.

The Reign of Songtsen Gampo

Due to the kindness of his [Namri Songtsen's] son Songtsen Gampo, the learned Indian Lichin was invited to Tibet, and Sambhotra,[8] the short man from Thon, created the Tibetan alphabet and translated sections of the *Precious Chintamani* and the *Sutra of the Ten Virtues*. King Songtsen Gampo also had many temples built, such as the four Border Taming Temples,[9] the four Further Taming Temples,[10] the four District Controlling Temples,[11] and the two central temples of Lhasa.[12] He had the statues of Shakyamuni[13] brought, established the stone pillar, and instigated five laws to keep the four root precepts. Adultery was punished with a fine for sexual misconduct, stealing was punished with repayment of the theft, killing was punished with payment of thousands of valuables, someone who attempted murder was punished with the obligation to support the victim's medical treatment as well as their relatives, and liars had to take an oath. Through this, the Dharma truly took root in Tibet and was predicted for five future generations. Songtsen Gampo's successor was his son Gungsong Gungtsen, who passed away at the age of nineteen, so Songtsen took over again and ruled the kingdom twice in one lifetime. Then it was entrusted to his nephew Mangsong Mangtsen. Mangsong's successor was his son Dusong Mangpoje, the king who was a magical emanation of the wind. These three kept up the former tradition, built several new monasteries, and expanded the kingdom. Dusong Mangpoje's son was Tride Tsugtsen, the bearded ancestor, who invited the old Hashang and others, and built five temples: Khartrag in Lhasa, Drinzang in Dragmar, Karchung and Namra in Chimphu, and Tritse in Ling.

His son Jangtsa Lhabon married a Chinese woman named Ongjo. When the prince died, his wife assumed power.

The Reign of Trisong Deutsen

During that time, the ancestor Trisong Deutsen's teachers—Thogje Lhabar from Chimtri, Kyepa Gyalgong from Chokro, and Shang-trompa from Nanam—caused a decline of the Dharma. Karchung and Dragmar were destroyed, the Shakyamuni statue was taken to Mangyul, and laws were established to prevent Dharma practice in the future. When the three of them had been punished, the king developed faith in the Dharma, and through his influence the people's minds changed. Pretending that he sent Ba Selnang to Mangyul as a minister, Trisong Deutsen had him trained as a translator. Then he had him invite Master Shantarakshita[14] to come to Tibet and bring the Shakyamuni statue back. From then on, representations of the Three Jewels were established again. When the king made plans to build the magnificent Samye, he called on some of his close ministers and subjects and advised them, "To accumulate relative virtue for me, you should build a monastery."

The ministers said that they couldn't accomplish his wish. They suggested that he gather the ministers and subjects and give them the choice of putting Hepo[15] Mountain in a copper shell, filling the Gegye sand plain with gold dust, inserting the Yeru River into a metal pipe, or building on top of Hepo Mountain a crystal stupa that could be seen from as far away as China. Some of them would then act against his orders saying that they couldn't accomplish such things, some would want to deprive the king of his power, and some of them would prefer to build the monastery.

The king, ministers, and subjects then gathered, and when these choices were suggested, the subjects claimed that they were unable to accomplish such things. The ministers spoke as they had planned earlier, and in the end they agreed to build the monastery. Master Shantarakshita was invited, he consecrated the land, and the construction was started. But at night, gods and demons tore down what the people built during the day, so they didn't want to continue building. The king became depressed and asked the master, "Don't I have sufficient merit? Are the master's blessings not strong enough? Or are the Tibetan gods and demons too vicious?" The master replied, "It is not that the king doesn't have sufficient merit or that my blessings are not strong enough. This is a peaceful activity, and the vicious Tibetan gods and demons can't be subdued peacefully, they must be subdued wrathfully. In the western country of Oddiyana lives a vidyadhara by the name of Padmasambhava[16] who has attained mastery over life and uses gods and demons as his servants. If you invite him, Your Majesty's wishes will be fulfilled." The king said, "It will be impossible to invite him!" The master replied, "There are three reasons that make it possible to invite him: he is now nearby in Yangleshod in Nepal, he is my abbot, and the three of us have a connection. This is the right time to invite him, and he will come when you do so."

Then Shubu Palkyi Senge, Nanam Dorje Dudjom, and Chim Shakyaprabha went as messengers to invite him, and Padmasambhava came to Tibet. He consecrated the site for Samye,[17] and construction was started again. At night, the gods and demons continued what the people built during the day, so the building of Samye was constructed spontaneously. The statues outside were being built at the same time as the temple, and upon their simultaneous completion, the statues actually walked around during the consecration and discussed the Mahayana teachings. At that time Shantarakshita, Ka,[18] Chok,[19] and others translated many teachings based on the cause, and Master Padma translated the *Guhyagarbha* and *Skillful Lasso Tantras*, the tantras of Hayagriva and Kilaya, as well as the tantras of Mamo and Yamantaka with the activities for guarding the doctrine.

The second transmission took place when Master Shantigarbha[20] was invited and the main translations were the Kriya Tantra Sections and the *Nopeka.* The third transmission was through Acharya Buddhaguhya.[21] He went to Mount Kailash[22] but was not invited to central Tibet, so Tsang Thelentra, Drenkha Murtri, and Jampal Gocha were sent there to translate the Bodhisattva Tantras, the Avadhara Tantras, the esoteric *Magical Vajra Activity Manual*, and many other texts. The fourth transmission was through Master Humkara,[23] who was known as Lord of the Secret Mantra. He was not invited to Tibet, so five monks and one servant— Nub Namkhai Nyingpo,[24] Dre Gyalway Lodro, Lang Palkyi Senge, Rupong Bhija Raja, Drugu Ebag, and Langdro Konchog Jungney—were sent. They cleared up their doubts and received the Vishuddha teachings from him. They also translated the Three Sections of Kriya Yoga, the Maha Yoga tantras and practices, and the *Heruka Galpo*, along with many other tantras and traditions.

As for the fifth transmission, though many teachings based on cause and effect had been translated, the king was not satisfied and felt like searching for teachings beyond cause and effect. Now in his previous life Trisong Deutsen had been a monk called Avadhuti, the son of Brahmin Sukhapala and his wife, Rishi Shoka, in the Indian region of Maduka. After Avadhuti had passed away, through the power of his previous life Trisong Deutsen, being an emanation of a bodhisattva, knew that there were teachings beyond cause and effect in India. Gathering all his ministers, scholars, monks, and subjects, Trisong Deutsen said, "The teachings based on cause and effect are completed, but in India there is definitely a teaching beyond cause and effect. Two people should go and search for it. Who will go? The virtue of such an act can't be contained in the realm of space!"

When all the ministers and subjects had calmed down, he said, "The building of the monastery as a support for the body representation has been accomplished, but Tibet lacks the speech support—the holy Dharma."

Master Padma told the king, "If you want to establish Buddhism in Tibet, you should collect sons of all the Tibetan people as taxes and train them as translators. Then, you should have them translate the Dharma. If you do so, the holy Dharma will flourish in Tibet."

The king was pleased and did what the master had told him. He summoned all the Tibetan boys. About one hundred thousand of them were quite bright, and among those, about one thousand were intelligent. These boys studied both colloquial and classical Indian languages with the two masters; but no matter how they were taught, they couldn't pronounce the language correctly. Teaching them "Namo Buddhaya," they could only say "Mamo Pupaya"; for "Namo Dharmaya" they would say "Mamo Pangmaya"; and when teaching them "Sanghaya," they could only say "Sataya." So Master Padma laughed, and the king despaired.

Master Padma, knowing past, present, and future, said, "Your Majesty, don't worry, there is a way! Shakyamuni's regent Ananda, who passed away and roamed around many sambhogakaya buddha-fields, made the aspiration to dispel the darkness of Tibet. He is now the son of Pagor Hedo and his wife, Drenza Karkyi, who live in a house near the temple of Nyemo Chekhar[25] in Tsang. His name is Genjak Tangta, and he is eight years old. You should ask his parents to give him to you, and they will certainly do so. He is an emanation and will be renowned as an undisputed great pandita."

When the king heard this, he was very happy and did countless prostrations. Then the king and ministers, surrounded by at least seven horsemen, left for the Nyemo district as quick as the wind. When the king and ministers arrived at Chekhar, the locals barricaded all the passages outside their doors. In those days people didn't know how to prostrate or how to show respect, and they were terrified of the king and ministers. In the afternoon many children returned to the village, herding different animals. Among them was a boy with a big head. The eyes below his prominent forehead were staring, his complexion was fair, his hands were clasped, and he was singing a song. The king rejoiced when he saw him and said, "Is Pagor Hedo at home? Do you know Drenza Dronkyi?"[26] The boy's answer was, "I do know Drenza Dronkyi, but right now she's gone to fetch eyes, and Pagor Hedo went in search of gossip."[27]

When the king asked, "Boy, whose child are you?" the boy answered, "I am my father's child." Upon being asked, "What is your father's name?" the boy replied, "It is the one you know." When the king said, "Then tell me your family name," the child answered:

> I have no other family but the Buddha family.
> I have no other name but Vairochana.
> I have no other country but the dharmadhatu.
> I have no other birth but Ananda.
> I have no other self but the self-existing vajra.
> I have no other purpose but to dispel the darkness of Tibet.

Hearing this, the king was delighted and said, "Come here! Bow down!" The boy said, "You show me how!" and as the king prostrated to teach him how to do it, the boy said, "What an auspicious coincidence!" The king said, "This is the very one that the master predicted. He is very eloquent and intelligent. Whichever way you observe him, he is adorned with the major and minor marks." Taking him on his lap, the king lifted him up many times and asked, "Will you come with me?" To which the boy replied, "All right, let's go!"

When they left a few days later, the boy said, "Majesty, come with me!" and the king, ministers, and attendants followed the child. The entire district paid respect to the king.

Before leaving, when his father had come back with beer, the boy said, "Father, tell your gossip to the king! Mother, put those eyes here!" The king rejoiced and said to Pagor Hedo, "This son of yours is indispensable to me. He is a bodhisattva on the tenth level, and without this holy one Tibet is like an animal realm. I shall send him to the noble land of India and have him translate all the vehicles into Tibetan, from the Hinayana up to and including the Ati. He will be the most sublime being in all of Tibet." Then the king gave Pagor Hedo ten ounces of gold and a gold bar.

The parents both fainted and when Pagor woke up from his faint he was startled. In tears of anguish he told the king, "He is the only one we old parents care about. He is the eye in our forehead, our heart within. He is only eight years old; he can't translate! Please don't order me to do this!" The king said, "He was predicted by the great Master Padma! You old people should also come with me. I'll take care of both parents and child!" Trisong Deutsen settled the parents at Yarlung Rogpatsa in the excellent central part of Yarlung, which has a wonderful view. Then he took Genjak Tangta to Samye and had him stay with the abbot and the master. For seven years he was given the three whites and the three sweets.[28] Through skillful means, within three years he developed his knowledge, improved his intelligence and memory, and became competent in languages.

Then the king invited the two masters to the Translation Hall of Samye; there, they paid respect to Vairotsana and requested, "Please turn the wheel of the Buddhist teachings on Secret Mantra!" Upon their request, Vairotsana started to translate. As the master taught the inner Secret Mantra teachings, Vairotsana translated them, and the king was happy.

After that, Vairotsana and the rest of the seven men to be tested[29] were ordained as *bhikshus*.[30] According to the sutras he was called Yeshe De, and according to the tantras, Vairotsana. The omniscient Padmasambhava taught all the sutras, mantras, tantras, and transmissions without exception to the outstanding scholar Yeshe De, the great pandita who was known under five names in one lifetime, and Yeshe De translated them for the king and the subjects.

While the abbot and the master completed the teachings, the king thought that although Master Padma had the Ati, which excels the teachings based on cause and effect, the Tibetan people wouldn't be able to understand it due to their disturbing emotions. He gathered the entire population of Tibet and asked if he should send the translator to India, or if they should request the master for the teachings. Then the story of how he had searched for the translator for thirteen days was announced to all the Tibetan people.

VAIRO'S FIRST TRIAL

The son of Genjak Dorje Gyal and his wife, Dron-makyi, was born near the junction of the Nyang and Tsang rivers, in a large and slightly protruding area. In his previous life he had been a bhikshu called Purna in Gyalmo Tsawarong.[31] Purna passed away and was born as a bright and intelligent boy called Genjaktag. At the age of eight the king sent for him, and from the age of nine for three years he served as outer and inner minister. At the age of twelve he became the king's attendant for three years, and although he had not yet reached the age of fifteen, he got up from the crowd and said, "Your Majesty, give your command and I'll go!" At that time, none of the others were able to promise such a thing. Now his first trial was to renounce his parents, country, home, friends, and everything else and make the very difficult promise to go to a foreign country with different languages and great danger from border guards and so forth.

A BRIEF HISTORY OF TSANG LEKDRUB

Also, in western India, there was a householder called Palkye, who had three bhikshu priests. When the householder Palkye went for prayer, one of his daughters stayed at home to guard the house. As the monks had not brought their prayer books, the bhiksu called Bhahula went to get them and saw the daughter and a son of the householder Dragshulchen engaged in sexual intercourse. The boy felt embarrassed and ran away, so the daughter grabbed the monk and said, "Don't be shy. Do it to me!" Bhahula said, "That is impossible; I am a monk." The girl said, "Then I'll kill myself, and it will be your fault!" and tapped herself with a knife. The monk thought that if he were to have intercourse with her, he would break his vows and go to hell, but should he not sleep with her, she would kill herself, and he would be responsible. Therefore, thinking that it would be better to die himself, he said to her, "Don't kill yourself. I'll make you happy! Close the door!" Behind her, he cut his jugular vein with a razor and passed away. He took birth as the son of Tsang Thelentra, who was also called Tsang Thegchen, and his wife, Kharchenza Tummo. He was an intelligent boy called Tsang Lekdrub and lived in the Deulung area. Rising from the crowd he said, "Majesty, give your command and I will accompany Genjaktag!"

The two boys were brought before the king, and a couple of gold bars were hidden in their hair. Some gold bars, spoons, and chains were hidden in their garments; a yak's horn full of gold dust and a package of gold were loaded on the horse Scarlet Bird Face,[32] along with some unusual garments and the claws of wild animals. As Tsang Lekdrub was very clever and knew some Indian colloquial languages and as Genjaktag, being a nir-manakaya, had been able to ride back and forth on the rays of the sun be-tween Genmo Mountain and Dragpoche since the age of eight and knew 360 languages without having studied them, the king believed that his aim would be accomplished.

This was the sixth chapter of the Great Image,
about the spreading of the teachings based on cause and effect,
and the plan to search for the pith instructions, due to the kindness
of the Dharma king.

7 ❖

The Trials of Vairotsana

Vairotsana Deals With Sixteen Trials

VAIRO'S SECOND TRIAL

Meanwhile, Vairotsana's uncle Hedo[1] invited the king and petitioned him very anxiously, "Please stop my nephew Genjaktag from going to India!" The king replied, "Whatever I do, I will not prevent the faithful from becoming monks or the diligent from practicing religion. I won't protect hunters and fishermen, and I won't support or assist thieves, rapists, or criminals!" Then he clasped his hands behind his back and walked to his residence.

Uncle Hedo said to his nephew, "Don't go; you'll die! You should get married and be our chief." But Genjaktag didn't listen. His uncle pleaded, "Don't go! Don't you care about the Lungmo Lungrig fields that have been sown and fully cultivated? In order to keep the land of your ancestors, you should beget sons!" In answer, Vairotsana sang a song:

> Uncle, don't speak like that!
> Hedo, don't say that!
> A wife is the swamp of samsara;

Sons are the dishwater of samsara;
A family is the gang of samsara;
And property is the prison of samsara.
Uncle, don't speak like that!
How pitiful to be interested in such things!

Uncle Hedo replied, "Boy, don't say that! My brother Genjak Dorje Gyalpo, our dear old father, Lochen Phagpa, and our noble grandfather also strove for the security of their sons, home, and fields and still tend them now. Boy, don't sell your parents!" In answer, Vairotsana sang this song:

Uncle, what are you saying?
Our ancestors spent their lives
Building a home,
But when they died, they weren't allowed inside
And were thrown out the door;
So what's the point of building a home?

No matter how you guard your land and home through
     misconduct,
When you die, you're not allowed
To stay in bed even for a short while;
So what's the use of guarding land and home?

Though our ancestors spent their lives
Cultivating fields,
When they died, their graves barely fit their corpses;
So what's the use of cultivating fields?

Nonetheless, our ancestors
Committed evil actions to feed their family,
Maturing the result in this very lifetime.
At home your wife and children only talk about this life,
Without considering death;
So what's the use of nourishing a family?

Though our ancestors spent their lives
Collecting property and cattle,

When they died, they had to go empty-handed and naked;
So what's the use of accumulating property and cattle?

Though our ancestors spent their lives
With friends and attendants,
When they died, they had to go alone.
Friends and attendants might have some good tendencies,
But they require scrutiny, arguing, and beating;
So what's the use of supporting friends and attendants?
Uncle, don't speak like that!

As Genjaktag gently advised him, Hedo asked, "What is actually so true and wonderful about the Dharma?" and again Genjaktag sang a song:

Uncle, listen! Hedo, listen!
Uncle, follow me!
Renounce the householder's life and practice the ten
    virtues!
As a result of performing the ten virtues,
You will be reborn in the higher realms as a god or human
    being.
The qualities of obtaining a human body
Are that you attain mastery over your hearing and thinking
And can receive the bodhisattva precepts.
By applying hearing and thinking,
If you meditate, you can attain unsurpassed enlightenment.

The sufferings of change are very intense:
Among them, in the higher celestial realms,
There are six types of gods in the world of desire,[2]
With superior forms and life spans.
They have an inconceivable variety of enjoyments—
Wish-granting cows, omniscient horses,
Crops that need no toil, bathing pools—
And the five sense pleasures are spontaneously fulfilled.
There is no business or profit,
There are no thieves or robbers,

And there is no harm from diseases of the five poisons.[3]
Uncle, if you are at all interested, be interested in that!

Yet those who always wander in samsara,
Direct their senses in the wrong direction.
Extremely diligent in the five conflicting emotions,
They'll never get out of samsaric states.

Uncle, listen to me this once!
In the seventeen regions of the world of form,[4]
Beings survive on samadhi. There is no sleep and no non-
    virtue;
There is no passion between male and female; and the five
    emotions do not exist.
There is no illness and there are no corpses; beings vanish
    like a rainbow.
If anything inspires you, let it be that!

Uncle, listen to me this once!
In the four perception spheres of the formless world,[5]
There is no old age, decline, coming, going, pride, or
    jealousy,
No wide or narrow, and no craving.
If anything interests you, let it be that.
For lower faculties the best support is a divine or human
    body.

Uncle, listen to me this once!
Concerning the eight vehicles based on cause and effect:
The Buddha Shakyamuni's way is to enter
The door of the four noble truths,[6] keep 250 vows,
And cross the five noble paths[7] and the eight levels
In order to attain the eight results of the shravaka[8] path.
If you have any interest, have it for that!

Uncle, listen to me this once!
The way of the noble *pratyekabuddhas*[9]

Is to enter the door of the twelve links of dependent
    origination[10]
And examine with one's own intellect, without needing
    a guru.
Through the yogic discipline of maintaining silence,
The result of one who is like a unicorn[11] can be attained.
If you are concerned about anything, let it be that!

Uncle, listen to me this once!
The bodhisattva's way is to enter the door of the two
    truths,[12]
Cross the five paths and the ten bhumis,[13]
And master the bhumi of Universal Light.
If anything inspires you, let it be that!

Uncle, listen to me this once!
In the Kriya of the Secret Mantra
One enters the door of the three purities,[14]
Regarding the three enlightened families as masters and
    servants,
So that one can reach the Lotus buddha-field.
If you yearn for anything, let it be that!

In Upa, which employs both,
One practices Kriya and accomplishes Yoga,
Like unexpected profit,
And can master the bhumi of Vajra Holder.
If you have any interest, have it in that!

Through the *sattvayoga*[15] of Yoga Tantra,
One enters the door of the five awakenings,
Where the five families and five wisdoms are equal
And used as friends in the practice
So one can reach the Densely Arrayed Realm.
If you are inspired by anything, let it be that!

In the Maha Yoga of the Secret Mantra,
One enters the door of the three samadhis.[16]

Though mind appears as a magical display,
By crossing the outer, inner, and secret paths,
One can reach the level of the Cloud Mass Wheel.[17]
If you are devoted to anything, let it be that!

In the Anu Yoga of the Secret Mantra,
One enters the door of space and wisdom.
Without definite number or color for body, speech,
    and mind,
Mind's expression manifests as the three kayas,
And one can reach the level inseparable from
    Samantabhadra.
Uncle, if you believe in anything, let it be that!
If you give any counsel, give that!
Yet if you direct your senses in the wrong direction
And exert yourself in the five conflicting emotions,
You will always fall into the lower realms!

After Genjaktag had said this, his uncle gave up. Believing his nephew's words, Hedo said, "All right, boy, do whatever you like!"

Then Genjaktag renounced his parents, relatives, friends, and possessions. Before reaching the age of fifteen, in the first spring month of the tiger year, on a Monday, the third day of the new year, he headed toward the south and reached the Arya Palo Temple. Together with his friend Lekdrub and his horse, Scarlet Bird Face, he prepared to depart for India. His second trial was the journey to India, which was difficult because of the long distance, the spies, and the toll collectors, and was extremely hard to travel to without a guide.

VAIRO'S THIRD TRIAL

After their departure, when they spent the night at the Arya Palo Temple, the revered Vairotsana had four symbolic dreams. First, he dreamt that an eight-year-old girl holding a shining golden knife cut open his stomach and took out his heart so that pus flowed out. At midnight, he dreamt that he took out the hearts of twenty-one Indian scholars and ate them. After midnight, he dreamt that a pale Indian man put a syllable A on the crown of his head; the A became a flame that suddenly burnt his body and made

it disappear. In the early morning, he dreamt that in India he uprooted a
large wish-fulfilling tree and brought it to Tibet. That was during one new
year's night. At daybreak, he related his dreams in a song:

> Friend, get up, we are lucky!
> Last night I had these dreams:
>
> In the evening, as I slept for a while,
> I dreamt that an eight-year-old girl
> Cut open my body with a shining knife
> And took out my heart so that pus flowed out.
>
> At midnight, I dreamt that I pulled out the hearts
> Of twenty-one Indian scholars and ate them.
>
> Past midnight, I dreamt that a pale Indian man
> Put the syllable A on the crown of my head, burning
>   my body.
>
> In the early morning, I dreamt that I uprooted an Indian
> Wish-fulfilling tree and brought it to Tibet.
> Friend, what do these dreams mean?

Thus he spoke. His friend Lekdrub had an intuitive understanding and
explained the meaning of the dreams:

> In the evening you dreamt of past propensities:
> The eight-year-old maiden with the shining knife
> Slitting open your stomach and pulling out your heart and
>   the flow of pus
> Mean that an emanation of Manjushri purified your
>   obscurations.
>
> At midnight, you dreamt of past karmic residue:
> Eating the hearts of the Indian scholars
> Means that you will discover the great bliss pith
>   instructions

Through your past karmic connections with the Indian
  scholars.

Past midnight, the pale Indian
Putting the A on the crown of your head and your body
  burning
Mean you will realize great bliss enlightenment,
As A represents the pure unborn dharmakaya.

In the early morning, the Indian wish-fulfilling tree
That you uprooted and brought to Tibet
Means you will completely reveal the great bliss pith
  instructions.
Your dreams are good! Let's go quickly!

As they continued without hindrances, they came to White Mountain
Pass. A lot of snow had fallen, so they stayed there for three days. In the
early morning, Vairotsana dreamt that both the sun and the moon rose in
Tibet from the west. The moon rose first but couldn't illuminate Tibet and
vanished in the center of the sky. The sun rose afterward; shining only on
Hepo Mountain, it went down in Tsawarong on the southeastern border.
From there a ray of sunlight rose and became luminous. Following this
ray, the sun rose, burnt Vairotsana's body, and illumined all of Tibet. When
he woke up, he told Lekdrub about it:

Friend, you who meditate on the true nature,
Get up; friend, get up!
As I slept for a while, I had these dreams!
I dreamt that the sun and moon rose in Tibet from the west;
The moon vanished in the middle of the sky,
And the sun shone on Hepo Mountain.
After that, it shone in Tsawarong.
Then I dreamt that a ray of sunlight manifested in Tibet;
Afterward, the sun appeared in Tibet,
Burning my whole body.
I dreamt that the sun illuminated Tibet and remained there.
Friend, what do these dreams mean?

Thus, he sang a song. Lekdrub explained the meaning of these dreams:

The sun and moon both rising from the west
Are we friends, the two brothers.
The moon disappearing in the center of the sky
Means that Lekdrub will die first, on the road.
Later, the sun shining on Hepo Mountain
Means that the instructions will dawn in the king's mind.
Then the sun shining in Tsawarong
Means that Vairo will be banished to Tsawarong one day,
And the doctrine will flourish there.
The sun again coming to Tibet and shining there
Means the ray of an incarnation will come to Tibet,
And Vairo, the sun, will go to Tibet
And spread the effortless doctrine there.
The sun burning Vairo's body and ashes
Means that you will burn up all your emotions and habitual
    patterns
And, without effort, attain perfect enlightenment in
    this life.
Your dreams are good! Let's go quickly!

Thus he spoke. Then they continued their journey, but as the path was blocked by snow, they couldn't pass. Vairotsana took the horse's reins and tried to break a path through the snow with a stick, while Lekdrub clutched the horse by its tail. Sure to die if they took one wrong step, it took them from dawn to dusk to cover a distance of about two miles. Risking his life in this way was Vairo's third trial.

VAIRO'S FOURTH TRIAL

They continued on the right track, but although they tried to avoid the hot valley of Nepal, they were forced to stop there for a day. The vicious yaksha called Ferocious, who lived off fresh human flesh, made obstacles by performing all sorts of mischievous miracles. Though they spoke words of truth to him in peaceful voices, the yaksha would not listen. Because Ferocious caused a lot of trouble through his demon power, Vairo displayed his magical power to control the yaksha and bound him by oath. This difficult escape from nonhuman obstacles was his fourth trial.

VAIRO'S FIFTH TRIAL

Continuing on from Nepal, they were afraid of robbers stealing their horse and gold, so they traveled at night. Since there was a lot of snow, in order to hide their tracks they tied a small cotton bag to the horse's hindquarters so its dung wouldn't be scattered. Vairo put wild animal claws on his hands and feet and went on all fours; Tsang Lekdrub did the same behind the horse, erasing its track. Thus, Vairo's fifth trial was escaping robbers who were difficult to evade by hiding his tracks in the snow and taking pains to erase his trail.

VAIRO'S SIXTH TRIAL

As they continued from Brown Rock Enclosure on the border of Nepal and India, they met many spies and vicious packs of wild animals that ate human flesh. The difficult escape from that mob was his sixth trial.

VAIRO'S SEVENTH TRIAL

When they arrived in India, they were caught by toll collectors on a narrow trail bordered by reeds, with nowhere to yield or make way. As the toll collectors were about to kill them and steal their horse and gold, Vairotsana performed a miracle. He transformed himself into a jewel chest with an iron razor inside. The chief toll collector, called Kuhara Wangdu, said, "Forget about that wondrous magician! Kill his companion and steal his gold!" Then Vairo transformed Lekdrub into a dumb Bhutanese tribesman and sang this song to the toll collector:

> The skylike mind is free of birth and death;
> Manifesting as the nirmanakaya, it illuminates obscurity,
> Just as the sun dispels darkness from the Jambu continent.
> As we are searching for the Dharma and need experience,
> Though this skylike mind, luminous and all-pervading,
> Is beyond killing, not killing, death, and no-death,

If you sever this illusory life, you commit an evil deed.
So I better reward you with some illusory gold dust
For showing me a little of the way!

Vairo then gave him a handful of gold dust. The toll collector was happy and showed him the right direction. The difficult escape from the strict toll collectors at the narrow pass was his seventh trial.

VAIRO'S EIGHTH TRIAL

As they continued along a fivefold dangerous trail, hindered by camels and evil spirits, they met many toll collectors who were difficult to understand. The guards swung at their necks with cane swords but couldn't cut them because of the gold bars hidden on their heads and necks. Though Vairo tried to approach them peacefully and bribe them, they refused to listen and kept hitting him and Lekdrub with their cane swords, so Vairo miraculously escaped. This difficult escape was his eighth trial.

VAIRO'S NINTH TRIAL

Then, at a narrow path of plantain trees, the horse Scarlet Bird Face looked at Vairo and Lekdrub with eyes full of tears and died. They both wept, too. Many jackals, wild animals, cranes, and other birds were attracted by the smell of the horse's corpse. After eating the corpse, they were about to kill Vairo and Lekdrub, who then buried the gold and fled. This difficult escape to save their lives was his ninth trial.

VAIRO'S TENTH TRIAL

Near Magadha[18] they were forced to go along a frightening toll bridge with no way around it and met toll collectors who were difficult to understand. "Do you have any gold?" the guards queried, then beat them up and tore off their clothes. Not finding any gold, the guards cut their shin muscles looking for gold, and for two weeks Vairo and Lekdrub were on the verge of death. This was Vairo's tenth trial.

VAIRO'S ELEVENTH TRIAL

Having convinced the toll collectors that they had no gold, they dug up the gold they had hidden and brought it with them. When they came to the Krisha area, they buried the gold again and went to a village to find provisions and inquire about the road. The people there said, "Some foreign spies have come!" Beating them, they tied them up and threw them into a pit full of snakes and frogs, where no one could survive more than a day. When after one week they hadn't died, the people said, "How amazing!" and released them. The extremely difficult escape from the frog pit in which he didn't die was his eleventh trial.

VAIRO'S TWELFTH TRIAL

Then they dug up their gold and brought it along to the Prasuta region of India, where in a place full of tigers, bears, and poisonous snakes they nearly died. There, they arrived at the Bhibhi Bira Grove, hid the gold, and went to the king's palace to beg for alms. Because they had entered the king's house without permission, he punished them by putting them in a pit for six days without food. Their noses dried up, and they almost died. The escape from the poisonous snakes, tigers, bears, and the king's punishment comprised Vairo's twelfth trial.

VAIRO'S THIRTEENTH TRIAL

They retrieved the gold and brought it along to the Magadha area, where they had to cross a poisonous sulfur lake. As there was no one to take them across, they went in a boat made from cloth and sticks. Being utterly exhausted while crossing the lake was his thirteenth trial.

VAIRO'S FOURTEENTH TRIAL

They continued to the Indian region of Avadhuti where, showering down upon them, many terrifying tribesmen beat them with sticks until the sticks broke. They nearly died from the beatings. The difficult escape from this place was Vairo's fourteenth trial.

VAIRO'S FIFTEENTH TRIAL

Next Vairo and Lekdrub went to the Indian Arya Palo Temple and were threatened by many masks of hide, metal, and snakeskin; the masks were so terrifying to look at that they barely escaped death. Continuing to the Krili Krana area, many poisonous snakes coiled around their bodies and licked them. Though they were exhausted and in extreme agony, they didn't die and escaped. The difficult escape from the masks and the poisonous snakes was his fifteenth trial.

VAIRO'S SIXTEENTH TRIAL

They proceeded to the Edhakesha area, where many women that were difficult to understand gave them poisoned food. For two weeks they were near death from the poison, which was difficult to overcome. This was his sixteenth trial.

Arriving in Central India and Searching for the Instruction Teachings

Upon reaching central India, they hid all the gold dust and spent six months in markets, towns, lodgings, temples, and so forth, trying to find out who was the most learned in the pith instructions, who were the abbots of the Dharma colleges, and who had attained spiritual accomplishment. They heard that although there were many general scholars, everybody agreed that Shri Singha[19] was the most accomplished. Meanwhile, they had arrived at the Indian Jakhavhuha area, where they met a king named Kumasha Dula. They asked him where the Dhahena Hall[20] with the bodhi tree was, and the king answered:

> Last night I had this dream:
> The son of the Indian Brahmin Pala,
> The monk Avadhuti, passed away
> And became the king of the snowy kingdom Tibet,
> A dark and gloomy world.
> This king is like a wish-fulfilling gem:
> In order to dispel the darkness of Tibet,

He sent two bodhisattvas abiding on the bhumis,
Who took the sun and moon from Dhahena
And illuminated the darkness in snowy Tibet.
It means you two monks are searching for the pith
    instructions!
I won't show you the Dhahena Hall!

To this, Vairotsana replied:

The nature of primordial uncontrived space,
Abiding in total evenness, beyond meeting and parting,
Appeared in the expanse of nondual enlightenment from
    the very beginning.

I didn't come to look for scriptures and pith instructions.
I asked you so that when I go back to Tibet,
I can explain what the southern countries of Nepal and
    Mon are like.

Then the king was very respectful and provided him with the proper directions to Dhahena. Around that time, in front of Dhahena, witnessed by everyone, the prostitute Dagnyima and the nun Kungamo were debating about the Unique Sphere[21] classified into three: tantras, scriptures, and pith instructions.

Then the panditas gathered and all compared the bad indications in their dreams, "Because the two nuns were debating, the pith instructions will be lost to Tibet! No one should be allowed to teach the pith instructions!" All the inconceivable tantras and pith instructions that were not commonly known were concealed in the minds of Prahe, Manjushri, and Shri Singha and remained there in complete perfection. The sixty great Tantra Sections with the pith instructions that were commonly known to the panditas and the king were hidden in Bodhgaya with three successive seals. It was announced that the king would punish anyone who secretly traded the pith instructions or acted as an intermediary. When the two Tibetan monks heard about this, they became very depressed.

As the two monks were sitting near the entrance of Dhahena, they met an old woman who was an emanation of Manjushri. When they asked her which ones were the first and middle halls of Dhahena and where Shri

Singha lived, the old woman said, "If you give me a reward, I'll tell you!"
Then they went to the shore of Kutra Lake and bribed her with gold dust.
The old woman went into the water, covered her face with sandalwood
leaves, and spoke through a long hollow reed:

> Manjushri Bhadra related this dream:
> Kungamo and Dagnyima both
> Divided that which is one in all aspects
> Into illusory tantras, scriptures, and instructions.
>
> As those of superior, mediocre, and common faculties
> Classified the true Dharma—
> Uncontrived, as it is, devoid of a self-nature—into three,
> Due to the deluded concepts of the three types of faculties,
> Tantras, scriptures, and instructions
> Were conceived as three in their state of oneness.
>
> Because of the tightness of their knots of illusion,
> These buffaloes, women, dogs, and so forth,
> Whose thoughts and energy are stirred by passion
> And who are chained by the five aggregates, such as that
>   of form,
> Under stressful pressure divide even
> The nature of samadhi beyond concepts into duality.
>
> That is why I dreamt that two bodhisattvas abiding on the
>   bhumis
> Poured the Secret Mantrayana,
> Oral explanations on the pith instructions of the panditas,
> Into the ears of the king who is an emanation of
>   Manjushri,
> In Tibet, the kingdom of the red ogres.
>
> This old woman heard what he said,
> And I'm sure you Tibetan monks will accomplish your aim!

Thus the old Brahmini spoke. She continued:

Kukkuraja Dhahuna said:
I dreamt that two worthy and fortunate monks
Came here to our country
To obtain future benefits for their kingdom.
They are yogis who, through karma and compassion,
Are connected with the Ati teachings beyond cause and
  effect,
Which give actual fruition in this lifetime.
Because so-called women of low caste could not restrict the
  secrets
And broke the root precepts by openly talking about them,
These teachings won't circulate on the plains but will go to
  the land of ice!
I dreamt that they took the Secret Mantra to the
  borderland!

This old woman heard what he said,
And I'm sure you Tibetan monks will accomplish your aim!

Dagnyima related the dream she had:
Mostly attached to the total equality of the nature of
  phenomena,
I couldn't resist the secret words.
Taking on a female body due to impure prayers,
I am fettered by illusory worldly phenomena.
Through the flaw of dividing total evenness into three,
The king of the red-faced Tibetan ogres,
With his skinny crooked form and thin dark skin,
Who takes the five conflicting emotions as food and wealth,
Sent a bodhisattva who took on a human body
And renounced the body of his last rebirth.
He will teach the Mahayana Secret Mantra instructions of
  the scholars
To the red-faced Tibetan ogres!
I dreamt that the Secret Mantra teachings went to Tibet!
Prahe's statements about
Not telling women the secret words is true!

This old woman heard what she said,
And I'm sure you Tibetan monks will accomplish your aim!

Kukkuraja the Younger spoke thus:
Unchanging awareness is the buddhas of the three times,
Inseparable from the wondrous essence beyond words.
But women by nature
Crave for mundane affairs that they can't give up;
After mastering the eighth bhumi they still risk falling into
    samsara!
Because the tantras, scriptures, and pith instructions were
    divided into three,
The great bliss instructions taught by the Buddha,
Authentic and uncontrived, will go to the king,
Whose pure skylike mind is primordially inseparable from
    evenness.
The Buddha's compassion never degenerates and is never
    exhausted,
But mind being deluded by illusory worldly phenomena,
Through the flaw of choosing to divide one into three,
The sun of Avalokiteshvara's compassion
Rose in the kingdom of Tibet, the extreme borderland.
The red-faced king who surpasses everyone
Sent monks, who are bodhisattvas
Abiding on the bhumis and are here now, with gold dust.
I dreamt that because the Secret Mantra was debated,
They swept away the pith instructions and left!

This old woman heard what he said,
And I'm sure you Tibetan monks will accomplish your aim!

Thus she spoke and then continued:

Rishi Bhashita related this dream:
Enlightened mind, the innate nature, not more than one,
Cannot be explained as tantras, scriptures, and pith
    instructions.

As it is beyond word, thought, and description,
It makes no sense to debate it. But as it became a subject
    for debate,
It is true what the Buddha said
About not giving the secret teachings to women.
I dreamt that because of that flaw,
A destined and compassionate king
Sent two worthy, fortunate monks
To obtain benefits for the kingdom he rules.
That is why they are in India.
As the root precepts and secrets were not restricted,
I dreamt that the Secret Mantra wouldn't circulate on
    the plains
But will be scattered and go to Tibet, the country formed
    of ice!

This old woman heard what he said,
And I'm sure you Tibetan monks will accomplish your aim!

Thus she spoke. Continuing, she said:

Shri Singha related this dream:
Women have a rough character, flatter,
Take illusory phenomena as absolute,
Don't discriminate the subject they talk about, easily betray,
And can't restrict the secret words but start quarrels.
Because of that, I had this dream:
There was a sun and a moon;
I put the sun under my arm and took it,
And the moon dissolved into me.
I am sure the pith instructions of the scholars will be lost
    to Tibet!

This old woman heard what he said,
And I'm sure you Tibetan monks will accomplish your aim!

Thus she spoke. Then she continued:

Kungamo related this dream:
All phenomena are enlightened mind.
Within the one innate nature, inherently uncontrived,
The attitude of women, controlled by conflicting emotions,
Caused a debate on dividing the Unique Sphere into three,
And spoiled the nature of great evenness. Due to that,
As I slept for a while, I dreamt
That the king of the dark borderland of Tibet,
Who is an emanation of Manjushri,
Sent two youths, who are emanations of bodhisattvas,
To India in search of the Buddha's teachings,
The undisputed great bliss pith instructions.
I dreamt that they removed a precious gem shining like
    a torch,
Which belongs to all the Indian scholars,
And took it to Tibet.
It is a sign that the secret pith instructions will be lost
    to Tibet!

This old woman heard what she said,
And I'm sure you Tibetan monks will accomplish your aim!

Thus, the old woman told them about the first bad dreams, and instructing them, "Stay at the entrance of the middle Dhahena Hall, where the Brahmini called Crystal Intellect will come to draw water. Meet her and give her a message to carry. Don't say that I told you!" she disappeared. Later on, even though they consulted oracles, they couldn't find out who it was that had said all this.

As they waited at the Dhahena water spring, they met the Brahmini when she came to draw water and sent a message with her. Three times she came back, only to tell them that she had forgotten the message; so they didn't receive an answer.

Then Vairo made the water jug stick to the ground with the mantra of illusory union, so that she couldn't take it away, and she said, "If you want to display miracles, I can do the same!" Revealing an eight-inch golden razor from under her armpit, she said, "VAJRA BANDHA PRABE-SHAYA PHAT!" and slit open her stomach. Inside of it were the *vajradhatu* deities, vividly clear.

Vairotsana said, "Namo Bhuddhaya, Namo Dharmaya, Namo San-ghaya," which translated into English means, "The Buddha is the excellent refuge and protector, the Dharma is the excellent foundation of the path, and the Sangha is the excellent community of those who have reached the tenth level. Homage to the Three Jewels!" Then they bribed the Brahmini with a bar of gold and a heap of gold dust, put a pebble in the water jug, and sent a letter with her. When she poured the water into a copper vessel, the pebble made a rumbling sound. The master heard it and said, "What is that?" "It is a reminder of two Tibetan monks who showed some slight power and sent you this letter," she replied, and she gave the letter to the master. In the letter it said, "MAHAKARUNA BUDDHA DHARMA SANGHA JNANAMOYA. BODHISATTVA KARUNA SAMAYA JNANA GARBHA KURU BHAMIN." Translated into English this praise they sent to Master Shri Singha means:

> Most exalted bodhisattva,
> You embody the merit of all beings of the six realms.
> Precious blazing gem of the Tripitaka,
> Endowed with the supreme power of compassion like a
>   wish-fulfilling gem,
> Under the sun of your radiant all-pervading compassion
> We obtained a human body in the stream of our births.
> We two bad Tibetan novices
> Always offer to the precious Triple Gem[22] to purify our ob-
>   scurations.
> If we could have a lengthy stay in your presence,
> Our darkness would be dispelled and our merit would
>   develop.
> Yet, not making pure prayers, we are not matured by your
>   compassion
> And are deprived of the sun of your noble face.
> Extend the abode of the exalted ones to the realm of sen-
>   tient beings,
> Illuminate the dense gloom,
> And skillfully show us the light,
> Holding us with the lasso of your compassion!

Shri Singha sent this answer, "SAMAYA APARIMITA JNANA." Translated into English this means:

If you supplicate me because of strong past *samaya*,
I can't avoid meeting you.
As the mind essence of sentient beings is the Tathagata
    family,
Even the tiniest insect is endowed with the seed of
    enlightenment.
Though beings of the six realms are equal to buddhas,
Feeling devotion as exalted ones making offerings to
    exalted ones,
To see the Three Precious Jewels, the unsurpassed objects of
    worship,
As sacred causes the accumulation of merit to grow.
I am delighted that you came here,
Having exhausted your limbs by the strength of your heart.
Let us soon meet to compare our knowledge!

He sent a reply with the Brahmini Crystal Intellect for them to meet him at midnight. When they met him at midnight, they did prostrations and circumambulations and offered a thousand ounces of gold. They told him the story of King Trisong Deutsen and pleaded, "Please give us the effortless Ati Yoga teachings to attain enlightenment in this very lifetime!" Master Shri Singha said, "Both the prostitute Dagnyima and Kungamo corrupted the teachings. Due to their debate all the panditas had inauspicious dreams. The panditas discussed it and burnt the teachings that were spoiled. All the teachings were restricted and hidden at Bodhgaya, where they are bound together with both the seal of all the scholars and the seal of the king who upholds the Dharma; therefore, it is difficult to reveal them. However, since the time has come for the Buddha's teachings to spread in the borderland, I shall examine my dreams." He analyzed his dreams while he meditated, and the signs were good, so he said, "The effortless doctrine will benefit Tibet. As the time has come to send it there, it must be sent; but we need to do so properly. If it is not done properly, the king will find out and have the three of us killed. I have also completely removed the pith instructions. You two should first receive all the teachings based on cause and effect from the other panditas. You should offer gold to the later panditas and receive the Secret Mantra teachings based on the result. Then I shall teach the effortless Great Perfection doctrine at night, so no one will be aware of it."

First, they received in their entirety all the teachings based on the cause, and then all the other Secret Mantra teachings. Then they received the outer, inner, and secret empowerments from the later seven scholars and listened to many of the inner Secret Mantra teachings. They met both nirmanakaya Prahevajra and Manjushrimitra, offered them gold dust and ornamented gold bars, did prostrations and circumambulations, and touched the crown of their heads to these masters' feet. Requesting the pith instructions, Prahe and Manjushrimitra gave them empowerments, blessings, and the complete pith instructions and proclaimed, "Receive them from Master Shri Singha!" So they went back to Master Shri Singha and requested the pith instructions.

First, Shri Singha performed a miracle in order to obtain the pith instructions: he transformed himself into the yaksha Meteor Face, Vairotsana into Shravasinha,[23] and Tsang Lekdrub into a wild goose. At midnight they went to take out the pith instructions that were hidden at Bodhgaya and bound with seals. As he broke the seals of the pith instructions and revealed them, all the outer and inner protectors of the Secret Mantra appeared, circumambulated Shri Singha and Vairotsana in clockwise direction, and touched their hands and feet to the crown of these masters' heads, and said,

> We nonhuman guardian protectors of the Dharma are in charge of the teachings. We look after these teachings and thoroughly follow them. Some of us feel as if our hearts have been torn out, some as if our father has been killed, others as if our mother has been killed, and still others as if our precious gem has been lost. Those who obtain and earnestly apply these pith instructions and practice them according to the texts are respected as lords and served as crown jewels by us nonhuman beings. All their intentions will be accomplished. Since we are watching over these teachings, cherish them and accomplish them according to the texts! As they are the most special among all teachings, you should practice them very secretly!

Then they disappeared. So Shri Singha and the two monks resealed the broken seals, and taking the oral traditions and pith instructions, they went to the Dhahena Hall. At that time the middle bad dreams occurred. The later seven scholars and the others met and told their dreams. Manjushrimitra related this dream:

Within spontaneously present great bliss,
Equal to the heart of all the conquerors, the summit of all
    vehicles,
Dwelling undistracted by the three thought *pranas*,
As a visionary experience I dreamt that
A precious shining offering lamp,
Needed by all the Indian scholars,
Was sealed in Bodhgaya and that
Two wandering Tibetan monks
Completely removed it.
Maybe they took the pith instructions from Bodhgaya!

Thus he spoke. The King of Dogs, Dhahuna, told this dream:

Relaxing within the vast expanse of great bliss, equal to
    space,
The self-existing, nondual original purity,
Unchanging and beyond cultivating,
As a visionary experience I had this dream:
The king of Tibet, an emanation of Manjushri,
Sent two monks who are emanated bodhisattvas.
From the foreheads of twenty-one Indian scholars
They pulled out the clear sense organs, the eyes,
And took them to Tibet!
Maybe they took the pith instructions from Bodhgaya!

Kukkuraja the Younger told this dream:

Within the nature of total evenness, uncontrived, as
    it is,
Carefree, nondual, and nonarising,
Realizing the nature beyond words,
In a meditative experience I had this dream:
Two young Tibetan monks,
Exposed the support of the Buddha's body, the bodhi tree,
The source of the Dharma, the basis of the doctrine in
    India.
Cutting the bodhi tree at its root,

They took the whole thing to Tibet!
Maybe they took the pith instructions from Bodhgaya!

Thus he spoke. The prostitute Dagnyima told this dream:

Within the nondual dharmadhatu, pure like space,
Free of thought, inconceivable, and without reference
    point,
Resting in self-existing great bliss that can't be cultivated,
As a visionary experience I had this dream:
The truth that all we scholars expound,
The wish-fulfilling gem that grants whatever one needs,
Was removed by a Tibetan monk,
A red-faced ogre, who took it to Tibet.
Maybe he took the pith instructions from Bodhgaya!

Thus she spoke. Rishi Bhashita told this dream:

As I rested lucid and undistracted
Within the self-existing, spontaneously perfect nature,
Unborn, free of reference point, and beyond words,
I had this dream as a vision:
Brandishing a knife, a monk from the borderland of Tibet
Chopped down the wish-fulfilling tree in India,
With its abundant leaves, flowers, and fruits.
As the wish-fulfilling tree fell from its root,
I dreamt that he left a piece of the root in India
And took the tree with the leaves to Tibet.
Maybe he took the pith instructions from Bodhgaya!

Thus he spoke. Shri Singha related this dream:

While spontaneously resting lucid and undistracted
In the great bliss of nonconceptual secret space,
The self-existing innate nature of whatever arises,
I experienced this dream:
Two monks from the dark border land of Tibet
Who are emanations of bodhisattvas

Swept away the precious nectar of the sacred Dharma,
The orally taught ocean of nectar
Hidden with five seals in Bodhgaya.
Maybe they took the pith instructions from Bodhgaya!

Thus he spoke. The nun Kungamo told this dream:

Resting undistracted within the realization
Of mind essence, the three kayas, equal yet distinct,
The wondrous core of the doctrine, the Ati teachings,
I had this dream as a visionary experience:
A precious volume, the innermost heart essence of the
    panditas
Who are learned in the nonarising nature
And have realized the mind essence of the buddhas of the
    three times,
Was sealed and hidden in Bodhgaya.
But I dreamt that two Tibetan monks who are emanations
Took that precious volume to Tibet.
Maybe they took the pith instructions from Bodhgaya!

Thus she spoke. Then they investigated whether any of the panditas
were absent and if any of them had been in Bodhgaya, but they couldn't
find out. They sent someone to Bodhgaya to ask the king of the assembly,
as well as the caretaker, whether anyone had come to the sealed place in
Bodhgaya. They were told that nobody had, so they discovered nothing.
The panditas discussed it and prepared a law that nobody was allowed to
take the pith instructions from Bodhgaya. The panditas and the king upholding the Dharma would punish whoever might take them.

 This was the seventh chapter of the Great Image,
about searching for the pith instructions.

8 ❁

Master Shri Singha Entrusts Vairotsana with the Entire Doctrine

E very day they listened to the Secret Mantra teachings based on the result from the later seven scholars and others. And every night they listened to Shri Singha's explanations on the pith instructions of the
effortless Great Perfection, the heart of the doctrine.

Inside his room Master Shri Singha put a clay pot on top of three big
stones and surrounded it with a net. He sat inside the pot and had the
opening covered with a big lid on which a pan filled with water was
placed. A pipe ran through a hole in the pot and crossed through a cleft
in the wall outside of the house. At midnight, Vairotsana and Lekdrub
listened outside as Shri Singha whispered the teachings through the tube.
They each had on a big deerskin hood, carried loads on their shoulders,
held walking sticks, wore their clothes backward, and had put on worn-
out pairs of boots the wrong way around. Lekdrub wrote down the
teachings in the waning moonlight with white goats' milk, while Vairotsana fully understood them by a mere indication and perfected the doctrine in his mind.

As a sign that the doctrine would come to Tibet, Shri Singha taught
Cuckoo of Awareness.[1] To express that everything is perfect, he taught

Shaking of Great Power. To express the meaning of meditation, he taught *Sixfold Sphere.* To express the conclusion of the view and conduct of all the vehicles, he taught *Soaring Garuda.* To show the superiority of Ati over the other vehicles, he taught the view of *Never-Waning Banner.* Then he asked, "Noble sons, are you satisfied?" And they answered, "We are overjoyed!"

Then, to show the unity of all philosophical views, he taught *Wish-Fulfilling Gem.* To show the greatness of the teachings and instructions, he taught *Supreme Lord.* To indicate the need to recognize earlier and later flaws and qualities, he taught *King of Mental Action.* To indicate the need to rely on the three types of knowledge, he taught *All-Embodying Jewel.* These are the four minor teachings.

To indicate that all knowledge should depend on the teachings, he taught *Infinite Bliss.* To show that the fruition is included in the body, speech, and mind, he taught the *Wheel of Life.* To indicate the need to depend on example, meaning, and symbol, he explained *Commentary on Mind* and *King of Space.* These are the four medium teachings.

Indicating how to help others through the provisional and definitive meaning, he taught *Jewel-Studded Bliss.* To indicate the need of distinguishing all vehicles, he taught *Universal Bondage.* To avoid the arising of logical contradictions, he taught *Pure Gold on Stone.* And because the conduct and the precepts are the yogi's life-force, he taught *Spontaneous Summit.* These are the four greater classes.

To check whether a teaching is mistaken or valid, he taught the *Marvelous,* and asked, "Are you satisfied with this?" They answered, "We are not satisfied yet. Please give us the tantras and oral instructions that the Buddha taught on these pith instructions!" Upon their request, Shri Singha explained the Eighteen Tantras with the pointing out instructions and asked, "Are you satisfied now?" Lekdrub, because he wanted to impress the king, said, "I am satisfied," and left. On the way (back to Tibet) he was killed by border guards and died at the age of forty-four.

Vairotsana said that he was not satisfied, and for three days he laid face down. Then Shri Singha asked, "Are you disappointed because your friend has left?" Vairotsana answered, "Why should I be disappointed when a traveler with similar karma goes his own way?" The master asked, "Well, are you sick?" and he answered, "Yes, I am sick." When the master asked, "What is wrong with you?" Vairotsana described his illness with this song:

Someone like me, Vairotsana,
Has no illness due to external causes.
My mind is ill because I have heard but not understood.
My mind is ill because I have seen but not grasped.
My mind is ill because I have experienced but not been
    satisfied.
My mind is ill because I haven't gained confidence
In the Eighteen Major Scriptures of the Mind Class.
As I am struck with this illness,
Please bear with me and provide me with the ultimate
    medicine!

In answer to his supplication Shri Singha said, "I have taught you everything. What is wrong with you?" Again Vairotsana sang a song:

The great bliss of self-existing wakefulness
Is stuck on the precipice of intense habitual tendencies.
That unprejudiced view
Is stuck on the precipice of my karma and thoughts.
That self-settled effortless meditation
Is stuck on the precipice of my drowsiness and agitation.
That conduct without accepting or rejecting
Is stuck on the precipice of my attitude.
That path that can't be traveled
Is stuck on the precipice of scriptures and reasoning.
The view of the buddhas of the three times
Is stuck on the precipice of my doubtful thoughts.
The effortless spontaneous perfection of Ati Yoga
Is stuck on the precipice of lacking signs and meanings.
The inherently present fruition of the three kayas
Is stuck on the precipice of conveying the meaning.
That free enlightened activity
Is stuck on the empowerment of direct anointment.
I couldn't cross the eight precipices
Of the Eighteen Major Scriptures of the Mind Class!

The master laughed and was very pleased. Then he taught *Ocean Expanse Instructions* and asked, "Are you satisfied with this?" But Vairo replied, "I am not satisfied." Then Shri Singha taught the tantras and pith instructions concerning the space class and asked, "Are you satisfied with this?" Vairo answered, "I am not satisfied."

Again Shri Singha taught the tantras and pith instructions concerning the Tantra Sections and asked, "Are you satisfied?" But Vairo replied, "I am not satisfied." Again Shri Singha taught many tantras and pith instructions, both vast and profound, from the Miscellaneous Cycle and the Concealed Cycle. Asked if he was satisfied, Vairo answered that he was still not satisfied. Then Shri Singha taught many tantras and pith instructions of the Distinguishing Brahmin's Cycle and the Resolving King's Cycle and asked if he was satisfied. Vairo replied, "I want to request something that enables me to see directly the self-liberating nature of these instructions right now, without having to make any effort," and offered Shri Singha a measure of gold dust and seven gold bars. Doing many prostrations and circumambulations, he pleaded:

> Magnificent glowing lion,
> You are the only refuge for this foreign monk.
> Inspired to search for you, I was able to risk hardships.
> As we met through a connection, you accepted me with
>   kindness.
> You taught me everything that was revealed of the doctrine.
> Now please directly show me the self-liberating nature!

The master, smiling, was very pleased. With the support of the Illuminating Blazing Gem mandala in the first Dhahena Hall, he bestowed the seven perfecting empowerments in their entirety, including the empowerment of direct anointment, clearly pointed out self-liberation through the *Three Meetings*, caused Vairo to reach fullness through the *Two Direct Perceptions*, cut his mental constructs with *Sixfold Sphere*, and distinguished his view through the *Five Greatnesses*[2] so that he realized the very nature of primordial buddhahood without effort.

Entrusting him with the five root tantras and the twenty-five branch tantras—thirty altogether—as well as the nirmanakaya Prahe's eighteen pith instructions taught by the Buddha, including *Ninefold Expanse*, *Four Important Writings of the Vidyadharas*, Kukkuraja's *Lustrous Essence of the Sun*, and Shri Singha's *Three Radiant Garlands* and *Lamp of Meditative Experience*, he authorized him thus:

As you requested the pith instructions,
Explaining the distinguishing and resolving tantras,
I clearly pointed out the instructions of the lineage.
In a solitary place, devote yourself to your mind,
And bring it to maturity, my heart son!

Then Vairo clearly recognized self-liberation and reached fullness through the *Two Direct Perceptions*. Through the self-liberating explanations he was freed in carefree space, and through *Sixfold Sphere* his mental constructs were cut. Through the *Five Greatnesses*, realizing his mind as the nature of buddhahood, he outshone all that appears and exists and accomplished the wisdom of great bliss, inseparable from samsara and nirvana. Expressing his gratitude to Master Shri Singha, he offered his realization:

In Bodhgaya, where the Buddha attained realization,
The essential truth was perfected.
I am very fortunate indeed that you introduced it to me,
Thank you for the self-liberation of my being!

Thus he offered thanks.

Then Shri Singha said, "These precious pith instructions clarify the whole of samsara and nirvana and actually make one see the essential truth. You should care for them like the apple of your eye. As they are the main point of all the teachings, the summit of all vehicles, revealing the heart essence of all the victorious ones, you should cherish them like your own life and heart. Since they grant all common and supreme needs and wishes, you should care for them like a wish-fulfilling gem. Likewise, you should constantly maintain the practices of Vishuddha, Medicine, and Kilaya, as well as the longevity sadhanas and so forth, according to the texts, keeping the samayas and staying free of all doubts. The Yamantaka sadhanas for guarding the doctrine, such as *Fierce Mantras* and so forth, and the Smashana, Mamo, and Putra sadhanas should be kept secret. They should be used to induce the key points and guard the doctrine, remove obstacles for practitioners, and accomplish needs and wishes." Thus, he conferred the instructions according to the original tradition. As Shri Singha had completed the teachings, he told Vairotsana that it was time for him to return to Tibet and sang a song:

Midday is past. You, sun,
It is time to light up another realm!
Midnight is past. You, full moon,
It is time to light up another realm!
Great courageous one, the arrow is ready to shoot;
It is time to hit the target that you aim for.
Vairo, you who perfect the tantras, transmissions, and pith
    instructions,
It is time to proclaim the doctrine in Ngari in Tibet!

Thus he spoke. Again Vairo requested:

Precious sun shining at midday,
Don't reduce your warmth for those without clothes who
    feel cold in the summer!
Precious barley growing in the garden,
Don't deprive of your fruit those who are hungry due to a
    barren harvest!
Precious king of healing and medicine,
Don't weaken the strength of your supreme medicine for
    those who suffer from the four diseases!
Precious beer pot filled with clear rice beer,
Don't dilute the potency of your beer for those who are
    dehydrated from the heat!
Precious mighty ruler and guide,
Don't lessen your skillful guidance of weak ones who are
    afraid of dogs!
Precious Shri Singha from India,
Don't reduce your compassion for the faithful ones that
    wander in samsara!

Thus, he sang a song. Again, Shri Singha told him in verse that since the
teachings were finished, he should resolve his mind and benefit beings:

The milk-sucking calf can't part from its mother,
But when the cow's milk has dried up, the calf adjusts.
The nectar-sucking bee can't part with the flower,
But when the flower is frozen, the bee acquiesces.

The barmaid can't part with the rice wine when she
    strains it,
But when there is no more flow, the barmaid complies.
The student can't part from the master with the pith
    instructions,
But when the tantras, scriptures, and instructions are
    completed, he consents.

Thus he spoke with tears in his eyes. Vairotsana was convinced and
consented to leave. He prostrated and did circumambulations, touched
the crown of his head to Shri Singha's feet, and offered him a handful of
gold dust and a gold bar. Preparing to go, he sang this song:

EMAHO! How wondrous and marvelous.
Whatever you say is like a flow of nectar!
Compassionate and loving protector,
With your immaculate healing nectar,
You cure all beings that suffer from the illness of obscuring
    emotions.
You are so kind to hand me enlightenment!
In future lives, may I never be separate from you!

Thus he prayed, and when he was leaving, Shri Singha sang this song
of advice:

If, for instance, the king's treasury
Is robbed by thieves who escape,
When their tracks are found, their precious lives will
    be lost.
Likewise, though the scholars hid the precious gems
Below Bodhgaya with a barrier, they weren't safe.
I took them and bestowed them to you, Vairo.
The first border guards killed your friend.
If they catch you, too, your precious life will be lost.
You should learn speed walking and go quickly to Tibet!

Giving Vairo some gold dust, he advised, "They say that your friend
didn't reach Tibet but was killed by the first border guards. Therefore, you

should find one of the chief swift-footed toll collectors, either Kuhara or Kumara, and make friends by bribing him with gold dust. You should go to the Iron Tree in the Kusha area to learn speed walking according to the sadhana of Three-legged Remati and leave for Tibet. Then the doctrine will definitely spread in Tibet without obstacles." Thus he proclaimed.

Then Vairo went to see all the great masters, including Prahe and Manjushrimitra, who taught him the nature of dharmata in an instant, and he fully comprehended it that very moment. Their wisdom became inseparable, and the entire doctrine was perfected in his mind, without exception. These great masters also advised him to go to Tibet for the benefit of beings.

 This was the eighth chapter of the Great Image, *about Master Shri Singha entrusting the entire doctrine to Vairo.*

9 ❈

Vairotsana Tames King Rahula Bhibhi's Arrogance

Vairotsana looked for the chief guard, Kuhara, but couldn't find him. He then gave Kumara, the speed-walking chief, a gold bar, and they took an oath to be friends. Vairo asked him to give the complete teaching of speed walking, but Kumara said, "Even a father wouldn't give the complete teaching to his son! I'll teach you enough to get you from here to Tibet!" which he did. The Indians have a kind of speed walking that is like a hawk snatching away food, but he gave Vairo one that is like an eagle cutting the mountain ridge. Then Vairo went to the Iron Tree in Kusha to practice the speed walking of Remati. Many old and young people from that area asked him, "Where do you come from? What is your intention?" In answer he said:

> I am Vairotsana,
> Whose wondrous and marvelous body was born
> Within the center of space that is inseparably united with
>   great bliss,
> The nonconceptual dharmadhatu, pure as the sky.

I came from the expanse of the mother, the utterly
    pure space,
To talk about something this world requires.
As the utterly pure all-ground, spontaneously perfect
    great bliss,
That pure skylike enlightened mind
Rose as a compassionate sun within the space of my
    awareness,
I discovered the intent of the conquerors of the three times.
The unborn nonconceptual syllable A
Is the only meditation to make into an object.
A is primordially unperceived and nonarising.
Because it is the source of whatever magical display one
    may need,
The syllable A is the origin of realization,
And I know the wealth that comes from it.
I have no other possessions but the pith instructions of the
    scholars.
I have no other masters but Prahe and Manjushri.
I have no other retinue but the eight types of spirits.
I have no other wife but Samantabhadri's womb.
I have no other friends but the mother dakinis.
I have nothing to eat but the food of dharmadhatu.
I have no other horse but the mental horse of the eight
    collections.
I have no other son but my son of awareness.
I have no other deity but my nature of mind.
I have no other magic but eradicating the three poisons.
I have no home and would like a place to stay for
    the night!

When he had said that, the people from Kusha were delighted; they all did prostrations at the same time and lifted him from his feet. He spent three days there practicing the Iron Mule,[1] which he accomplished. Then he went to the sandalwood area of Takey, where the king of Takey, Rahula the Bald, inquired, "Tibetan monk, could you tell me what this so-called nonarising Dharma is?" and offered him a goatskin jacket. Putting it on, Vairo answered:

I am Vairochana,[2]
Who, intending to be the visible sun
That encompasses all types of beings,
Went through sixteen trials without difficulty.
My illusory body has become old,
But the buddhas' compassion has risen in me;
As I make it appear for everyone,
My name is Vairochana.
My name and aim are similar;
Having realized the depth of the pure skylike dharmata,
There is nothing that does not have buddha-nature.
As the Buddha's representative, I will explain this to you;
Majesty, listen and reflect carefully!
Nonconceptual enlightened mind
Is free of subject and object.
Giving up mental constructs of conventional words,
Cognizant of the very essence, undistracted,
That is the nonarising dharmata.
That itself is the meaning of the view.
If you get used to that essence, without forgetting,
You definitely won't have to take rebirth.

When he said that, the king of Takey was very pleased and asked, "When the mind is not attached to the five sense pleasures and they are naturally purified, is that the same as enjoying the sambhogakaya or not?" Vairotsana answered:

The perfect enjoyment without relinquishing the sense
    pleasures
Is to realize the nonduality of giving up and not giving up
The sense pleasures in the expanse of buddha-nature;
Such practice is the highest enjoyment.

Then the king asked, "Can you explain how the all-ground consciousness can be the dharmadhatu?" Vairotsana replied:

The all-ground consciousness is your own mind;
The dharmadhatu is nothing but your uncontrived mind.

There is no difference between the expanse and the
    all-ground,
So when you cut to the root of the ground, they are
    nondual.
Not to alter this nonduality is the transmission that perfects
    everything.

Again the king asked, "Can you explain the meaning of 'Awareness
wisdom doesn't shift from the expanse; even when tainted by ignorance,
it is not different from the expanse'?" Vairo replied:

When you are aware, original wakefulness appears as the
    expanse.
When you are not aware, original wakefulness appears as
    samsara.
Though there is a big difference between awareness and the
    lack of it,
There is no shifting elsewhere than in the vast expanse
    itself.
There is an immense difference between awareness and
    ignorance,
But when you are aware, the great bliss dharmakaya
Is nothing other than the basic space of the all-ground
    consciousness.

Thus he taught. Then the king asked, "How can one practice this secret that is the innermost secret yoga of Mahayana within the great path of
the view?" To his question, Vairo answered:

Though you actually face the unique Mahayana Secret
    Mantra based on the result,
These extraordinary highest secret teachings,
They are hard to realize.
The wondrous Secret Mantra is the heart of the doctrine.
When all phenomena are directly introduced
As self-display in unbiased evenness, partiality and doubts
    are cut.
This outstanding Secret Mantrayana is said to be the best.

When he had said that, the king asked, "Is there any difference between Yoga, Maha Yoga, Anu Yoga, and Ati Yoga on the ultimate level or not?" At this request, Vairo replied:

> If the nonconceptual dharmadhatu nature is not realized,
> Even though the view and conduct of the three yogas are
> not in conflict,
> As the ultimate depth of the luminous dharmata is not
> understood,
> View and conduct cannot be accomplished when they
> are apart.
> Enlightenment in Ati Yoga, the Great Perfection,
> Is complete without action, free of view and conduct.
> As it is uncontrived and primordially pure,
> Unimpeded by anything, it spontaneously perfects
> great bliss.
> View and conduct are just conventional names;
> Expanse and wakefulness are beyond words.

Thus he taught. Again the king asked, "Which view is higher, that of the two masters[3] or that of Ati Yoga?" Vairotsana replied:

> In the dharmadhatu their ultimate view is originally one,
> But they are not the same from the start.
> The three types of emptiness meditation, such as that on
> shunyata,
> Are skillful ways to lead beings to the destination,
> So how can the result be attained right now?
> The causal teachings, which ultimately give realization of
> emptiness,
> Skillfully make one renounce samsara
> And purify the two types of obscurations through the
> aspect of emptiness.
> Yet, though over eons one has taken
> The Mahayana vow to attain enlightenment,
> How can the utmost depth of the Great Perfection be
> understood?
> The summit of the Great Perfection, Ati Yoga,

Is the ultimate vehicle of perfect liberation.
This inherent, spontaneously perfect, wish-fulfilling
    gemlike kaya
Forms the basis of everything, like space.
Though the two views are equal and distinct, the difference
    is inconceivable:
The view and conduct [of Ati Yoga] are superior in all
    aspects
To those great masters who refer to shunyata;
Because the view is beyond words of emptiness,
And the conduct is a perfectly free play that encompasses
    everything.
Both view and conduct are uncontrived and spontaneously
    perfect.

Thus he taught. Again the king asked, "How does one meditate when practicing Maha Yoga?" Vairo answered:

From the unborn expanse appear a variety of displays.
By visualizing phenomenal existence as *mudra* deities,
Bodily movements are perceived as mudra forms,
Whatever is said is the Dharma mudra,
And whatever is practiced is the samaya mudra.
When the world and beings are both illumined
As Mahamudra deities,
Visualized in the inherent unaltered expanse,
That is the ultimate view of Maha Yoga.

Thus he taught. Again the king asked, "If all vehicles are perfected in the Ati, Ati Yoga being beyond words from the beginning, if one is awakened, how does one become familiar with the three world systems as awakened?" Vairo answered:

The unaltered all-ground is spontaneously perfect from the
    beginning;
Unchanging, the all-encompassing all-ground is primor-
    dially awakened.

The all-ground of sentient beings is originally without
    reference point;
Spontaneously perfect from the beginning, it is primordially
    awakened.
Within the unaltered dharmata, as all beings rest
Uncontrived in that state, it is similar to that itself.
This is known as becoming familiar with the three worlds
    as primordially awakened.

Upon his saying that, the king's pride was broken; he did a thousand prostrations and requested, "Please give me a method to realize the concise meaning of these teachings right now!" Vairo replied:

I pay homage within the state of enlightened mind!
The three worlds are primordial pure lands.
The five degenerations are the primordial solitary places.
All that appears and exists in samsara and nirvana is the
    child of enlightened mind.
And the world and its beings are all pure in their own
    nature.
The primordially pure three worlds are the basic space
    of mind.
With this view you should realize the three worlds as pure.

Feeling overjoyed, the king requested, "Please explain this further!" Vairo replied:

As the wide expanse of space includes the three worlds,
The great vastness of phenomenal existence being every-
    where,
It is utterly purified as nonarising enlightened mind.
Within the immense expanse of pure mind essence,
All beings of the three worlds, without exception, that
    appear,
Are also purified as the essence of one's own mind.
Therefore, I pay homage to the primordially pure form,
In the utterly pure open space of great bliss.

Thus he taught. King Rahula the Bald was delighted, and placing his head at Vairo's feet, he did prostrations. As he offered Vairotsana a gold statue of Arya Maitreya, he said:

> Though the Buddha's compassion is unbiased
> And the buddhas of the three times cannot be made into
>   statues,
> To [Buddha] Vairochana, supreme embodiment of the three
>   kayas,
> Who purified the two obscurations and perfected the two
>   accumulations,
> In order to purify this king's obscurations,
> I offer a rupakaya to the dharmakaya.
> Please make the compassion of the expanse arise
>   within me!

 This was the ninth chapter of the Great Image,
about Vairotsana taming the arrogance of King Rahula the Bald.

10

Vairotsana's Arrival in Tibet

THEN, AS VAIROTSANA prepared to go to Tibet, all the Indian scholars had inauspicious indications in their dreams, and there were bad omens. All the flowers turned toward Tibet; all the fragrance of sandalwood and other medicinal plants drifted toward Tibet on the wind, and all the dogs faced Tibet when they barked. Then the Indian king upholding the Dharma, the seven scholars, and others talked about their various inauspicious dreams. Gathering at the entrance of Nalanda University, the source of learning, in the city of Kapilavastu, they discussed why the indications and signs were negative. "It is simply those Tibetan monks who took our pith instructions!" they said. Then they looked at the seals in Bodhgaya and finding that they had been broken, they cried, "Who told them? Who took them?"

Even though they investigated through the Nigu[1] and others, they could not find out. Consulting an oracular mirror[2] they were told, "The instructions were leaked by someone with a long iron beak who is sitting on three rocks and whose body is made of rock and filled with eyes.[3] At his head is a large valley with a lake in the center. Outside are two beings wearing deerskin hoods and holding walking sticks. They have eyes on their necks and are listening to these leaks, each carrying a load. Very strange; I don't know whether they are gods, humans, or miraculous beings." Then the scholars and the king upholding the Dharma got together to discuss the situation: "The marvelous heart of the doctrine, the mind essence of all the victorious ones, the summit of all vehicles, the teachings of the effortless Great Perfection have been taken to Tibet! Our Indian elixirs and merit will also be lost to Tibet! Our positive qualities, the heart of the doctrine, will be lost to Tibet without anything left! We should send speed-walking messengers to capture and kill the thieves who have taken them!" The speed-walking chief Kumara heard this; running to his friend Vairotsana, he told him about the dreams of the seven scholars:

> Bodhisattva friend, listen!
> The King of Dogs Dhahuna told of a dream he had:
> "I dreamt that the marvelous heart of the doctrine, the
>   highest vehicle,
> The teachings on the unaltered nature of primordial
>   buddhahood,
> The pith instructions to attain enlightenment in this
>   lifetime,
> Which were sealed and hidden in Bodhgaya, were taken
>   to Tibet!
> I dreamt that the king of Tibet, who has the Dharma eye,
> Sent two boys who are emanations of bodhisattvas,
> With gold dust. They came here,
> Tore out the hearts of twenty-one Indian scholars,
> And took them to Tibet!
> The panditas should send speed-walkers immediately!"

> When those present heard this, they said,
> "If they have attained accomplishment, they will still
>   get away!"

> Kukkuraja told this dream:
> "In a visionary experience about
> The great bliss pith instructions from the king of vehicles,
> Which is the highest and utmost Vajra Vehicle,
> The instructions to attain fruition in this lifetime,
> I dreamt that the secret instructions hidden in the mind,

Which are like the sun that treats everyone equally, were
    not there!
The king of Tibet, who is an emanation of a bodhisattva,
Sent two yaksha-headed beings who had purified their
    obscurations.
They came to our country, India,
And putting the sun in their pocket they took it away!
The panditas should send speed-walkers immediately!"

Manjushri Bhadra related this dream:
"For the sake of the highest destined ones, the Buddha
    taught
True enlightenment that spontaneously perfects
    great bliss.
In order to transmute the five conflicting emotions,
We seven scholars should also keep in mind
These esoteric instructions to attain fruition in this life,
So we can dispel our ignorance.
I dreamt that the king, an emanation of Avalokiteshvara,
Who practices this primordial self-perfection,
Sent two Tibetan monks abiding on the bhumis
With gold dust, and they came here.
Through the blessings of Vajrasattva's compassion
The sun of perfect compassion had risen here;
But the two monks put that wish-fulfilling gem needed
    by everyone
In their pocket and took it to Tibet!
The panditas should send speed-walkers immediately!"

Dagnyima related this dream:
"As all that appears and exists is awakened in the unaltered
    all-ground,
I dreamt that the Mahayana Secret Mantra teachings
That were hidden in Bodhgaya with five seals,
Which spontaneously perfect the inherent uncontrived
    dharmata,
Unaltered as it is, were taken to Tibet!

I dreamt that the king of Tibet, an emanation of the three
  families,
Put the essence of all organs, the eyes
Of the scholars learned in the meaning of cause and result,
The great fruition teachings of true enlightenment,
In his pocket and took them to Tibet!
The panditas should send speed-walkers immediately!"

Rishi Bhashita told this dream:
"The teachings on primordial buddhahood beyond cause
  and effect,
Which are the ultimate view of the conquerors of the
  three times,
The highest vehicle of great bliss, spontaneously perfecting
  equality,
Were sealed and hidden in the space of realization.
But I dreamt that the king of Tibet, an emanation of
  Manjushri,
Sent two Tibetan monks abiding on the bhumis
With gold dust. They came here
And uprooted the wish-fulfilling tree in central India
With its abundant elixir, flowers, and fruits and took it
  to Tibet!
The panditas should send speed-walkers immediately!"

Shri Singha related this dream:
"For the benefit of fortunate beings with the highest
  faculties,
The naturally uncontrived supreme vehicle
Was hidden in Bodhgaya with five seals
For the sake of future destined ones.
But I dreamt that Trisong Deutsen, an emanation of the
  three families,
Decided to mature and liberate fortunate beings
Through the pith instructions to attain fruition in this life.
He sent two yaksha-headed Tibetan monks
With gold dust, who came here,
Took the heart out of the impermanent illusory body,

And brought it to Tibet!
The panditas should send speed-walkers immediately!"

Kungamo related this dream:
"The unmistaken true path of perfect dharmata,
The great bliss pith instructions of the Indian scholars,
Were hidden deep within enlightened mind.
But the king of Tibet, who in his last life
Was the son of Brahmin Shri in India,
A monk called Avadhuti who passed away,
Emanated, took on the body of the king of Tibet,
And now steers the Tibetan kingdom.
In order to spread the true great bliss in Tibet,
This incarnated bodhisattva sent gold dust
With two monks whose wisdom bodies are fully matured.
They came here, and through a terrifying hurricane
    from Tibet,
They uprooted the bodhi tree at Bodhgaya!
The panditas should send speed-walkers immediately!"

When the people who were present heard this, they said,
"If they have attained accomplishment they will still
    get away!"

Thus Kumara spoke, and putting his head against Vairotsana's breast,
he wept. Vairotsana answered:

How wonderful! Trustworthy friend!
You took birth as a human, superior to other births;
Through pure prayers you were born in India.
You attained the miraculous accomplishment of speed
    walking
And are from a noble family that makes fine offerings to
    the gurus.
As you kept your precepts, all your wishes will be fulfilled.
Purifying your obscurations, you told me what the noble
    ones discussed.
Since you are straightforward, everyone will rely on you;

Your body completes whatever is needed, so I asked for
    your help.
My parents gave me birth, but you prolonged my life.
Making friends with you, I gained true enlightenment.
I shall dispel the darkness of ignorance from Tibet,
And the merit of maturing and liberating beings,
Which is equal to eons of training for the purpose of
    enlightenment,
I shall dedicate to Kumara.
I have accomplished speed walking, so I am leaving now;
See me off to Nepal, so I can give you some heartfelt
    advice!

Thus speaking, he gave Kumara a heap of gold dust and three gold
bars, and taking the golden statue offered by the king of Takey, the two
friends continued together. Vairotsana wore a big deerskin hood over his
head and worn-out boots backward on his feet. The collar of his garment
was put on backward, and he went along holding a white willow stick.

The first toll collector they met was the speed-walking chief Kuhara,
and since he was a friend of the speed-walking chief Kumara, the two
friends bribed Kuhara with a handful of gold dust and two gold bars and
said, "When the speed-walkers come here tonight and ask if you have seen
a Tibetan monk, you should say that you didn't see anyone resembling a
Tibetan monk, but that someone came by wearing a big deerskin hood on
his head and worn-out boots backward on his feet who wanted to reach
central Tibet and was so unusual that you don't know whether it was an
emanation, a man, or a yaksha." They made the guard swear to do this.
Then Kumara went to the gate of Kapilavastu City, called all his speed-
walking friends, and said, "Did the Tibetan monk Vairotsana come by
here? He should be killed!" The king upholding the Dharma and the seven
scholars also said that anyone who met him should kill him.

At the first border post the speed-walkers asked the toll collector, "Did
a Tibetan monk come by here?" The toll collector replied, "No Tibetan
monk came by, but someone wearing a big deerskin hood on his head,
worn-out boots backward on his feet, and the collar of his clothes on his
back came by. He was headed toward central Tibet and was so unusual that
I don't know whether it was a man, a demon, or an emanation." When he

said that, the speed-walkers turned back. Then Vairotsana continued on to Brown Willow Grove in Khotan, where he met the nun Litsa Tsultrim Dron and asked her for a place to stay:

> Patroness of this place,
> This monk has no place to stay
> And no food or drink
> And is begging for a gift.

Upon hearing this, the nun replied, "I don't have anywhere to stay either. I myself wander around in towns and depend on others; but I shall give you an offering. Monk, what gift do you want?" When she said that, the master said:

> For this old monk traveling a difficult road,
> A place to stay behind the door is fine, as long as I'm
>   comfortable.
> It is fine to wear torn clothes as long as they keep me warm.
> It is fine to eat leftover food, as long as it fills my stomach.
> No matter what you say, I am not going!

The nun thought that he might be the learned Vairotsana who was supposed to be in the area; if it were he, he would be extremely exhausted. Asking where he had been and what his story was, she found out that he was Vairotsana and asked, "Venerable great guru, how can one realize the nature of mind?" Vairotsana replied:

> The nature of mind is like the expanse of space:
> The expanse of space has neither center nor limit;
> The expanse of space is impartial;
> The expanse of space is unchanging;
> The expanse of space is free from foundation and root.
> Enlightened mind is without limit or center;
> Enlightened mind is impartial;
> Enlightened mind is unchanging;
> Enlightened mind is free from foundation and root.
> True enlightenment is the perfect buddha.

When he said that, Litsa Tsultrim Dron was convinced. Offering him a horse called Golden Duck, she requested the pith instructions. As she practiced the instructions, the correct realization dawned in her mind, and she remained in the nature of the view.

Then, when Vairotsana arrived in Nepal, he met a pandita called Prajna Siddhi at a place called Takshaka. The pandita asked him, "Vairotsana, what is your level of realization? Tibetan monk, how can one realize one's mind? In which vehicle should one be skilled to attain fruition? Which offerings please the exalted ones?" To the first question Vairotsana answered:

> Mind's definition is primordially devoid of self-nature;
> It doesn't depend on a cause and can't be defined with
>   examples.
> This luminous nature of nonconceptual purity
> Is understood by the conquerors but can't be pointed out.

To the second question he answered:

> The entrance to the one view of the ultimate nature of
>   things
> Is clearly distinguished for those of higher and moderate
>   capacities.
> Understand that you can attain fruition by realizing
> Any of the sacred Dharma vehicles taught by the Buddha.

To the third question he answered:

> Regarding everyone as equal
> Within the primordially pure vast space without reference
>   point,
> Unattached to the originally luminous, simple buddha form
> And without being stingy of retinue, place, or material
>   things:
> That is the best of offerings.
> Consider that the exalted ones will like it most.

The scholar Prajna Siddha was overjoyed and made him the resident monk for one winter month. Then, going into Nepal, the Indian goddess

Remati Sister sent snow in order to find out whether Vairotsana's teachings were true or not, so he sang this song:

> The past, present, and future are one's own mind;
> Free of birth and death, one's own mind is the buddhas of
>   the three times.
> In order to make the mind's sun rise
> For fortunate ones of highest intelligence,
> With an intention as good as gold,
> Between India and Tibet
> I risked sixteen trials,
> But none of these hardships prevented my obtaining the
>   instructions.
> This snow is about to hinder me.
> If my teachings are true, stop this blizzard!

When he said that, the red goddess revealed her form from between the clouds, prostrated, and promised to serve him. Suddenly, the snow stopped, and the sun became very warm. Then Vairo offered the golden statue to the Swayambhunath Stupa and said:

> The forms of the past, present, and future conquerors have
>   no obscurations,
> Their words of strong compassion are like the sky of the
>   Jambu continent.
> Though the Buddha's compassion is unbiased,
> Worldly affairs are as endless as the sky.
> For the sake of liberating the ocean of samsara through
>   compassion,
> I ask the forms of the conquerors of the three times for
>   forgiveness.

Thus speaking, he offered the statue. Then, he went to teach the Dharma in the Nyangro Meadow and arrived at Samye toward the evening. The king's subjects and attendants were all outside, while King Trisong Deutsen himself was sitting in a tent. Vairotsana disguised himself, sneaked into the tent from the northern side, and whispered into the king's ear, "I've got the pith instructions you told me to get, but the Indians are very jealous; if you have heard any slander, you shouldn't listen to it!" Giving him the main points of the instructions, he made the king take an oath and withdrew. Then, the king went to his nine-storied mansion, and while he was there, Vairo sent a message with his main attendant Mithingte:

> Great king of Tibet!
> Disheartened with worldly affairs,
> You yearned for the unmistaken, perfectly true teachings
> And sent us with gold dust to search for them.
> Passing the borders was like going through hell,
> But due to pure karmic fortune I met many scholars
> And learned arts, shastras, medicine,
> And various other useful things required in this life.
> I have the various protective deities that liberate samaya
>   breakers
> And the weapons of logic to refute opponents.
> I have all the vehicles of cause and result without
>   exception,
> Including the respective stages of the gradual path for those
>   of different faculties.
> I have the wondrous essence of the doctrine, the highest
>   vehicle,
> The heart of all the buddhas that spontaneously perfects
>   great bliss,
> The entire effortless Great Perfection beyond cause and
>   effect, without exception.
> When I meet you, please listen to my advice!
> I haven't seen you for so long; are you in good health?
> Your Majesty, I hope to see you soon!

He sent this to the king, who replied with this message:

> I am like the commander of the great ship of samsara.
> Though my health is steady,
> I can't bear that some day my five aggregates
> And eighteen major constituents will perish.
> You found the best antidote against the decay of aggregates
>   and constituents:

The essential truth beyond cause and effect
That excels all outer and inner teachings based on cause
    and result.
I am delighted that none of the border guards, yakshas,
    fearful bears and savages,
Or other terrifying vicious obstacles
Were able to harm your physical body,
Which is like a wish-fulfilling gem!
As you have come and brought
The true, unmistaken, blissful sacred teachings,
The effortless Great Perfection beyond cause and effect,
I shall meet you and pay my respects!

That is what the message said. Then, the venerable Vairo sent a message to Queen Margyen:[4]

Your Majesty Margyen, precious queen,
Not realizing the unborn dharmadhatu of great bliss,
You are attached to the worldly affairs of apparent
    existence.
Today I heard from your attendants
That you have not been unbalanced
By the eighty-four thousand obstructing forces and the five
    elements
And that the three sons you gave birth to
Were born without obstacles.
Having developed the thought of enlightenment in order
    to be a lamp of the doctrine,
I nearly died from all kinds of hardships.
Vairo's body completes whatever one might need,
And I respectfully request an audience with Queen
    Margyen.

Queen Margyen sent this answer:

You, Vairo, developed the unsurpassed supreme enlightened
    mind
To dispel the ignorance of samsaric gloom.

You went through hardships to find the pith instructions
That spontaneously perfect great bliss without effort.
I am very happy that you have returned without hindrance;
I received your message and shall meet you as you wish.

That was the message she sent.

 This was the tenth chapter of The Great Image,
about Vairotsana's arrival in Tibet.

11 ⚬

Vairotsana Is Banished to Tsawarong

OR THE NEXT three days Vairotsana and King Trisong Deutsen didn't
meet. On the morning of the third day, when they met and the king was
about to prostrate, Master Vairo said:

> I have revealed the mind essence of the conquerors of
>   the three times,
> The self-existing, naturally perfect, enlightened mind of
>   great bliss.
> Come all you arrogant ones who have fallen into worldly
>   delusion
> And faithfully submit obeisance!

Upon hearing this, the king, queen, and their retinue prostrated and
circumambulated him and touched their heads to his feet. When they
went inside, the king untied his hair, spreading it over the threshold so
that Vairotsana could walk over it. Then, Trisong Deutsen presented him
with the horses Red Spark and Golden Duck, adorned with golden
turquoise-inlaid saddles, jewels, gold, silver, brocades, wolf skin coats,
fine food and drink, and so forth, then said:

145

KYEHO! Master, please accept these offerings
Of Red Spark and Golden Duck
With their beautiful golden turquoise-inlaid saddles,
Precious materials, coats of lynx and wolf fur,
Fine food and drink, and so forth
And teach me the king of pith instructions,
The effortless great bliss that gives instant
    enlightenment!

Upon his request Vairo replied:

I don't want these gifts! I don't want horses;
I gained accomplishment in speed walking,
So what would I do with domestic horses?
I don't want it! I don't want precious wealth;
I gained mastery over the dharmadhatu treasury,
So what would I do with illusory wealth?
I don't want it! I don't want silks and garments;
I have the ornament of samadhi realization,
So what would I do with silks and garments?
I don't want it! I don't want food or drink;
I drink the essential nectar of dharmata,
So why should I crave food?
I won't sell the king of pith instructions, the Great
    Perfection,
For the king of animals, the horse.
I don't trade Dharma for wealth;
To do so would contradict the Buddha's teachings.
I shall give the king of pith instructions
Only to disciples who are very modest and respect
    their guru,
Who observe the sacred commitments correctly and are
    very intelligent,
Who have faith and cherish the Dharma more than
    their life,
Who have a good character and practice the teachings.
I won't trade Dharma for wealth!

Thus he spoke. Again the king requested:

> The Tibetan people's modesty is no greater than the water
>   in a vase,
> But the king's modesty is the size of the ocean!
> Whatever you teach, I'll observe the sacred commitments
>   correctly
> With sincere one-pointed devotion to the master.
> I request the pith instructions without caring for my life or
>   for wealth or food,
> And regarding them as precious gold, I shall undertake
>   them in the correct manner.
> Please teach me the king of pith instructions!

Offering the horses and wealth, he did prostrations and circumambulations, placed his head at Vairo's feet, and wept. As he kept pleading, Vairotsana said, "If His Majesty has this much faith and will study and practice the pith instructions in the correct manner without concern for his body or life, I shall teach the pith instructions at midnight so that your wicked subjects and ministers won't be aware of it."

At this promise, the king prostrated to Master Vairotsana and placed his head at the master's feet. Trusting that Master Vairo possessed the sacred Dharma in general and the Ati Yoga pith instructions in particular, everyone did full prostrations, and he became known as the King's Master, holder of the pith instructions. Then all the subjects and ministers proceeded, saying, "Our king, Trisong Deutsen, also has a master!" So Vairo was called the King's Master. Then the Triple Gem became the highest object of veneration; the Sangha was more powerful than the king and was respected as the sublime object of offering. During the daytime, Master Vairotsana translated the teachings based on cause and effect for the king, ministers, and others; at midnight he translated the pith instructions for the king himself.

First, he translated the four sets of Scriptures on Vinaya along with their commentaries. Then he translated the *Prajnaparamita in a Hundred Thousand Verses*, the *Sutra Requested by Maitreya*, *Stories of Sadaparudita* up to the ninth section, the *Jewel Mound Sutra* up to the thirty-fifth section, and the 108 sections of the *Great Volume of the Buddha*. Of the

Parinirvana Sutra, he translated 250 sections, leaving eight untranslated. He also translated fifteen sections of the *Sutra of the Descent to Lanka* (*Lankavatara-sutra*). Thus, he translated the teachings based on the cause with their respective commentaries.

Of the scriptural Dharma, he translated the tantras of Yamantaka, *Jewel Light Tantra*, *King of Mastery Tantra*, *Blazing Like Kalpa-Fire Tantra*, and *Wrathful Pundarika Tantra*, as well as the Sixteen Tantras and others. At midnight, he taught the Secret Mantrayana. During the daytime, he translated many sutra teachings, and he occasionally taught the pith instructions. Then he consented to propagate the pith instructions and taught *Great Space Tantra* to be the fine shirt adorned with *Entering into All Objects* as the fringe, *Cuckoo of Awareness* and *Shaking of Great Power* as the sleeves, and *Six Topics of Enlightened Mind* as the collar.[1]

Of the tantric scriptural Dharma, he translated the *Tantra of Yamantaka's Words*, *Precious Discourse Tantra*, *King of Mastery Tantra*, Five Tantras including *Great Space Tantra*, the *Marvelous, All-Creating Monarch Tantra*, *Ten Sutras*,[2] and *Ocean Expanse Instructions*.

Of the inner Secret Mantra he translated the Eighteen Tantras and the Sixteen Maha Yoga Tantras. Of the teachings he himself composed, he taught the tantras and sutras that are the quintessence of the oral transmission.

He translated the first teachings on the Four Noble Truths, the middle teachings on metaphysics of the Causal Vehicle, the final teachings on absolute truth, and all the other teachings contained in the eight sciences taught by the Buddha.

He translated the tantras, scriptures, and instructions of the five families, Vajradhara, and the lords of the three families,[3] as well as everything contained in the eight charnel grounds.[4] He translated all the commentaries and oral instructions of the supreme Six Ornaments[5] and the twenty-five vidyadharas, including Prahe, Manjushri, and Shri Singha. Day and night for five years he turned the wheel of the Dharma, compiling 590 volumes of teachings by Master Padma, Master Shantarakshita, the twenty-five Indian scholars, and others, as well as Indian astrology, Chinese divination, Bon, Taoism, healing and medicine, and various other arts. In brief, he taught all topics of knowledge without exception, connecting the upper and the lower, such as the king and Yudra Nyingpo, Mutig Tsenpo and Mipham Gonpo, Tsawarong and central Tibet, and so on.

At that time the king felt like showering the Dharma on the entire population of Tibet. He wanted to organize a Dharma celebration to express his gratitude, but the great lord had a bad omen in his dream and said:

> I dreamt that the sun and moon simultaneously rose in
>   Tsawarong;
> That all the books went up into the sky;
> That the ten laws affected me, Vairo;
> And that the king and ministers died.
> It is not a good sign: Majesty, postpone the festival!

When he said that, he threw flowers at the books three times, Dharma melodies resounded naturally from all the volumes, and the sky was filled with offering substances such as canopies, victory banners, flags, a rain of flowers, and special music. Gods, nagas, *kinnaras*,[6] and others gathered and brought joy, love, and respect. The outer ministers turned their backs and were furious, but the king and one hundred thousand Sangha members and others did countless prostrations and circumambulations.

At that time, manifesting as Shakyamuni, I caused all sorts of visual appearances, such as Ananda, Vairo Yeshe De, a *tirthika*, a Bonpo, a sorcerer, and so forth.[7]

Meanwhile, the learned Indian panditas and the Indian king upholding the Dharma became suspicious of each other. The panditas believed that the king had broken the seals and sent the pith instructions to the king of Tibet. The king thought that the panditas had broken the seals and sent the instructions with the Tibetan monk. At that time the king was powerless to teach the tantras, pith instructions, and quintessence of the Ati Yoga teachings, the inconceivable special instructions that remained in the minds of the panditas, and for a while he remained in meditation. The panditas and the king then compiled the commonly known Eighteen Major Scriptures of the Mind Class into one, and compiled the Sixty Tantra Sections as esoteric instructions. The king said, "Conceal them as treasures in Bodhgaya," and it is said that they were hidden there. Another version has it that these teachings were hidden at Vulture Peak Mountain, and elsewhere it is said that they were hidden in the Asura Cave. The king sent copies of the books to a place where they vanished without a trace; like putting a jewel into the throat of a crocodile, they were hidden as treasures until the end of the eon.

Then the Indian king and the wicked ministers conspired and decided to send malicious gossip to Tibet so that Vairotsana would be killed. To proclaim the slander, they sent conspirators to Tibet, who declared to the Tibetan king, ministers, and subjects, "That Tibetan monk Vairotsana didn't find any pith instructions! He took the Indian evil spells, black magic, sorcery, and other destructive things to bring ruin to Tibet. He should be punished under Tibetan capital law!" This is what they proclaimed.

Then the wicked Tibetan ministers assembled and went to complain to the king: "You sent that monk Vairotsana to search for the Dharma, but that is not what he found! They say that he brought evil spells and other black magic to destroy Tibet! He is bound to ruin the Tibetan kingdom; you should have him killed!" The king refused, saying that it wasn't true. Insisting, each of the ministers then talked to him privately, but he wouldn't consent. Minister Ngam Tara Lugong[8] complained, "He even wants to use up our wealth! By secretly teaching the Dharma to the king, he has created a lot of jealousy!" Ngam Tara Lugong summoned the ministers and said, "If Vairotsana is not killed, Tibet will be ruined, and the government will collapse!" So they decided to ignore the king. Then the king said, "If it has gone this far, to murder him won't do; he should be drowned!" He had a beggar who looked like Vairo caught, dressed him up in Vairo's clothes and boots, and put him in a closed copper vessel, which was thrown into the Tsangpo River at the Yarlung junction. Then it was declared that the king had had Vairotsana drowned, and the king pretended to beat his chest, lament, revolt, and shed tears.

The king then ordered the construction of a pavilion for sitting in the sun and had a thick pillar made. He dug a cavity inside the pillar, put a plank over the entrance, and let Vairotsana stay inside. At midnight, when the attendants and servants up on the roof were asleep, the king took the plank off the pillar and listened to the Dharma. One night Tsepongza Margyen happened upon him, and through her the wicked ministers discovered what the king was up to. The ministers said to the king, "Your Majesty! You smeared your ancestors' gold and silver on clay, saying you were making a temple! You cut up the brocades, saying you were making canopies! You said you were practicing the Dharma, but you caught a beggar and threw him in the river! Your Majesty, you don't have compassion, you are wrong! Now you say you made a pavilion for sitting in the sun, but you have hidden Vairotsana inside, causing evil to increase! This is not good! Once again the government is threatened!" The king replied, "Before you couldn't perceive as much as a ray of sun from a bodhisattva's countenance, and you still can't. That slander is a lie, and you are wrong! But if you insist on having it your way, it would be better to banish him than to kill him." Upon hearing this, the ministers agreed it was a better solution and they decided to banish Vairo. While the king, ministers, and subjects had a meeting, Vairo, thinking that he might not be banished if he told them about the hardships he had undergone, sang a song about his sixteen trials:

> King, ministers, and subjects, listen to me!
> When the compassionate Trisong Deutsen
> Needed someone to search for the pith instructions,
> He couldn't find anyone to go.
> Traveling to the frightening borderland,
> A promise that no one else could make was my first
>   trial.
>
> Then, when I started my journey,
> In fearful places with border guards speaking different
>   languages,
> Finding the road without a guide was my second trial.
>
> While it snowed on the White Pass,
> Where I would fall into a deathtrap if I took a single
>   misstep,
> Nearly dying from exhaustion was my third trial.
>
> When I was forced to spend the night
> At the dwelling of Yaksha Ferocious in the hot valley
>   [of Nepal],
> Escaping the flesh-eating yaksha was my fourth trial.
>
> Crawling on my hands and feet like a wild animal
> In order to erase our tracks in the snow of Nepal, while
> Hiding during the day and walking at night, was my
>   fifth trial.

At Brown Rock Enclosure in a place full of spies,
A pack of wild beasts were about to eat me;
Performing a miracle to escape from being eaten was my
    sixth trial.

Traveling in India along narrow paths with nowhere to
    give way,
My escape from toll collectors, who were bound by law to
    kill me,
By deceiving them with a miracle was my seventh
    trial.

While proceeding on a narrow blocked trail without
    shoulders,
Evading toll collectors I met who were hard to interpret
And who beat me with their cane swords was my
    eighth trial.

At a dangerous narrow path of plantain trees, Scarlet Bird
    Face died.
Escaping the terrifying roars of
A wolf pack that ate his flesh was my ninth trial.

At a fearful metal toll bridge near Magadha,
Tribesmen wanting gold, who were hard to interpret,
Cut my shin muscles to get gold. Escaping them was my
    tenth trial.

Arriving in the Kriya Krisha area,
People claimed I was a foreign spy.
Escaping the dreadful frog pit into which they threw me
    was my eleventh trial.

Reaching the Prasuta area and a place called Bhibhi,
Terrified by poisonous snakes, bears, and the king,
For six days I was close to death. That escape was my
    twelfth trial.

Proceeding to the Magadha region,
I risked my life trying to cross a poisonous lake
In a boat made of cloth and sticks, which was my
    thirteenth trial.

On my way to a place called Avadhuti,
I evaded suspicious tribal people from Mon
Who beat me with a shower of sticks, which was my
    fourteenth trial.

On the way to Arya Palo and the Krisha region,
Trying to escape terrifying hide, metal, and snakeskin
    masks
And the bite of vicious poisonous snakes was my
    fifteenth trial.

Overcoming the poison
That a group of women in the Edhakesha area
Had put in the food they gave me was my sixteenth
    trial.

Having gone through these sixteen hardships,
I deceived an old Brahmini who was hard to fool
And met the learned Indian panditas,
Including Prahe, Manjushri, and Shri Singha,
Who are difficult to encounter even after eons of
    purification.

I discovered the essence of the doctrine, which is hard
    to find,
And realized my mind as the buddha, which is hard to
    realize.
For the sake of dispelling the darkness of Tibet,
I went to the king and ministers to satisfy them.
As I accomplished all these hardships for the sake
    of Tibet,
Vairotsana shouldn't be banished!

Thus he sang. Relating all these stories in detail, he became discouraged and burst into tears. The ministers and subjects lowered their raised heads, their faces dim, and made no reply. Vairotsana thought that perhaps they might listen if he reminded them that he had been sent to search for the pith instructions after the king, ministers, and subjects had all discussed it and that he had risked his life after renouncing his parents, relatives, and friends, so he sang this song:

> Majesty, ministers, and subjects, please listen!
> From the age of eight I stayed with the king:
> For three years I worked as an outer, inner, and middle
>   minister, and
> For three years I was the king's attendant.
>
> Then the king, ministers, and subjects all gathered
> And planned the search for the great bliss instructions
> In the foreign country where death was almost certain.
>
> In order to fulfill the king's wish,
> I renounced what no one else could bear to leave for even
>   an instant:
> The parents who gave me birth and cherished me more
>   than their own eyes,
> The relatives I am linked with in life, death, and grave,
> And the home I connected to through prayers and karma.
>
> Enduring hardships without concern for my body or life,
> Between Tibet and India I nearly died from exhaustion
>   fifty-four times.
> I have all the teachings of the Buddha without exception and
> Discovered all the oral instructions on great bliss
> Hidden in the minds of the Indian scholars.
>
> Since all of you had discussed and agreed upon this from
>   the beginning,
> Don't you feel sorry for banishing me,
> The lamp that can clarify Tibet's darkness of ignorance, to
>   Tsawarong?

Having sung this, he cried. The ministers lowered their faces and looked dejected. The king and those subjects who were devoted to the Dharma wept, and the king said, "We should all consider that Vairo is right about having endured many hardships for the sake of Tibet, and he has come back after revealing the depth of all the pith instructions. Let us decide not to banish him; let him stay here!" When he said that, the ministers departed with angry faces; they looked away and didn't say a word. The next morning the king and all the ministers had another meeting, and Vairo was told to leave no matter what. Hoping that they might not banish him if he told them about the qualities he possessed that were valuable for Tibet, Vairo sang this song:

> Majesty, ministers, and subjects, listen!
> First I developed the aspiration toward supreme
>   enlightenment,
> Risking my life by enduring various hardships.
>
> Vairo's body indeed completes whatever is needed:
> I have all nine diagrams of divination to find human food
>   and horses' fodder;
> I have the healing and medicine practices to cure disease;
> I have the profound stream of wealth, without fear
>   of hunger and thirst.
>
> I have the shravaka vinaya rules to eradicate the three
>   poisons;
> I have the truth of the interdependence of cause and effect
>   to stop the *kleshas*;
> I have the Bodhisattva Vehicle to travel the five paths and
>   ten bhumis;
> I have the three sections of Kriya and Yoga to purify
>   obscurations and ward off sudden accidents.
>
> I have the Maledictory Fierce Mantra to eliminate
>   breaches;
> I know the three sadhanas of Mamo, Yamantaka, and Kilaya
>   to guard the teachings;

I have the three types of supreme and common accomplish-
    ments; and
I know the Great Perfection, which delivers enlightenment
    into the palm of one's hand.

Therefore, it is not right to banish me, Vairotsana, who
    embodies all needs,
To a foreign place with different languages.
You should banish those who are dishonest to friends,
    short-tempered to relatives,
And unfaithful to the king!

When he said that, nobody answered, and they all sat there with angry, gloomy faces. Again, Vairo thought it might help if he reminded them of the best things, so he sang this song:

Listen! I am going to sing a song about the nine best things:
The best father is the vajra master.
Did you know that other, ordinary fathers are the oceans
    of samsara?

The best mother is clear knowledge.
Did you know that other, ordinary mothers are the fetters
    to samsara?

The best son is a worthy disciple.
Did you know that common sons are the welcome party
    of samsara?

The best wealth is the seven noble riches.
Did you know that illusory wealth is deceptive
    seduction?

The best ornaments are the qualities of learning.
Did you know that ornaments to adorn the body are
    attachment?

The best fourfold conversion is the dharmadhatu.
Did you know that the fourfold conversion of the ministers
and subjects is an illusory net?

The best magic is Mamo, Yamantaka, and Kilaya.
Did you know that the magic of evil mantras is a wicked
murderer?

The best teaching is the supreme Ati Vehicle.
Did you know that the vehicles of cause and result are the
expedient meaning?

The best buddha is the realization of one's own mind.
Did you know that peaceful and wrathful buddhas are
mere wishes?

Upon his having said this, the king thought that they should recon-
sider letting the learned Vairotsana stay. He summoned the subjects and
ministers and advised them not to banish Vairotsana, but the wicked ministers said, "If this Vairotsana, who knows black magic and all kinds of dis-
astrous things, is not banished, Tibet will be ruined. Expel him!"

Vairotsana then sang a song saying that Tibet would be ruined if the
king and ministers banished him:

Majesty, ministers, and subjects, listen once more!
Instead of listening to the king's command, which is like
the sun,
You believe in irrelevant rumors from abroad,
So the king and subjects of our homeland will be spoiled
and ruined.

You banish Vairotsana, who teaches the truth,
And employ ministers, who burn everyone physically and
mentally,
So the king and subjects of our homeland will be spoiled
and ruined.

You give up the precious Dharma that benefits this and
  future lives, and
Listen to schisms from abroad that were spread to ruin
  Tibet,
So the king and subjects of our homeland will be spoiled
  and ruined.

Even though he spoke in this way, he received no answer. Instead, they all asked him to leave. Then Vairo blamed Tsepongza Margyen, saying, "It is your fault!" and sang a song about her going to hell due to breaking her sacred commitment:

I, Vairotsana, who will take no further rebirth,
Intending to mature the Tibetan kingdom,
From the age of fifteen up to fifty-seven
Left all association with my parents, relatives, and friends
  behind.

I have told the queen and her husband
How much hardship I endured to bring Tibet to spiritual
  maturity.
I have the means to prolong their lives,
So they can attain fruition and stabilize the monastery;
But Minister Lugong provoked evil in Tibet,
And I blame the queen for indirectly supporting him.

Whatever she does, her feelings are far from love.
She offends the Three Jewels and doesn't respect them;
She doesn't keep her samaya and associates with bad friends.
Look in the sutras and tantras translated by the learned
  translators
Whether there is anywhere else to go but the three lower
  realms!
Study *Rampant Elephant* and other tantras
To know the effect of breaking one's precepts!

Not growing weary even if she lives for a hundred years,
She wanted a relationship both now and later.[9]

With words, a woman's character can lead one astray,
    and
I blame the queen for never sticking to what she says.

Thus he spoke. The queen prostrated to Vairo, and with folded hands she replied:

Learned master, listen to my answer!
Though between the age of fifteen and fifty-seven
You left your parents and relatives
And endured countless hardships,
Cherished like a jewel from the sea through all these
    years,
Trisong Deutsen, a descendant from the border region
    of Mon,
And the foreign subject Tara Lugong,
Who scatter the Tibetan kingdom into ruins,
Want to banish the sun of Tibet! What a pity!

Saying this she grasped Vairotsana and wept. Vairotsana replied, "Now the queen says not to banish Vairotsana! Her words are inconsistent!" Crying, Queen Margyen replied:

Great scholar, don't speak like that!
I am the king's wife
And the mother of his three sons.
A woman's character is very selfish;
It's impossible to forget that!
Those words slipped from my mouth when I was angry
With Trisong, who comes from a foreign Mon family.
Master, you are right; please forgive me!

Then Vairotsana sang a song to the king about not being attached to worldly affairs:

I, Vairotsana,
Have realized the depth of dharmata's ocean,
So what use do I have for illusory wealth?

All that appears and exists is a celestial palace,
So what use do I have for an ego-clinging country?

My father is the Triple Gem,
So what use do I have for an ego-clinging father?

My mother is the pure dharmadhatu,
So what use do I have for an illusory mother?

Whatever appears is my friend of awareness,
So what use do I have for sentimental relatives?

Thus speaking, he prepared to go.

Then a king from Nawoche came to pay his respects to Trisong Deutsen. He asked where Vairotsana had gone and what he was doing. Minister Tara said, "Vairotsana has been banished to Tsawarong." The king from Nawoche paid his respects to Trisong Deutsen, and weeping, he said, "Now that Vairotsana has been banished to Tsawarong, won't the sun of Tibet set? How do you dare banish someone like that?" Trisong Deutsen agreed, and gathering the subjects and ministers, he said with tears in his eyes:

Listen! Close and distant ministers and subjects, linked
    by karma!
I met a foreigner speaking a different language
Who said that the sun of Tibet would set.
Weeping, he asked how I dared banish someone like
    Vairotsana!
Please let us agree to let this great scholar,
Who perfects all needs, stay in Tibet!

All the wicked ministers said unanimously, "If we don't banish Vairotsana, his black magic and evil spells will spread!" Minister Lugong, particularly, started evil gossip, deceiving the king with a false letter from his subjects:

Majesty, listen! The ministers have full authority!
His Majesty should listen to them!

Vairotsana may be an expert in the Secret Mantra,
But the nature of that Secret Mantra is like a match.
Meeting causes and conditions, with grass and flint one
    may start a fire,
But a mountain wind could burn down the forest and blow
    away the ashes.

Likewise, endeavor in the Secret Mantra recitation is
    like fire.
Flawless, it burns obscurations but is hard to control.
Imperfect, it burns body and mind. Why can't you see that?

In the Tibetan kingdom, which is vulnerable and sensitive,
People grow weary, are temperamental, dishonest, and
    without samaya.
If the Secret Mantra is mistakenly taught in Tibet,
It will burn all the weak practitioners.
If so, who would take the highest place as king of the
    central government
And who would serve as the king's attendants?

As a result of practicing the Secret Mantra in a
    perverted way,
In this life one will experience leprosy, blisters, and
All kinds of discomfort and misery,
And the result in one's next life will be to experience all
    types of suffering.

If it is practiced in Tibet, the Tibetan kingdom will be
    ruined.
So we had better ask this wish-fulfilling gem Vairotsana
To go to Tsawarong.
With his strong Secret Mantra compassion he might even
    subdue the Tsawa country!

That is what the letter said. The king was powerless against the
curse of the ministers, so the king and ministers requested Vairotsana to

leave for the land of Tsawa. As Vairotsana was leaving, he sang a song
to them:

> Majesty, ministers, and subjects, listen!
> Whoever goes to Tsawarong is sure to die.
> Long ago I stayed there, and now once again,
> Vairotsana will confront death there.

> As the intrinsic nature has no fixed place,
> I am embraced by the entire realization of the Buddha.
> Vairotsana is going to die in the land of Tsawa.

> Within the unaltered dharmata, all phenomena are
>   nonarising.
> Confident in the dharmata's view of great bliss,
> I am going to die in the land of Tsawa.

> Having realized the self-existing, naturally perfect unborn
>   nature,
> I am beyond the extremes of death, immortality, arising,
>   and ceasing.
> Vairotsana is going to die in the land of Tsawa.

> Since I have the self-existing, spontaneously perfect
>   mansion of great bliss,
> I am not attached to illusory countries and houses.
> I am going to die in the land of Tsawa.

> I, Vairotsana, virtuous in body and speech in Tibet,
> Am going to keep the Vinaya rules in the land of Tsawa.

> Skillful in making all that is seen,
> I am going to perform all kinds of crafts in the land
>   of Tsawa.

> I, the physician who can cure all illness,
> Am going to practice medicine in the land of Tsawa.

Knowing how to teach the commentaries on the expedient
   meaning,
I am going to guide the lay people of the land of Tsawa.

Holding the basis of the doctrine, the Tripitaka,
I am going to propagate the teachings in the land of Tsawa.

I, the *tantrika* who eliminates breaches,
Am going to guard the doctrine in the land of Tsawa.

Knowing nineteen hundred different languages,
I am going to translate the sacred Dharma in the land
   of Tsawa.

Realizing all the supreme and common accomplishments,
I am going to bestow accomplishment in the land
   of Tsawa.

Explaining the pith instructions, the Buddha's meditation
   teachings,
I am going to point out the instructions in the land
   of Tsawa.

Gods and Dharma protectors staying above,
Come to meet me, Vairotsana!

Spirits and yakshas staying in-between,
Come to meet me, Vairotsana!

Nagas and earth lords staying below,
Come to meet me, Vairotsana!

With these words, the gods from above, the nagas from below, and
the eight types of gods and demons staying in between, including the
spirits, directly showed their form, circumambulated Vairotsana, and
promised to obey him. Then, the exalted one sang a song about the seven
regrets:

King and ministers of Tibet, listen!
Vairotsana pays homage
To the abbot Shantarakshita from Zahor,
To the glorious Padmasambhava from Oddiyana,
And to the twenty-five learned Indian panditas!

At the age of eight I came here to be trained as a translator,
    and
At the age of fifteen I had learned sixteen hundred different
    languages.
I translated all the secret Indian Dharma treasures into
    Tibetan,
But the sun to dispel Tibet's darkness has been expelled.
The time will come when you'll regret it,
When intelligent people with understanding arrive!

From the age of fifteen up to fifty-seven,
I wandered around India for the sake of sentient beings.
Though I turned everything in Tibet into virtue,
This Tibetan monk, whose body is adorned with good
    qualities, is expelled.
The time will come when you'll regret it,
When the Tibetan boys come back from India.
Without having mastered the Tibetan language, it is
    impossible to be a translator!

In this snowy kingdom with its high mountains and
    clean soil,
The king lives in divine luxury;
But this bodhisattva, like an actual incarnation
From a flock of golden ducks on a precious golden island,
Is banished alone to Gyalmo Tsawarong.
The time will come when you'll regret it,
When you study and discuss the sutras and tantras!

Many wondrous common accomplishments will occur, and
The ears, eyes, and minds of the king and subjects will
    be lucid,

But they won't understand Sanskrit, the Indian Dharma
    language.
Though an extensive temple was built as a foundation for
    the Dharma,
The accomplished Vairotsana is banished to the borderland.
The time will come when you'll regret it,
When you remember his great qualities!

Even though the king and his subjects practice virtue, it
    turns negative;
Only Vairo can practice Dharma without being carried away
    by vanity.
In spite of the perfect compassion of the buddhas and
    aryas,
Due to the power of the unwholesome, the *maras*[10] have
    won.
Keep this in your heart, Majesty and subjects: Are all your
    wishes fulfilled?
The time will come when you'll regret it,
When the true scholar and master arrives.

The one time that the sun of the Dharma rises in Tibet,
The outer and inner ministers and the queen make it set.
Having experienced everything except death,
I, Vairotsana, go alone and unattached.

Having realized all that appears as dharmakaya,
I am endowed with the true Great Perfection.
Knowing the cause and effect of the three kinds of vows,
I possess the true sutras and tantras;
But this wish-fulfilling pile of gems is expelled.
The time will come when you'll regret it, when I don't
    return!

Thus he spoke.

Then, they gave Vairotsana two measures of camphor and many cool-
ing medicines as a parting gift, and bringing a horse with provisions, they
requested him to leave for Tsawarong. Vairotsana said, "In a previous life-

time I was the prince of Tsawa, a monk called Purna, who passed away. It
seems that the time has come to spread these instruction teachings in
Gyalmo Tsawarong." When he came from the Arya Palo Temple and stood
at the door preparing to leave, Queen Margyen requested Vairotsana to
stay, saying that the king and ministers had made the wrong decision.
With great devotion she pleaded:

> Master, you are the essential teacher of the Jambu
>   continent;
> Staying with you for one hundred years I still won't grow
>   weary!
> Lord, you who illumine the darkness of ignorance,
> Queen Margyen would like to tell you what she thinks!
>
> It seems that there is no one capable in Tibet, so Lugong
>   has to be minister.
> While he destroys Tibet, the king is easily influenced!
> It seems that I, Margyen, mad from breaking my vows,
> Am banishing Vairotsana, the sun of Tibet!
>
> While I took a nap, I had this dream:
> I dreamt that the sun and moon rose from the top
> Of the triple-storied central temple
> Of Samye, Trisong Deutsen's wish,
> And that the sun set in Tsawarong!
>
> I dreamt that a poisonous snake suddenly killed the king!
> I dreamt that the triple-storied central temple's roof
>   collapsed!
> If Vairotsana is expelled, the king will surely pass away!
> As a punishment, Minister Lugong will definitely die!
> The stability of the Dharma in the king's temple will
>   certainly deteriorate!
>
> Please request Vairotsana to stay!
> To tell you frankly, if Vairotsana doesn't stay,
> Tibet will be ruined, and you'll regret it!

When the sun of Tibet sets, there will be darkness:
We had better decide to let Vairo stay!

Saying this, she wept. Vairotsana answered that he didn't want to stay:

Majesty, ministers, and subjects, listen to me!
I'll give you some metaphors about how bad things are
    in Tibet!

The king is so easily irritated that he's like Yarlha Shampo.[11]
The ministers are so wicked that they're like deadly poison.

The queen is so sneaky that she's like a dog jumping a wall.
The youths are so timid that they're like ravens chased
    by hawks.

Religion and politics endure so briefly that it's like a
    summer stream.
The study of the shastras is so naive it's like a reading class.

The tantrikas conspire so much that it's like a shamanic
    ritual.
The ganachakra[12] headed by samaya-breakers is like
    washing blood with blood.

The conceited translators explain mantra so much that
    it's like giving an order.
Vairotsana swears he won't stay among such people
    anymore!

Then the king prostrated, lamenting, "Alas, guru and patron must part, due to the subjects! Please give me some short, kind advice!" The master said:

Majesty, give me your hand!
If I don't die and Your Majesty stays in good health,
I sincerely pray that we may meet again soon.

In the town of Kapilavastu in India,
King Indrabhuti has five hundred panditas in his service:
Among them the most learned ones are Vimalamitra[13] and
    Buddhaguhya.
You should invite them to Tibet and devotedly supplicate
    them.

At that time you should let them verify my teachings.
You should also invite many other panditas, and
Have all the Dharma translated, without judging if it's better
    or worse.

Thus speaking, he left. The king, queen, the two types of Sangha, and all the ministers and subjects escorted him for a short distance. When Vairotsana mounted his horse, they brought him a silver plate with food, saying, "Great master, on your way to the Tsawa country, some of us would like to accompany you for a short distance and others for longer." Vairotsana replied with this song:

The king, who emanated through the blessings of
    Manjushri,
Intending to illuminate the dense gloom in the Tibetan
    kingdom
With the sun of compassion,
Sent me off with gold dust to find it.

Crossing the border, I wandered in the four directions:
I walked all over the east and west of India, on foot,
To Indra's Lion Castle and to the Kashmiri Arya,
And risked my life enduring all kinds of hardships.

I discovered crafts, shastras, healing and medicine practices,
And all the vehicles based on cause and effect without
    exception.
I fully perfected all the teachings of
The supreme Ati Vehicle, the core of the doctrine,

The pith instructions that grant enlightenment in this
> very life
And that are the heart essence of all the Indian scholars.

This precious lamp that completes whatever one needs
Is going, going to Tsawarong!

Then most of the people escorting him for a short distance turned back, but the two types of Sangha,[14] the king, queen, ministers, and nobility went with him up to Ngamo Gung on the Nyan Pass. King Trisong Deutsen asked Vairotsana, "Lord, now that you are leaving for the land of Tsawa, what should we do?" Vairo said, "Now that your skillful advisors are banishing Vairotsana, who embodies all needs like a precious shrine, you will be ruined!" and he sang this song:

Majesty, ministers, and subjects, listen!
Since the ministers are the most important, Tibet will be
> ruined!
Because the king is easily influenced, Tibet will be ruined!
As the queen is very jealous, Tibet will be ruined!
Because a common girl is queen, Tibet will be ruined!

Vairotsana, a wish-fulfilling gem that perfects all needs,
Has been banished to Tsawarong,
So Tibet's wealth will be reduced to ruin.

Because of banishing the heart-son of Prahe and Manjushri,
It will be difficult to attain the result in Tibet.
Because of expelling the pith instructions that give
> enlightenment in this very life,
It will be hard to attain fruition even if you practice
> for eons.

Because you have banished me, a bhikshu who is the life
> tree of the doctrine,
Eventually there will be quarreling among the main gurus.

Because of banishing me, who binds gods and demons into
   servitude,
The vicious king, ministers, and subjects will be punished.

Because of banishing a guru like me, a stream of em-
   powerments,
The king's rule and power will quickly degenerate.
As punishment, the gods and demons will be disturbed
So that the Tibetan kingdom will be like fire extinguished
   by water.
The law will be corrupted and Tibet will fall to pieces.

Because of expelling me, Vairo, who has been very kind
   to Tibet,
Tibet will be ruined. That is what you get for banishing me!
I am going, going to Tsawarong!

Having said this, he left. On the way to Ponga Sinbukye, the king,
ministers, and subjects asked, "Great master, how can we Tibetans make
our grandsons, our kingdom, and our gurus flourish?" Vairotsana sang
this song:

Majesty, ministers, and subjects, listen!
When His Majesty and the ministers and subjects all
   go back,
This precious tree is expelled to the land of Tsawa.

Because a Tibetan king like you,
Who is easily influenced and makes decisions without
   reflecting,
And Lugong, who is minister because there are no capable
   men in Tibet,
Have sent away someone as learned as I,
Like the sun in the dark Tibetan kingdom,
Minister Lugong will die in twenty-one days,
And the king will die after three winter months.

Majesty, after this life,
For sixteen lifetimes you will subsequently
Suffer from leprosy, ulcers, insanity, and other diseases.
At one point your close disciples, who have seen the
    profound treasures,
Will lose faith and cast abuse on you.

Because the victorious ones have appointed me as doctrine-
    holder,
The result of breaking your precepts will mature at
    that time.
During the rule of your grandson, Tibet will fall to pieces,
And eventually the spiritual teachers will be stirred up as
    enemies.
Because of banishing this old monk, the sun and moon
    will set.
I am going, going to Tsawarong!

Having said this, he arrived at the top of Mang Pass. The king didn't believe him. He prostrated to Vairotsana and held on to his foot, saying,
"Please give us—king, ministers, subjects, and two types of Sangha—some
advice. Leave us a testament!" Vairotsana turned toward Five-Peaked
Mountain in China,[15] and with his eyes gazing into the sky, he said:

Homage to the youthful Arya Manjushri!
Listen! Reflect on this!
Generally, we sentient beings from the three worlds of
    samsara
Are caught in a tight cyclic prison from which there is
    no escape.

Tied with the knot of belief in a self and
Controlled by the chains of dualistic fixation on wrong
    ideas,
We fall into the bottomless abyss of the three lower
    realms.

As we are caught in the stream of the four rivers of birth,
    old age, illness, and death,
The opening for seeing the wisdom lamps arise is blocked,
    and
The bridge to the liberation path of enlightenment is cut off.
Don't you see that the suspending rope of compassion to
    guide us is severed?

Yet we sentient beings in samsara
Have a grunting black pig of ignorance groaning within,
A poisonous black snake of anger wrapped around
    our waist,
A red-beaked cock of lust sitting in front of us, and
A black bull of pride rubbing his horns inside.
Don't you see the jealous old watchdog that keeps on
    barking?

Through the force of Mara we can't block the womb
    entrance;
Even the Sugata's compassion can't divert the journey
    to death!
Medicines of youthful doctors still don't cure our genetic
    illness, and
Even tied to an anchor we can't avoid getting old.
Afraid to meet enemies, we're like a small bird endangered
    by a hawk.
Scared to separate from kind relatives, we're like a mother
    who is losing her child.
The misery of seeking what we lack is like a hungry ghost
    longing for food and drink.
Don't you see that the frustration of not being able to guard
    what we have is like an old woman tending sheep?

Yet, when we think of the Dharma, our gloomy ignorance
    warms up.
When we think of wise men, the fire of our anger flares up.

When we think of beautiful girls, the water of our passion
   is stirred.
When we think of our own virtues, the horns of our
   pride grow.
When we think of others' qualities, the wind of our
   jealousy swirls.
When we think of our own wealth, the palm of our stinginess contracts.
Don't you see that we beckon ill will when we think of
   others' possessions?

Yet our arrogance is overwhelmed by the godly son
   demon.[16]
Physically harassed by the demon of the aggregates, we
   are miserable.
Our life is short because it is taken by the demon of the
   Lord of Death.
Don't you see that we are on the wrong path
Because the truth is clouded by the ignorant demon of
   the emotions?

The ripening of our angry killing and beating
Is suffering in the hot and cold hells;
The maturation of our proud arguing and quarreling
Is the agony of the fighting demi-gods;
Don't you see that the maturation of alternating virtue
   with sin
Is the misery of birth as a god and a human?

Yet we turn our back on the Buddha, Dharma, and Sangha
   like our neck hair.
We take demons, black magic, and heretics on our lap like
   our favorite child.
We hurl vows, precepts, and discipline like stones.
We keep desire, hatred, and ignorance on our body like an
   amulet.

We throw our father, mother, and guru out the door like
    an old dog.
Old age, sickness, and death follow behind us like
    shadows.
Don't you see that the hells, hungry ghosts, and animals are
    waiting in front of us like an appointment?

Yet our form aggregate is like an empty valley, and
The life span possessed by our life-force is like a woolly
    lamb.
Don't you see that the demon of the Lord of Death is like
    a blue wolf?

Yet if we don't rely on the Buddha, what refuge can we
    depend on?
If we don't respect the guru, who is there above him?
If we don't practice the Dharma, how can we feel at ease?
If we don't offer to the Sangha, to whom can we offer?
If we don't befriend our fellow practitioners, with whom
    can we associate?
If we don't keep our vows, how can we be at ease?
If we don't practice generosity, whom can we pay back?
How indulgent not to be weary of samsara!
What a shame not to be afraid of demons!
How insensitive not to fear death!
How numb not to feel old age!
How pitiful to forget our mortal illness!
Don't you see that negative behavior and breaking samaya
    are mistakes?

Yet the thief of our stinginess sidetracks our generosity;
The enemy of immorality smashes the ornament of our
    discipline;
The fire of anger burns the garment of our patience;
The horse of our diligence is trapped in the shackles of
    laziness; and
The food of our concentration is lost to the foe of
    distraction.

Don't you see that our sword of wisdom is knocked into
    hell by the hammer of stupidity?

Yet we reject the limitless kindness that is like a
    mother.
We forsake the limitless compassion that is like a loving
    sister.
We ruin the limitless joy that is like a lover.
Don't you see that we postpone the limitless equanimity
That is like a king who treats everyone equally?

Yet if we don't attain the dharmakaya, this form aggregate is
    like a water bubble.
If we don't acquire a Brahma-like voice, the sound of our
    voice is like an echo.
If we don't perfect the accumulation of wisdom, our think-
    ing process is like a poisonous snake.
If we don't build the Mahayana castle, our home is like a
    gandharva city.[17]
Don't you see that unless we master one of the bhumis on
    the way to enlightenment,
The indicated object is just like a dream?

Yet we are more courageous in killing than wolves;
We copulate more diligently than donkeys;
We are more clever in lying than actors; and
In stealing we are craftier than rats.
Don't you see that we drink more wine, which stirs up
    emotions, than spirit kings?[18]

Yet for some of us Dharma practice is just supporting old
    people and children.
For some of us Dharma practice is simply giving soup to
    our children.
For some of us Dharma practice is no more than preventing
    sudden accidents.
Don't you see that for some of us Dharma practice is merely
    prestige?

Upon saying that, Vairotsana looked up at Tibet. All the mountains of Tibet looked like vulture peaks; the high mountains and clean soil were like sunrise. Looking down toward Tsawarong, the low, dark gray mountains were like dusk. Looking upward at Tibet, he said:

> In the Jambu continent, supreme among the four
>   continents, the land of Tibet
> Grows whatever is needed and, surrounded by glaciers,
>   is fearless.
> The Tibetan people communicate with pleasant speech,
> And the people's divine king is like a wish-fulfilling tree.
>
> From a flock of golden geese on a precious lake,
> Like a wish-fulfilling gem that provides whatever one
>   needs,
> This lonely goose is sad to go!

Thus speaking, he wept; the two types of Sangha, as well as the king and ministers, also wept. Then, in order to relieve the king's worries, Vairotsana sang this fearless song:

> Since a homeland is not certain, I am not afraid to be
>   banished.
> Since mind is free of birth or death, I am not afraid to
>   be killed.
> Since qualities appear as illusions, faults have no
>   substantial basis.
> Since I am not attached to friends, I am not angry with
>   enemies!

And walked on.

The king, queen, and two types of Sangha grasped hold of Vairotsana, and crying, they pleaded, "Great master, let the government collapse by itself and Tibet fall to pieces; but master, please don't go! Please come back!" Vairotsana sang a song about preferring to leave and not staying:

> Can one strong man reverse a rock
> Rolling down from a very steep mountain?

Can the milk of a cow that calved last year
Fatten the skinny calf whose mother died?

Can a drop of seasonal rain satisfy
A big fish from a dried-up ocean?

Can one person with faith in Vairotsana
Make him return to Tibet, where everyone rejects him?

Having said this on the point of leaving, the king asked how he should
act, and Vairotsana said:

Even though you enjoy the inconceivable innate nature,
Don't interrupt your good deeds.
Even though you realize the nature of things as evenness,
Don't ignore the cause and effect of karma.
Even though you realize your mind as the Buddha,
Have incessant devotion to your guru!

Preparing to go he said:

I, Vairotsana, who embodies all needs,
Am going, going to Tsawarong!
This precious lamp is going to Tsawarong;
The sun of Tibet will set!
Tibet will become a dark place;
The doctrine will flourish in Tsawarong!

King and ministers of Tsawarong,
All inhabitants of that deep ravine,
Respect and take good care of me!
All you eight classes of gods and demons,
All dakinis, Dharma protectors, and vow-holders,
Listen to this yogi's command:
Support the Buddhist teachings!

Then he left like a flying hawk, without looking back. The two types of
Sangha, the king and the ministers, the gods from above, the nagas from

below, and the gods and spirits from in-between all burst into tears, which poured down their faces as they cried. Then the king, ministers, and all the others wiped their tears, and doing full prostrations facing Gyalmo Tsawarong, they all prayed and then headed back.

This was the eleventh chapter of the Great Image,
concerning Vairotsana's banishment to Tsawarong,
because there was no worthy recipient for the instructions in Tibet.

12 ❈

Vairotsana Arrives in Tsawarong and Entrusts Yudra Nyingpo with the Pith Instructions

VAIROTSANA DIDN'T dare to go straight down to Tsawarong, so he halted on top of a mountain. The people from Tsawarong saw him there and said, "There is a Tibetan spy!" Led by the son of King Phen of Doshen,[1] they insisted on putting him into a frog pit. After three days, the queen and her subjects approached the entrance of the hole. Vairotsana called from the bottom, "Respectable inhabitants of this country, listen to me from this frightening frog pit! This Tibetan monk wants to tell you something!" Then, led by Palshe from Gyalmo, the nobility went to the entrance of the hole, and from the bottom of the frog pit Vairotsana said:

> King, ministers, and noble citizens of this country!
> From the age of fifteen to fifty-seven,
> In order to make all of Tibet virtuous,
> I brought to Tibet the pith instructions of the view
> From the twenty-three Indian scholars,

The summit of all vehicles, the fruition teachings of the
    Buddha.
But the ministers who bring the kingdom ruin,
Queen Margyen, insane from breaking her precepts, and
The king, who easily changes his mind and evidently
    lets Tibet fall to pieces,
Listened to the slander of vicious Indians
And banished me, the learned sun of Tibet.
This Tibetan monk possesses
The pith instructions to attain fruition in this very life,
The wrathful mantras to eliminate breaches,
The sadhanas to dispel the darkness of ignorance,
And the commentaries on the result, which are like
    a heap of jewels.
Please take me out of this frightening frog pit!

As he spoke thus, the king said:

That sinful king of Tibet, Pugyal,[2]
Does a lot of things that are not very efficient.
When he marries, he takes a foreign maid as wife;
For ministers he appoints those with the strongest
    kleshas;[3]
For food he eats all sorts of raw meat;
As clothing he wears foreign garments from Mon;
For wealth he considers common stones as precious;
As work he steals and leads wars;
For deities he relies on yakshas and *rakshas*;[4] and
For friends he seeks out vicious nagas.
Only looking afar, he doesn't see what's nearby;
That red-faced ogre king is very greedy,
And I don't trust him. As for you, magician,[5]
I shall consult the ministers and all the nobility.
From the frog pit we'll throw you into a louse pit,
And if no army shows up after seven days,
We'll believe and respect you.

As they took him out of the frog hole in order to throw him into the louse pit, Vairotsana, his body covered with frogs clinging to him up to his eyes, said:

> In a previous life
> I was born as a mongoose in this country,
> Eating snakes and frogs as food.
> Now the effect of it has matured.
> May this karmic retribution be completed!

With these words all the frogs and snakes dropped off his body and left. Then he was put in the louse pit. As no war occurred, after seven days the locals came to look and were amazed to find him unharmed and looking magnificent. They took him out of the louse pit, and Vairo apologized to the lice:

> In a previous life
> I was born as the prince of this country,
> A monk called Purna.
> When my shirt became infested with lice, I let the birds
>   eat them,
> And the effect of this has now matured.
> If there is any slight karmic debt left over,
> May it ripen in this lifetime!

As he apologized to the lice, the lice departed one by one. Then, the people from Gyalmo asked him for forgiveness and said, "How can so much suffering come to a bodhisattva like you?" He answered:

> I kept the precepts in my previous life,
> But from my births as a mongoose up to Purna, I
>   broke them,
> And the misery of breaking my precepts has matured
>   here.
> Through Vajrasattva, Prahe, and Manjushri,
> I realized the secret of mind, true wisdom,
> The unborn nature of effortless enlightenment.

Whoever realizes nonarising enlightenment
Is sure to attain perfect buddhahood here and now.

Queen Dru grasped him and cried, saying, "In the past I had an uncle called Purna, who was a monk, but I didn't recognize you as his incarnation. I am sorry that I subjected you to this!" Then the king and his retinue felt regret and apologized, saying:

Since there is no one else in Tibet, a covetous man is king.
You, bodhisattva, who remembers past and future lives,
Traveled all over the Jambu continent for the sake of
    beings.
In particular, in the red-faced ogre land of Tibet,
You acted for the welfare of living beings.
The time to tame the wicked ministers
Hasn't come yet, so you have come here.
Bodhisattva, you act for the welfare of sentient beings.
Engaging in the two activities and giving up the extreme
    of enlightenment,
You demonstrate all possible things to benefit beings!
Bodhisattva, please forgive us!

Then, as the queen and her retinue did full prostrations and placed his feet above their heads, Vairo suddenly exclaimed, "Don't let him be harmed!" and hit the ground with his hand, saying, "A A TRA KA SA LA A A TAT KA SA LE NA GA." When they asked why he did this, he answered:

I taught and explained the great bliss instructions of
    unborn enlightenment
To the king of Tibet,
But he didn't understand them and expelled me.
I don't want the king of Tibet, Trisong Deutsen,
To die in three winter months
And told the king please not to let that happen.

Feeling sad about Trisong Deutsen, he burst into tears, and the king and ministers also wept. Then, they requested the master to sit on a raised

seat made of nine layers of cushions, and headed by King Dru, the king
and all the ministers, holding coins of gold and silver, gold bars, gold dust,
brocades, and many other things, prayed:

> Your body is a bodhisattva benefiting the six realms;
> Your speech teaches whatever vehicle of the Buddha is
>   effective;
> Your mind is like a wish-fulfilling gem, granting all needs,
> Pointing out the unperceived mind of the victorious ones.
> Great ancestor, summit of the Tripitaka,
> You naturally perfect the three kayas of the conquerors of
>   the three times!
> Protector of beings, you who treat everyone equally without
>   duality,
> We offer you silver coins and golden flowers.
> Thinking kindly of us, take us across the ocean of existence
>   and
> Hold us with the lasso of your wisdom compassion!

Having said this, they threw flowers and the master said:

> The long days of spring will have three cold spells and three
>   hot spells.
> The long winter months will have three periods of pleni-
>   tude and three periods of hunger.
> A long journey will have three joys and three sorrows.
> The long human life will have three pleasures and three
>   sufferings.

Then Queen Dru and all the others, including the king and ministers, respectfully listened to the Dharma. In order to test him, Prince Yudra Nyingpo sent a couple whose only son had died to see the master. They asked
him, "Great master, if we practice the Dharma, will we meet our son or not?
If we will meet him, we'll practice the Dharma!" The master answered:

> Since all of us here were born, we are sure to die;
> Just like your son, you will also die.

Nobody knows whether we will die today or tomorrow,
And our best friend when we die is the Dharma.

Then Yudra Nyingpo sent an old couple that was near death. They requested some teaching to benefit old people, and the master replied with this song:

Under the influence of old age,
All of us old people here are sure to grow frail.
Earlier, when our skin was beautiful,
All we thought about was dressing up and having fun.
No question about the sacred Dharma,
We even forgot our mealtime!
Then, when we got married,
All we thought about was children and wealth.
Let alone the sacred Dharma,
We even forgot about our parents!
Now that we are old and frail,
All we think about is eating and drinking.
No question about the sacred Dharma,
We even forget our kind relatives!
Since we are old, we are sure to die,
And our best friend when we die is the sacred Dharma.

Then some young people in fancy dress were sent, and asked him, "Is the Buddha happier than we are?" The master replied with a song:

Boys and girls, listen!
After a year or two,
Your nice glossy skin will be wrinkled by age.
You won't be able to stop the dripping and flowing
Of your spittle, snot, or tears.
As you get old, you are sure to die.
Keep that in mind and practice the Dharma.
The only lasting happiness is the Dharma!

Prince Yudra and all the others believed in him when he said this, and they arranged a high throne. The master was seated upon it, on many lay-

ers of cushions, and everyone did prostrations, threw flowers, and requested the Dharma. Taming beings according to their needs, he taught
crafts, healing, and medicine, as well as commentaries to develop faith.
During the daytime he taught the Five Sutra Collections, including the
Jewel Mound Sutra, as well as the three outer tantras. In the evening he
gave the inner Secret Mantra teachings. Prince Yudra Nyingpo offered the
master a fine horse, adorned with silk scarves and a gold saddle inset with
turquoise, and requested the pith instructions. The master replied, "I am
not selling the king of the view, the *Great Space Tantra*, for the king of animals, a horse." Then the prince offered a lot of wealth in gold and silver
and requested again, but the master refused him, saying:

> I am not selling the essence of the doctrine,
> The Great Perfection, for illusory wealth.
> If I sold it, the victorious ones would punish me.
> I shall give it to worthy recipients who have high morals.

Yudra thought the master might teach him if he insisted, so when the
master went to the toilet, he followed him into the trees and persisted in
his request, but the master said, "Instead of requesting the Dharma respectfully, do you think you will get it by insisting?" Then Yudra eaves-
dropped on Master Vairotsana, and when the master was reciting the *Great
Space Tantra*, Yudra memorized it. He even stole the master's book and
said, "I've already got this!" so the master said:

> The true meaning of the Secret Mantra
> Taught by Vajrasattva, Prahe, and Manjushri,
> The extremely profound view of the victorious ones,
> Such a path to enlightenment can't be found in written
>   words.

Then, Prince Yudra Nyingpo offered many silver and gold coins, prostrated and circumambulated Vairo, bowed at his feet, and with tears in
his eyes said, "Great master, I shall do whatever you say, but please give
me all the pith instructions you possess!" As Yudra continued to supplicate him, the master believed that Yudra wasn't just testing him. He decided that if Yudra truly wanted to get the teachings by any means, he
would have him do the nine purifications and the thirteen hardships to

train him as a vessel for the pith instructions. So Vairotsana said to him, "If you want to attain the great bliss of effortless enlightenment, you should practice the nine purifications and thirteen hardships for me." Yudra answered, "Whatever the great guru says, I shall do. Please give me the nectar drops from your lips!" Then Vairo said:

> Future yogi,
> As you want liberation from the six realms of samsara,
> You should practice these nine purifications:
>
> Use your body and mind to work
> For the guru's land and residence;
> It will purify obscurations acquired over eons.
>
> Without regarding your body and life,
> Fight and kill the enemies
> Who control and harm the guru;
> It will purify obscurations acquired over eons.
>
> If it serves the guru's purpose,
> Please him with your own flesh, bones, and blood;
> It will purify obscurations acquired over eons.
>
> For the guru's enemies
> You should recite all the fierce mantras
> To kill, make hail, and so forth:
> It will purify obscurations acquired over eons.
>
> To the guru's opponents
> You should lie and speak whatever rough words you know,
> Violently putting them down:
> It will purify obscurations acquired over eons.
>
> Don't speak about the guru's faults,
> But mention his different qualities.
> When you walk, move around, or lie down,
> Always venerate the guru on the crown of your head:
> It will purify obscurations acquired over eons.

Though you constantly meditate on the *yidam* deity,
Always visualize the guru on the crown of the yidam's
     head:
It will purify obscurations acquired over eons.
Never forget to respect the guru with a yearning mind,
And always treat him like your inner heart.

If it benefits the guru,
Offer your children, wife, land, and servants,
Your kingdom, and your own body,
All the wealth of which you are so fond,
And whatever might please the guru's mind:
It will purify the obscurations acquired over eons.

To scold your guru's enemies
With one harsh word is more virtuous
Than to read and recite as many mantras as you can;
Hundreds of them don't approach even a fraction of it.

It is more virtuous to please the guru by benefiting beings
Than to make different images of the victorious ones
Out of gold, turquoise, and other precious stones
All over the billionfold universe
And doing as many prostrations and circumambulations as
     possible to them;
Hundreds of them don't equal even a fraction of it.

It is more virtuous to please the guru for an instant
Than to practice the virtues of the shravakas and pratyeka-
     buddhas
In all the worlds of the ten directions
And please all the bodhisattvas as best as one can.
They say hundreds
Because it is more important to please the guru
Than the buddhas of one hundred thousand eons.

I go for refuge to the gurus,
The embodiment of all the buddhas,

The root of the Triple Gem,
The essence of the vajra-holders.
Train in these nine purifications
And you will progress in the effortless instructions of the
    Great Perfection.

Yudra did a thousand full prostrations and prayed:

Guru, spiritual friend,
You are our father, our mother, our protector!
You are the lamp to dispel the darkness,
You are the compassionate hook to pull us out of the depths
    of samsara.
I'll do whatever you say,
If you drag me out of the depths of samsara with your
    compassion!

Vairo replied:

Listen to me, Yudra Nyingpo!
The cyclic ocean of the six realms is frightening!
The suffering of the three lower realms is dreadful!
The anguish in the eighteen hells is terrifying!
For countless eons we have gone through life spans.
You, Yudra, want to be free from it,
But can you cope with the thirteen hardships?
If you can't, it will be hard to escape samsara's ocean!

Yudra answered, "I would rather deal with them in this lifetime than
suffer for eons in the lower realms. I shall certainly do whatever the guru
says!" So Vairo said,

Then listen to me! Requesting without faith and respect, do you expect great bliss enlightenment by annoying me, trying to get it by
force? These mantras have the Buddha's seal of secrecy! If I give
them to an unsuitable recipient like you, the eight classes of gods
and demons will punish me! If you can, take two measures of gold

dust and go to Oddiyana in the southwest. Offer one measure of gold dust to Prahevajra, who is Samantabhadra's successor, equal to the Buddha himself, and I'll give you something very much cherished by Prahevajra. Give precious gold dust to the other twenty-three scholars, including Manjushrimitra, and do one thousand full prostrations. Then I'll give you the replica of the Indian scholars. Offer half a measure of gold dust to Shri Singha in Bodhgaya and do one thousand full prostrations. Then I'll give you the sixty-four Tantra Sections.

Nowadays, at Samye in central Tibet, King Trisong Deutsen has invited the learned Vimalamitra, who is the master of the Dharma assembly. He has established an institute for many scholars where the Dharma wheel of the Lesser Vehicle[6] is turned. I am criticized a lot, so you, Yudra Nyingpo, should go there and discuss the view of the victorious ones, translate the transcripts of the scholars, refute them with logic, display magic and miraculous powers, and proclaim Vairotsana's life story; then I'll give you the empowerments and all the instructions. Leave your wife and children at the palace, and serve me for nine years; then I'll give you the pith instructions in their entirety. Cut off your braided hair adorned with gold and turquoise; take off your gold and silver rings and jewelry; wear yellow robes dyed with roots; drink soup made of leaves, barley, and flour; give up pride and arrogance at all times; and turn your back on your royalty, country, and servants. If you can cope with that, I'll give you the pith instructions of effortless great bliss.

Then he explained the pith instructions. He acted in this way to benefit others so that his common followers would start to practice the Dharma, cut through their errors, purify their obscurations, and wouldn't be presumptuous about the teachings but would be keen to request them.

In fact, in his past life Prince Yudra had been Tsang Lekdrub, who had passed away. Because of his connection with Vairotsana and because he was clairvoyant, as soon as Vairo came to the land of Tsawa, Yudra hugged him and wept. When the others threw Vairo into the frog pit and he was reciting the *Great Space Tantra* and the *Marvelous* inside the hole, the prince came to listen at the hole's mouth; just by hearing the *Great Space*

Tantra once he knew it by heart without mistaking a single word. When the prince recited the *Great Space Tantra* before Queen Dru and the king and ministers, they asked him who had spoken these words, so he told them that the Tibetan monk sitting in the pit was saying them. When they had taken the master out of the hole and they had all done prostrations, the prince sat there reciting the *Great Space Tantra,* as well as other tantras. So Vairo asked him where he had heard these words; he replied that he had heard the master recite them from the frog pit.

Then, as mentioned above, Queen Dru and the others prostrated and encircled the master, throwing flowers and apologizing with an infinite offering of wealth. They all respected him like a crown ornament and made him the court priest.

As the master saw that Prince Yudra was a destined disciple, he said to Yudra's father, King Rinchen, and his mother, Queen Tsogyal, "Your son could be a good practitioner; you should give him to me." His mother replied, "He is our family lineage-holder, so I won't give him to you!" To please her, the master gave her much wealth, and as he continued to ask, the mother conceded.

Then King Dru, the subjects, and two ministers decided to build a house for Master Vairotsana. Demonstrating his miraculous power, the master summoned the gods and demons and made them build a lofty and very large house, with a stupa outside and a temple inside, from excellent stones immovable even by giants. They finished it overnight. During the daytime, he taught the teachings based on the cause, as well as the outer sections of the Secret Mantra teachings, which Prince Yudra understood instantly. In the evening, he gave the inner Secret Mantra teachings, and Yudra realized them immediately. At midnight, he taught the pith instructions to Yudra and some special disciples. Concerning these, he first taught the cycle of Eighteen Tantras of the Mind Class with the pointing-out instructions. Then, he gave the tantras and pith instructions from the cycle of the Space Class. Then he gave the Cycle of Tantra Sections, the Brahmin's Cycle, the King's Cycle and so forth, together with the tantras and pith instructions. Yudra offered many gems and brocades, did countless prostrations and circumambulations, and requested, "Great guru, though I know many translations, logic, and pith instructions, I haven't realized the essence. Please give me a pith instruction that directly points out the essence, without depending on words," and in verse he said:

Though I can utter the Sanskrit syllables
And have discovered the scriptures and pith instructions,
I don't have confidence in my own awareness.
Please introduce me to the essence of the lineage
Without depending on conventional words!

Vairotsana then gave him the general tantras, transmissions, and pith instructions, both vast and profound. After completing these infinite teachings, he especially gave him the essence of all the pith instructions, which all the spiritual forefathers cherished as their own hearts, the oral instructions to clearly point out self-liberation. Manifesting the Illuminating Blazing Gem mandala, he gave the complete seven streams of empowerments, including the genuine empowerment of direct anointment. He gave the thirty root tantras with the pith instructions, the eighteen minor teachings of the nirmanakaya Prahe, the teachings of the vidyadharas, and the two teachings by Kukkuraja, the three teachings by Shri Singha, and the three essential oral instructions by the master himself. Upon finishing these teachings, he entrusted them with the three seals:

Having requested the pith instructions,
You should fully accomplish self-existing
    enlightened mind,
The king that is always perfect.
Not transcending fresh realization,
Concentrate on that and naturally mature the
    fortunate ones!

Then Prince Yudra Nyingpo realized the nature of his own awareness beyond any words, and his mind became inseparable from the master's. Offering his realization and gratitude to the master, he spoke these words:

Giving up on finding truth through verbal explanations,
I fully experienced self-liberation through your pointing-
    out instruction.
Thank you for instantly illuminating eons of dense
    darkness!

Thus he offered his thanks. Then Yudra went to Gyalmo Kyitarong, where he meditated on the essence for five years so that his mind penetrated the unconditioned nature of great bliss. The minds of master and disciple became one, and they remained there, benefiting beings.

 This was the twelfth chapter of the Great Image, *about spreading the doctrine in Tsawarong and entrusting the pith instructions to Prince Yudra Nyingpo.*

13 ⟡

Going to the Pure Lands After Completing the Instructions in Tibet

Trisong Deutsen Invites Vimalamitra

As soon as Vairotsana was banished to Tsawarong, Trisong Deutsen thought, "Since Vairotsana, the trunk of the Secret Mantra, who is like a precious stupa, was banished during the time of the wicked ministers and the Indian slanderers and now is gone, as evidence that Vairotsana's teachings are unmistaken and to bring out his greatness and make the doctrine flourish in Tibet, I should invite a scholar from India who is learned in the general teachings based on cause and effect and especially in the pith instructions and install him as the court priest."

He gathered all the ministers and attendants and said, "Since in the dense darkness of Tibet we have banished to Tsawarong the lamp giving effortless enlightenment in this very lifetime through the teachings of cause and result and especially through the pith instructions, we should invite a scholar learned in the teachings based on cause and effect to Tibet. Who will go to invite him?"

The king and all the ministers agreed to send Khon Lui Wangpo,[1] and giving him two measures of gold dust and some gold bars, they sent him along with two servants.

Khon Lui Wangpo gave the Indian king two measures of gold dust and seven gold bars and in return asked him to send a pandita learned in the teachings based on cause and effect and the pith instructions. The king presented the gold dust to the panditas, and from among them he sent the learned Vimalamitra to Tibet.

Twenty-one days after Vairotsana was banished, Minister Lugong died. The king died within three months, before Vimala arrived. He had three sons, and during their reign Vimala came to Tibet and stayed at the glorious Samye, giving teachings. Vairotsana heard about this and said to Yudra Nyingpo,

Both King Trisong Deutsen and I made the aspiration to spread the doctrine in Tibet and especially to spread the instruction teachings. I went through all kinds of hardships, and like a god, a demon, or an animal, I traveled unknown roads in foreign countries with different languages. I found the depth of the pith instructions of the Indian scholars. Upon my return, I impressed and satisfied the king. Yet, through the power of my karma, the Indian slanderers, and the evil Tibetan ministers, I was banished here. Since both the king and I intended to spread the instruction teachings in Tibet, you must go there, regardless of the difficulties. The great scholar Vimalamitra has now come to Tibet. You should compare your realization with him, and demonstrating the power of my teachings, you must spread the pith instructions there.

You should act with such compassion that the queen, princes, and wicked ministers develop strong regret, and let them apologize. For the cut-off type of individuals who are uninterested, you should sow virtuous seeds and make a connection through prayers. For those who have no interest but are clever talkers, you should teach the shortcomings and dangers of samsara. You should inspire those who have faith but are not very intelligent to enthusiasm and teach them in stages. For those who mainly fixate on this life but yearn for the Dharma, you should elaborately explain the commentaries of the texts with the instructions. For those who like conventional words, you should teach logic and designations.

If there is anyone who is able to meditate, you must teach one of the complete cycles of pointing out instructions and give practical guidance on the nature of reality. To fortunate ones who practice the two greater vehicles, you must give the complete teachings and the mind-mandate transmission. You should gradually guide those who are convinced by terminology through infinite skillful means. Anyway, as my country Tibet is as good as blind, think with loving kindness of those blind men who have no wise leader, and don't let them get lost!

Vairotsana Goes to China and Receives Teachings from the Chinese Scholars

Then Vairotsana decided to go to China from Tsawarong:

> How wonderful! I, the vagabond Vairotsana,
> Came to Tsawarong by the strong force of past karma.
> Having filled the Tsawa kingdom with Dharma,
> I am going to compare my realization with the Chinese
> scholars!

Saying this, he left for China.

He met the Chinese ascetic Bhoti Garba, who taught him the *Five Topics on the True Meaning*: wisdom dawning as total immersion, like the sun; dharmata arising as an encounter, like a king; thoughts appearing as original wakefulness, like fire spreading in a forest; signs self-occurring and self-liberating, like the space of the sky; and samadhi beyond emerging and entering, like going to a land of gold. This is how he explained these five topics on the meaning:

> First, just like the sun always remains beyond clarification
> or obscuration,
> All samsaric and nirvanic phenomena are enlightened
> mind:
> Whatever arises, is thought of, or appears in enlightened
> mind.

Since there are no qualities of good and bad or accepting
    and rejecting,
Awareness is totally self-arising, dawning as total immer-
    sion in wisdom.

Second, seeing a king, the recognizing mind is encountered
    simultaneously;
Likewise, whatever arises, is thought of, or appears in a
    yogi's five faculties,
Is self-display of mind itself, self-occurring.
That is the real nature dawning as an encounter, self-
    manifesting.

Third, when a forest catches fire, all that is dry, wet, big,
    or small,
Beings, earth, rocks, and so forth help the fire to burn.
Likewise, knowing all samsaric and nirvanic phenomena
    to be mind itself,
Whatever the body does and whatever happens to it,
Whatever the speech does and whatever happens to it,
Whatever the mind thinks and whatever happens to it,
Existence and non-existence, phenomena, emptiness,
    all deeds,
Whatever occurs, whatever arises, whatever is thought of,
    and whatever is felt
Spontaneously arises as the real nature:
It is nothing other than that.

Fourth, whatever appears within the space of the sky—
    clouds, steam, mist, thunder, lightning, light, rainbows,
    thunderbolts, hail, rain, wind, day, night, black, and
    white—
Is self-occurring, self-existing, self-appearing, and self-
    liberating.
None of them are the slightest bit other than the sky itself.
Likewise, enlightened mind itself is not different from
    buddhas and beings,
Samsara and nirvana, and all the six realms.

Samsara and nirvana, happiness and suffering,
And the conflicting emotions are all enlightened mind,
    primordially free.

Fifth, if one goes to a land of gold,
Everything big, small, oblong, round, thin, thick, or
    square,
Whether it is dug up or not, is gold.
Likewise, all samsaric and nirvanic phenomena
Are the self-existing, original wakefulness of mind from
    the beginning,
Free of altered or spoiled cause and conditions.
As there are no phenomena other than mind,
There is neither practicing nor any samadhi to practice;
There is no emerging from or entering into samadhi.

To a yogi who has such realization,
Since original wakefulness dawns as total immersion,
He is convinced, without the veil of straying.
Since the dharmakaya arises as an encounter,
He decides without accepting or rejecting.
Since thoughts manifest as original wakefulness,
He resolves flaws and qualities without attachment
    or aversion.
Since signs occur as intrinsic freedom,
He is sure not to need contrived meditation.
Since his samadhi is without emerging or entering,
He determines there is no need for any effort.

Though he met the Chinese mystic Bhoti Garba, his own realization was infinitely beyond that, but not everyone could understand it. Then, he met the learned Chinese mystic Dharmabodhi, who taught the *Six Vajra Lines* on the natural state beyond effort to the monk Vairotsana:

When the view is resolved, it transcends dense gloom.
When meditation is resolved, it cuts one's life.
When the conduct is resolved, one fluctuates aimlessly, like
    an infant.

When birth and death are resolved, sentient beings are
    killed.
When the fruition is resolved, the rope of hope and fear
    is severed.
Sweeping away cause and conditions, wisdom is resolved.

Thus he instructed the monk Vairotsana. Though Vairo met the Chinese scholar Dharmabodhi, his own realization was infinitely beyond that. Then, Vairotsana met the learned Chinese mystic Vajra Sukha Deva, who taught him this instruction on the indivisible three kayas:

Arising is nirmanakaya,
Cessation is dharmakaya, and
Their nonduality is sambhogakaya.
Any thought related to the five sense objects that occurs in
    the mind is the arising of nirmanakaya.
Whatever happens, whatever appears, it is devoid of
    self-nature.
Ceasing as dharmakaya and arising as nondual
Is primordially dwelling in sambhogakaya.
Self-occurring, self-manifesting, and self-ceasing—
These three are indivisible in the three times;
Nonarising and uncompounded, they are beyond any
    concept of meditation.
Whatever arises is the three kayas, as it is, beyond any
    concept of conduct.
The spontaneously present three kayas are originally
    awakened, beyond any concept of fruition.

Though he met Vajra Sukha Deva, Vairo's realization went infinitely beyond that. Then, Vairotsana requested teaching from the Chinese mystic Pandita Barma, who gave him an instruction on directly watching awareness:

Watch your own mind. Does it have any cause, conditions,
    color, or substance?
You will see that it is free of birth and death, indestructible.
Watch the skylike nature.

Then, while observing outer objects,
Whatever is perceived is your own mind.
Looking within, you won't find an ego or a self;
There is nothing to be practiced.
Whatever appears is self-occurring;
There is nothing to affirm or negate,
Nothing to be attained and no attainer, which is the
    fruition.
To be without reference point, unprejudiced, is resolving
    the view.
To be without grasping or fixation is deciding on
    meditation.
Knowing whatever appears to be the self-occurring dharma-
    kaya is dealing with the conduct.
Being without hope or fear about samsara, nirvana, or cause
    and effect is settling the fruition.

Though he met Pandita Barma, Vairotsana's realization was infinitely deeper. Then, Vairotsana requested the learned Chinese hermit Tsandha for instructions. He replied:

You should fully comprehend realization,
Control perceptions, attain mastery over them,
And let them remain in their natural state:
This is to be mindful of interrupting samsara!

Though Vairo personally met the learned hermit Tsandha, his realization was infinitely superior. Then, the learned Chinese mystic Mahabodhi gave Vairotsana an instruction on thought occurrence and awakening:

Watching the movement of thought occurrence, it
    clears up;
Awakening and freeing are simultaneous.
One may wonder about its duration;
While thought occurrence arises suddenly,
The movement appears like a flash to the self-arising
    awareness.
Observing it, it is nonarising and totally open;

While letting go, holding on to it is naturally liberated.
Occurring, appearing, and awakening
Are liberated, unborn, and wide open.
In this way everything is freed into the essence itself.
Dharmakaya cannot be created as an object of mind;
It is awakening in the great state beyond concepts.

Though he met the learned Chinese Mahabodhi, he excelled him in realization. Then, Vairotsana requested the learned Chinese yogi Shri Ani, who gave him an instruction to naturally clear up the three winds:

Appearances occur because of the choking outer wind;
Let the watcher naturally clear up!
Vivid clarity occurs because of the inner swirling wind;
Let the watcher naturally clear up!
Emptiness occurs because of the secret entwining wind;
Let the watcher naturally clear up!
If you don't know how to do this,
As the wind vigorously moves outward from within,
Fixation and attachment occur.
Not knowing how to clear up the winds naturally,
You will wander within the three worlds.

Though he met the learned Shri Ani, Vairotsana's realization was infinitely beyond that. Then, Vairotsana requested instructions from the learned Chinese mystic priest Bhiti, who taught him the *Six Vajra Words on Conviction*:

As all that appears and exists stays within space,
Be convinced that substance is not inherently existent.
As the essence of samsara and nirvana is within mind,
Resolve that enlightenment is not elsewhere.
Since happiness appears as an illusion,
Decide that suffering is devoid of self-nature.
As empty luminosity is inconceivable,
Be convinced that wisdom shines self-existing.
As original wakefulness is free from arising and ceasing,
Resolve that death is not frightening.

As the core of samsara and nirvana is within mind,
Exhausting cause and conditions,
Decide that you won't take rebirth.

Then, Vairotsana requested instruction from the learned Chinese yogi Dharmabodhi, who said:

Monk, watch the sky!
Clouds, lightning, thunder, and rain occur and clear up
    spontaneously.
Today's clouds are not yesterday's clouds,
And tomorrow, today's clouds won't be there.
Monk, observe your own mind!
The thinking mind spontaneously occurs and clears up.
Yesterday's thoughts are not the same as today's;
Today's thoughts won't remain tomorrow;
Thoughts occur and clear up spontaneously.
Give up concepts of hope and fear;
Emotions and original wakefulness occur and clear up
    spontaneously.
Just as there is nowhere to paint in empty space,
In empty awareness there is nowhere to accumulate sin.
As many big or small rivers as there are,
In the ocean they are all of one taste, with no difference.

Thus he spoke. Then Vairotsana requested instructions from the Chinese yogi Surya Ghirti, who said:

Recognize awareness,
Let awareness be,
Let awareness flow freely, and
Transcend awareness:
Be endowed with these four pith instructions.
Recognizing is like a king;
Thoughts are identified as original wakefulness.
Letting be is like a mirror;
Thoughts are recognized as original wakefulness.
Flowing freely is like a spring,

Joy and sorrow of samsara and nirvana are realized as
    equal, and
You have attained the view of self-liberation.
Instant transcending is like cutting up silk:
Everything is realized as the essential nature.

Thus he spoke. Then, the learned Chinese yogi Shata Sati taught Vairo
about the real nature, as it is:

Everything is the single awakening, inconceivable
    luminosity;
Stopping thought occurrence, it pervades everywhere.
Without inside or outside, it is unimpeded.
Everything is self-existing original wakefulness:
This single realization is total openness.

Thus he spoke. Then, the Chinese cemetery hermit Goni gave Vairo
this instruction:

Realize the essence, enlightened mind, as it is.
If you think that you have realized it,
Then that thought, too, is a mental concept.
To attain confidence, the rope of hope and fear must be cut.
At that time it is nondual, inexpressible, and inconceivable;
It can't be traversed;
It is intangible.
The innate nature is not the realm of mind.

Then, the Chinese yogi Patipa taught Vairo about resolving the natural state:

First, search for the mind's origin;
In between, search for the mind's location;
In the end, search for the mind's destination.
First, as mind has no origin, it is something without cause
    or condition.
In between, as mind has no location, it is something
    without path.

In the end, as mind has no destination, fruition is some-
   thing that cannot be achieved.
Realizing that is the view;
Stabilizing it is meditation;
Being convinced about it is the conduct;
And being beyond attainment is the result.
It is primordial total purity, primordial total liberation,
Totally all-encompassing, totally unborn,
Totally free, basically awakened.

Then, the learned Chinese mystic Yogi Barma taught Vairo this:

Determine that the view doesn't exist,
Determine that there is nothing to meditate on,
Determine that conduct is without indulging or
   rejecting,
Determine that fruition is without attainment:
That is the realization of the highest yogi.

Again, Yogi Barma gave some advice for beginners:

By means of the watcher, identify that which observes;
It is indescribable.
By means of a meditator and a meditation object,
Identify that which meditates.
Through the feeling of meditation,
Not seeing a meditator, observe the nature of things;
It transcends the realm of the mind.
By means of the conduct,
That which acts is free from any identification.

Then, Vairo requested instructions from the learned Chinese mystic
City Yogi, who taught him the *Instruction of the Three Entrances*:

As to the way things appear,
The way things arise,
And the way things are:
Knowing appearances to be self-occurring,

The outer entrance is ascertained.
Knowing arising to be self-occurring,
The inner entrance is ascertained.
Knowing the true nature to be unborn and nonarising,
The secret entrance is ascertained.

As one's own body can't search for itself,
There is nothing that connects body and mind,
And nowhere else to go but enlightenment.
Knowing appearance to be personal experience,
Ignorance arising from intrinsic conditions is purified.
Knowing arising to be self-occurring,
Ignorance from intrinsic causes is purified.
Controlling the strength of the natural breath energy,
Ignorance arising from both is purified.
Cutting attachment to both body and mind,
One is free from the three obscurations,
And there is nowhere else to go but enlightenment.

Then, the learned Chinese yogi Hesandhu taught Vairo this instruction on the nonduality of arising and ceasing:

Look beyond the unceasing display of phenomena;
It is definitely nonarising.
Look between both;
Can it be expressed?
It transcends conceptual mind.
It is free of fixation, unobstructed, without origin,
Indescribable and inconceivable.
AHANILATSAG!

Then, Vairo requested instructions from the learned Chinese mystic Yogini, who said:

If you want to attain enlightenment, settle in endeavor.
If you want to watch your mind, observe your breath.
If you want original wakefulness, always depend on
    mindfulness.

> If you want bliss, try to find the nature of the five
> poisons.
> Wanting to attain enlightenment will ruin you.

Thus the dakini advised him. Then, Vairo requested instructions from the learned Chinese yogi Prajna Ghirti, who said:

> Knowing the natural state,
> Knowing it to be distinct,
> Knowing it to be free,
> Knowing it to be nonexistent,
> Knowing it to be unborn,
> Knowing it to be nonconceptual,
> Knowing it to be intangible,
> Knowing it to be unmoved,
> And knowing it to be naturally pure:
> With these nine points you will be liberated.

Then, Vairo asked the Chinese female hermit Chudun about the true meaning. The yogini answered:

> Once one has realized that which is clear as the sky,
> Good and evil are a mere distinction, and
> Suffering and samsara have never existed.
> Nonarising phenomena are effortless;
> Since nothing is bound, there is nothing to liberate.
> What is called supreme enlightenment is primordially
> nonexisting.
> Those naive ones who don't understand this
> Uselessly follow after enemies,
> Completely giving up virtuous qualities.
> Confused by strong attachment and fixation on worldly
> affairs,
> They go to the lower realms.

These are the instructions from the scholars, siddhas, dakinis, and realized ones. May those who have extinguished their obscurations and completed their lives encounter them.

Then Vairo returned to Tsawarong and advised Yudra Nyingpo:

I, Pagor Genjak Vairotsana,
Was born at the junction of the Nyang and Tsang Rivers.
I alone know 360 languages,
As well as 360 different scripts.

I laid bare the heart treasures of
All the Indian, Chinese, and Oddiyana scholars.
I, Vairotsana, spent a month in China,
Taking teachings from yogis living in mountains, forests,
    and cemeteries,
Such as Hashang Garbha and others.

Except for a few destined devotees,
It is extremely difficult to realize the meaning of those
    instructions.
Without having realized your own mind,
Reciting the initial syllable of the buddhas,
The A, before getting from KA to KHA,[2]
You slander the realized beings.

Going astray due to evil deeds and obscurations, you
    go to hell:
For a hundred thousand eons you won't be liberated
And will surely fall into Vajra Hell.
Therefore, I entrusted the pith instructions of the Great
    Perfection
To you, Yudra Nyingpo;
Keep them completely hidden in your mind,
Sealed with samaya commitments.

Firmly concealed by the precepts,
If you don't find a destined disciple,
Keep them secret even at the cost of your life.
Test whether they deceive you

By skillfully stealing your books in hope of receiving
    instructions.

Not requesting teachings with devotion, they annoy you
    in different ways.
They don't respect the master; they fail to prostrate or use
    polite language.
Unable to part with the wealth they cherish,
Tied by attachment and miserliness,
When they get the instructions, they will drop hints to
    show them off,
Boast about them and sell them like merchandise.

If the instructions are lost to such people,
You and others will be ruined.
Dharmapalas and the eight classes of gods and spirits will
    be disturbed,
Frost and hail will cause harvests to fail,
Suddenly a time of poverty will come,
And there will be various epidemics and evil patterns.

So keep the Ati pith instructions extremely secret.
If they are spread everywhere,
Samaya breakers will practice them,
And not accomplishing them, the doctrine will perish.

If the pith instructions are practiced by non-
    Buddhists
And get into the hands of unworthy recipients,
It is like giving weapons to mad people,
Helping to destroy the doctrine.
So, my heart son Yudra Nyingpo,
You better keep the pith instructions hidden!

Then, in Gyalmo Tsawarong, Vairo gave the instructions he received
from the learned Chinese to Yudra Nyingpo.

Vairo Sends Yudra to Tibet, Where Yudra Debates with Vimalamitra

Yudra gave these teachings to Nyag Jnana Kumara, who gave them to Sangye Yeshe and Sogpo Palkyi Yeshe. Prince Yudra Nyingpo now knew thirty-six languages, had many extraordinary powers, and could demonstrate various miracles.

Yudra then obeyed his master and went to the glorious Samye, where Master Vimalamitra was about to explain the eight chapters of the *Prakarana* in the monastery courtyard. Yudra went directly inside, and raising his face to Vimala, he stared at him and said, "KAKAPARI KAKAPARI." Then he stared at the king and said, "AKAPARAMITHA." Vimala nodded his head and answered, "DHATHIM DHATHIM," upon which Yudra left. Then the king asked Vimalamitra, "That foreigner who came, what did he say. and what did the master answer?" Vimala answered, "He said, 'Will the yelping of a fox become a lion's voice? Moving with a raven's gait, can one traverse the universe? Expounding the childish Hinayana teachings, can one attain the effortless result?' And I answered, 'It seems that all phenomena are indeed evenness.' What he said to the king of Tibet was, 'AKA-PARAMITHA,' which means, 'The embodiment of unborn, naturally acquired enlightenment, the one who possesses the effortless great bliss pith instructions of the twenty-three Indian scholars that result in buddhahood in this very lifetime, the heart of the pith instructions, was banished to Tsawarong. What a pity for the stupid, ignorant king and ministers!' He is blaming us, to make us feel ashamed."

Another time, Yudra wrote four verses of the *Great Space Tantra*, beginning with: "Vajrasattva, Great Space, is the vast dharmakaya, perfectly free," on a skullcup in a place where Nyag Jnana Kumara used to walk. When Jnana looked at the skullcup, he was amazed and asked who had been there. He was told that aside from a foreigner who had come the other day and picked up the skullcup, saying, "Let's get the barmaid to make some wine!" no one else had come. The syllables he had written in Sanskrit were from the *Vajrasattva, Great Space Tantra*. Then Nyag looked into the four directions, paid homage, and raised the writing above his head. When Nyag tried to find Yudra, he was told that a foreigner was drinking wine in a liquor shop and that they hadn't seen anybody else. Then Nyag sent ingredients for making wine to the barmaid and invited the foreigner to come and talk to him when the wine was delivered. When Yudra came to talk,

Nyag prostrated and took off his clothes to make a seat for him. As Yudra sat down, Nyag offered him a golden cup full of wine and asked from where he had come. Yudra told him what had happened to Master Vairotsana.

Jnana was extremely inspired and requested the pith instructions, but Yudra said that Vimala would be sufficient for him. Jnana then explained that he was very inspired by Vairotsana's teachings and asked Yudra to please give them to him. Master Vimala also requested them, so they asked him to teach both of them together. Then Yudra promised to give the teachings, and the two masters got together at the glorious Samye. They didn't agree about who should prostrate and where they should sit. Jnana and the king and ministers told Yudra that since the great Vimalamitra was the most learned Indian scholar, Yudra should prostrate to him. But Yudra answered, "The emanation Vairotsana perfected all the pith instructions from the great Indian scholars, such as Prahe and so forth. I am from a royal family; I have completed all of Vairotsana's teachings, know many languages, and have many talents, so it is not proper for me to prostrate!" and refused to listen. Then Jnana, the king, and all the ministers told Vimala to prostrate to Yudra. Vimala said, "I am from a royal Indian family; I am a great scholar and an expert in the five sciences, so I can't prostrate to some king's child," and also refused to listen. Then Jnana and the king and ministers decided that whoever was the most learned in the Dharma and had the most magical power should receive prostrations. The two masters tested each other in languages, and Yudra proved to be more learned. Then, they debated on the absolute teachings, and Yudra was again the more learned. Vimala then said that they should compete in miracles. They had a miracle match, and Yudra transformed himself into a sparrow and playfully flew to the top of a willow tree. Vimala transformed himself into a hawk; flying straight up into the sky, he swooped down and hit the little sparrow, which changed into a golden hammer and sped into the sky, while Vimala hid himself in the trees.

Everyone said, "Yudra excels in Dharma and miracles, but Vimala is authentic and older, so they should prostrate to each other and sit opposite," and they arranged rows of seats on the right and the left. While Yudra and Vimala compared their understanding and realization experiences, the virtuous Dharma protectors and gods threw flowers from the sky, the earth shook, and a curtain of light appeared in the sky. Everyone was inspired and said, "He has the special pith instructions that can't be taught to everyone. Let's request them!"

At the head of the right and left rows they built equal thrones for the two masters, and a small throne for Jnana between them. As the two masters taught the Dharma simultaneously, Jnana listened intensively and thoroughly understood them at the same time. Yudra gave the teachings that had been expounded to King Trisong Deutsen previously, such as the *Great Space Tantra* and so forth, which became known as the Five Early Translations. Vimala taught *Spontaneous Summit* and others, which became known as the Thirteen Later Translations.[3] The two appeared like the joining of a mother hawk and her son, and everyone had faith in them and wept with regret for having banished Vairotsana. Then, the king and all the ministers, the two types of Sangha, the scholars Nyag Jnana and so forth, all unanimously praised Vairotsana, describing his qualities:

> Your unsurpassed supreme body represents the Buddha,
> Homage to Vairotsana's body!
> With the voice of Brahma you expound the ocean of the
>   doctrine,
> Homage to Vairotsana's speech!
> Your omniscient great bliss wisdom is the mind of the
>   victorious ones,
> Homage to Vairotsana's mind!

Thus praising him, they enumerated his qualities:

> Knowing your past and future lives and
> Striving for the benefit of sentient beings,
> You have true compassion and bodhichitta.

> Discovering the pith instructions without remainder,
> Which can't be found when searched for,
> You are the perfect incarnation.

> Leaving Tibet for India before you turned fifteen
> Without knowing the road
> Shows that you have authentic divine eyes.

> That you were unharmed by savages and vicious wild
>   animals

On treacherous paths
Is indeed a sign of not returning to samsara.

You covered the distance from India to Tibet,
Which takes thirteen months, in one day:
Showing such a miracle, you truly accomplished speed
    walking.

Though you were thrown in a well of frogs and a louse pit,
You were not eaten or harmed:
You attained the perfect zeal of patience.

Just by hearing the pith instructions,
You understood and realized them:
You have seen the actual truth of the dharmata.

Skilled in languages by traversing the four borders,
You actually purified the two obscurations.
Having acquired the essential instructions from all the
    Indian scholars,
You attained the perfect accomplishment of the tathagatas.

Knowing all the vehicles signed by the Buddha,
You are the Buddha's true representative.
Possessing the four miraculous powers,
You are a perfect bodhisattva!

Thus praising his qualities, they all cried and did prostrations facing
Tsawarong.

Yudra Nyingpo Tames Nyag Jnana's Arrogance and Returns to Vairotsana in Tsawarong

Then Jnana thought that there was nobody greater than him in Tibet, since
he had received the Eighteen Major Scriptures of the Mind Class and many
other teachings from the two masters so that now he possessed the teachings of both masters. Both the masters saw this, so they each gave Jnana a
vase, telling him to fill each vase with water from the Tsangpo River. Jnana

filled the two vases with water and gave them to the two masters. The two masters each poured a drop of water on Jnana's palms, and Vimala said, "The Buddha's doctrine is like the water of the Tsangpo River. We two know about as much as this vase full of water; you know about as much as the drop on your palm."

Jnana felt that the masters had clairvoyance, and his pride was broken. Jnana then received the esoteric Secret Mantra teachings and especially many Ati teachings. From Vimala he received many Secret Mantra tantras, especially the rituals for cremation, empowerment, and consecration as well as *Magical Net Tantra*[4] with the pith instructions. From Yudra, Jnana received the Five Early Translations as well as the Thirteen Later Translations. He received the pith instructions of the Eighteen Tantras of the Mind Class, the earlier and final tantras of the *All-Creating Monarch*, and the Root, Scripture, and Commentary Sutras.[5] From the cycle of the Space Class he received the Four Space Class Tantras with the pith instructions as well as many others.

Jnana was now able to listen to the Dharma intensively and had a great talent for languages. Through the previous transmissions, he mastered most of the teachings and was an expert in the teachings based on cause and effect. More than anything else, the heart of the doctrine, the effortless Ati nature, inspired him, and as he was very intelligent, Yudra thought he might be worthy to receive the instruction teachings, so Yudra said:

> If the destined highly qualified one called Jnana has faith,
> I have the ultimate instruction that directly introduces
>   self-liberation,
> Not mere words about the general meaning.

Because Jnana was obscured by philosophy and by the fame of his knowledge of Dharma and languages, he thought that nobody could have instructions superior to the ones he already knew and that the foreigner was claiming to have another instruction because he wanted wealth. Therefore, Jnana answered:

> What can a transmission add to one's mind,
> Which is endowed with enlightenment itself,
> The foundation of all Dharma statements?
> It would contradict what you have already taught.

Yudra understood that Jnana wasn't a worthy recipient for the pith instructions and said:

> The mind transmission beyond words,
> Direct, uninterrupted self-liberation,
> Is only for a few worthy disciples.
> Adding alum to gold will turn it toxic.

Upon uttering those words, he disappeared into the sky. Then Jnana felt regret; as he prostrated and prayed with tears in his eyes, Yudra came back and asked why he was calling so much. Jnana answered, "Please teach me the instruction that clearly points out self-liberation." Yudra said:

> The nectar stream of accomplishments
> Is blocked by a mountain of arrogance.
> If you think the master's teachings are contradictory,
> You misinterpret the warmth of the self-liberating
>   instructions.
> You should pray with fervent devotion to meet me again!

Thus speaking, he left to go to his master.

On the way, he met Pam Sangye Gonpo. Giving Pam a complete transmission of tantras and instructions in the tradition of the three entrustments, Yudra matured him. When Yudra continued on his way, Pam said that he had heard a lot about Master Vairotsana's greatness and accomplishment and had much faith in him; he asked if he could come to Tsawarong to meet Vairo.

Praying to Master Vairotsana, Pam went to Tsawarong to meet him; later on he spread the pith instructions and hid tantras and instructions as treasures.

Then Yudra met Gya Lodro Shonnu. Seeing that he was destined, Yudra entrusted him with all twenty-five classes of tantras with empowerments and instructions, and then moved on. As Gya Lodro Shonnu was worthy, he received a complete cycle of pith instructions that matured him. He hid some tantras and pith instructions as treasures and took some of them with him. He meditated in the Tsami region and realized the stainless wisdom mind. In lower Do Kham he spread the instructions to some fortunate ones.

As Yudra continued, he met Bes Dorje Gyaltsen in lower Do Kham. Bes Dorje Gyaltsen, who knew a little about the teachings on cause and effect and had done some Kilaya practice, was watching the cattle and driving them home. Yudra said, "Tantric brother, have you got a practice that keeps you from getting hungry?" Bes answered, "I don't have a practice that keeps me from getting hungry when I work. Who would have such a thing? What is it like?"

Yudra said:

> Having recognized self-arising awareness
> Through the nectar instructions of the hearing lineage,
> Self-manifesting mindfulness is the view and meditation.
> Resting naturally, the essence will arise.

Bes thought this was a wonderful instruction; he prostrated, placed his head at Yudra's feet, and asked for instructions. Yudra saw that he was worthy and said, "Are you able to give up all the fame and craving for this world? Are you able to let go of all your wealth for the sake of virtue? Are you able to practice the profound instructions on the meaning of realization?" Bes answered, "I can do whatever the master says. By all means, please give me the pith instructions and take care of me!" Yudra promised to teach them and gave him many general Ati tantras and pith instructions. In particular, he gave him the complete empowerment of direct anointment. Then Bes offered all his property to his guru; starting with a nine-pronged vajra made of refined gold, he offered thirty-five hundred possessions. Yudra then gave him the complete empowerments, tantras, and instructions and said:

> In response to your request for the pith instructions:
> Mind is beyond meditation and nonmeditation
> In your inherently awakened wisdom of awareness;
> Letting go of everything, free of fixation,
> Just don't lose your mindfulness.

Then for Bes Dorje Gyaltsen the time of realization had come. He actually saw all outer and inner phenomena as self-cognizant awareness and experienced direct self-liberation. Offering his realization to the master, he said:

Just as a house built by children collapses,
My obscurations acquired over eons have been exhausted.
Due to the guru's kindness I realized my mind,
Which is like a torch that naturally lights up a dungeon.

Later, Yudra met Pam Sangye Gonpo and Gya Lodro Shonnu again; both of them were authorized as holders of the pith instructions. Bes received the mind essence and the pith instructions from Yudra and nurtured the actual state of realization for three years at Dentig Monastery. Realizing his mind as inseparably united with the nature of unconditioned great bliss, he spread the pith instructions in lower Do Kham.

Then Yudra went to Master Vairotsana in Gyalmo Tsawarong and told him what had happened. He precisely related how they had praised Master Vairo with the eleven perfections. Master Vairotsana was very happy and sang this song:

I, the monk Vairotsana,
Possess the eleven true perfections.
Because I had not purified some slight cognitive
    obscurations
And the time to tame the fortunate ones had not yet come,
I, Vairo, was banished to Tsawarong.
I matured you, the most worthy one,
And turned the land of Tsawa into virtue.
On the tree sprouted from bodhichitta
The unsurpassed fruit of enlightenment has ripened!
Now I shall return to central Tibet.

And so he decided to go to Tibet.

The Tibetan King and Subjects All Agree to Invite Vairotsana to Tibet

Meanwhile, the Tibetan king and his subjects agreed to invite Master Vairotsana from the Tsawa region, make confession, and put him in charge of the major Dharma College. Master Vimala also urged them to invite Master Vairotsana. Of King Trisong Deutsen's three sons, Mutig Tsenpo had killed Shang Tsenpo Uring for the price of [the region of] Namar and had been banished to Tod Ngari, so he was absent. When Mune Tsenpo was ruling Tsang, the local folk poisoned him,[6] and he died. During the time of Tride Tsugtsan, also known as Lord Saynalek Jingyon, the king, ministers, and subjects were in harmony. Having agreed on the funeral ceremony for Mune Tsenpo and the religious activities, Master Upadesha, Thangzang Palkyi Dorje, and Gang Palkyi Nyingpo were sent to invite Vairotsana. So they went to Tsawarong and met Vairotsana. When they requested him to come to Tibet, the master was pleased; he promised to come and said, "Escape to Tibet without saying you have invited me. If the people here hear about it and you haven't fled, you will be killed." So the three messengers went ahead.

Master Vairotsana gathered the king and ministers of Tsawarong, including the religious subjects, and told them, "Since I am going to Tibet, you should each ask for the teachings you need and clarify any doubts you have."

He then completed whatever teachings he hadn't yet given. As the master prepared to go to Tibet, Queen Dru and the others offered jewels, gold, turquoise, brocades, delicious beverages, and so forth, prostrated, and kept praying to him with tears in their eyes, "Great master, the king of Tibet is very hostile, and the place is evil, too. Please don't go!" Vairotsana said, "First, King Trisong Deutsen and I aspired toward supreme enlightenment. In order to spread the effortless doctrine in Tibet, I endured hardships between India and Tibet that brought me near death, searching for effortless enlightenment. As the time to subdue Tibet had not come, I came here. Now the time has come, so I am going to Tibet." Replying to everyone without preference, he said:

> All phenomena are enlightened mind;
> Like the example of space, it is free of all bias.
> Once one has realized the depth of the pure skylike mind
>   essence,
> There is nothing that doesn't become the essence of
>   buddhahood.
> How pitiful to maintain preferences of good and bad
> Within the vast expanse of the innate nature, equal
>   to space.

In answer to their request to look upon them with compassion, he said:

> In the skylike dharmadhatu, without center or limit,
> The sun of Vairotsana's awareness rose,
> Illuminated the darkness of ignorance in Tsawarong,
> And fulfilled the wishes of the king and ministers.
> Wisdom clouds gathered in the sky of the true nature, and
> Stainless Dharma nectar rained down continuously.
> The sprout of enlightenment matured in Tsawarong:
> May the devoted fortunate ones nourish it!

Thus speaking, as he prepared to leave, Queen Dru and the others offered him the five precious things,[7] brocades, gems, delicious dishes, and so forth and earnestly prayed over and over again, pleading, "Master, please regard us with compassion and stay here!" But the master said, "The time has come for me to convert Tibet; I definitely must go."

Queen Dru and the others said, "It is impossible to disobey the master, but please promise to come back again! We have offered the master gems, gold, silver, brocades, horses, and many other things for going. Please give us some concise instructions! Please leave the Tibetan monk Sangye Gonpo here as our guide and resident monk! Master, please come back here again!" Master Vairotsana then said, "There are no teachings or instructions that are greater than the ones I have already given. Yet, this is what you should do," and he gave them this advice:

> Since this life's wealth, relatives, friends, joy, and
>   sorrow
> Are impermanent and illusory, let go of attachment.
> Remember the refuge of all, the Triple Gem,
> And the guru of all beings. Never forget them.
> Care for everyone with great compassion, like your
>   own child,
> And take your own mind as witness for the teachings of
>   cause and effect.
> Whatever occurs is personal experience, your mind's
>   projections,
> So observe inherent clarity within, without prejudice.

Always rely on mindfulness, without emerging or entering,
>   and
Act at ease within the conduct of self-existing compassion.
Enlightenment is nowhere else, so sever your hopes
>   and fears!

Then Vairotsana left Pam Sangye Gonpo as the resident monk and
Dharma master and promised to return. When Master Vairo was leaving,
the people from Gyalmo brought offerings of gold and silver on plates. He
told them he had no need for gold and other wealth and gave it all back.
Because they insisted, he took three silver coins, two measures of gold
dust, and the king's blazing life-supporting turquoise; then he left. The
Gyalmo people escorted him for a short distance up to Mang Pass, and
everyone did many prostrations and circumambulations, receiving his
blessings while touching their heads to his feet. Then Master Yudra and
Vairo both left for Tibet like a flash of lightning. The Gyalmo people,
Queen Dru and the others, all wept, their faces wet with tears, and did full
prostrations facing Tibet. For three days they prayed and did prostrations
toward Tibet and then returned to Gyalmo Tsawarong.

On the way to Tibet the master met Pam Mipham Gonpo, a gray-haired
old man who was a hundred years old. The old man gave them a place for
a night's rest and asked, "From where do you two monks come, and where
are you going?" Yudra replied that they came from Gyalmo Rong and were
headed to Tibet. The old man said, "You two guests must be misinformed.
I heard that the learned Vairotsana is staying in Tsawarong and made the
sun of the Dharma rise there. Why don't you stay there and listen to his
teachings?" When Vairotsana revealed himself, the old man stared at him,
propping his eyelids up with small sticks to see better. He embraced
Vairotsana and cried for a while, saying, "I am old and decrepit and have
wasted my life without Dharma practice. Though I am an old man, I can't
die, and I suffer from my conflicting emotions. Master, what a wonder that
I met you; I am so happy! Please give me a teaching to help me at the moment of death!"

Seeing that he was destined, Vairo uttered an indication as he put his
hand on the crown of the old man's head, but this did not liberate him.
Vairo thought that as the old man was a fortunate disciple, this must
be because Tibet was a deficient place. Placing a stick to support the old

man's posture and tying a meditation belt around his waist, Vairotsana gave him instructions. The old man immediately became realized and liberated simultaneously, and attaining enlightenment, he changed into a sixteen-year-old youth. He acted for the benefit of the doctrine and sentient beings like the sun and the moon.

The three people who had gone to invite Vairo thought that it would be incorrect for them to arrive before the master. Wanting to arrive in the king's presence at the same time as Vairotsana, they proceeded slowly. Master Vairo and his disciple, meanwhile, miraculously arrived at the upper retreat place of Samye Chimphu in an instant. It was the time of King Mune Tsenpo's funeral, and Vimala and Nyag Kumara were leading the ceremony. The two monks arrived flashing like sparks of molten metal in the funeral crowd, so everyone wondered who they were.

When Jnana Kumara got up and looked, he recognized them and prostrated; it then became known by the king and ministers that Master Vairo had come. While Master Vimalamitra and Vairotsana very excitedly showed each other respect, Jnana and the other Tibetan scholars, the two types of Sangha, and the king and ministers fell to the ground doing full prostrations. They all vied to offer each of their ornaments, gems, gold, turquoise, horses, garments, and so forth, piling them up in front of Master Vairo like a mountain. Meanwhile, the three messengers who had gone to invite him also arrived.

Then a high throne was arranged with garments and other things, and Master Vairo took his seat. On either side they made two smaller thrones for Vimala and Yudra to sit on. The scholars, the two types of Sangha, the king, ministers, and subjects all gathered in front of Vairo. Some of them wept and prostrated, some encircled him, some pitched canopies, some raised tassels, some blew conches, some made music with drums and other instruments, some sang songs and danced, some did pantomimes, and they all recited joyful verses of praise. Then Vairotsana and Vimalamitra meditated while Yudra, Jnana, the three messengers, and others conducted an elaborate funeral ceremony for King Mune. Vairo sang this carefree song:

> Attending the guru with the three services[8]
> Is like Vairotsana meeting the great panditas.
> If my masters are pleased with me,
> Even if no one else is satisfied, I'm at ease!

Studying sutras and tantras with the threefold knowledge,[9]
I am like a merchant reaching a land of jewels.
Having given up my body, life, and possessions for religion,
Though this life has been poor and uncomfortable, I'm
    at ease!

Pleasantly adorned with the three trainings,[10]
I am like a royal princess arriving at her wedding.
Firm and straightforward in my practice,
Even if others slander me, I'm at ease!

Observing what is in the three pitakas,[11]
I am like a torch raised above a land of darkness.
Showing patience toward enemies who provoked my
    disgrace,
Even though they claim I can't benefit others, I'm at ease!

Serving the Dharma with body, speech, and mind,
I am like a distant traveler returning to his homeland.
Never distracted from my virtuous practice,
Though the king told me not to return, I'm at ease!

Using original wakefulness as an antidote for the three
    poisons,
I am like camphor that alleviates fever.
As I think of nothing but the holy Dharma,
Though they say my mind is wild, I'm at ease!

Hearing, reflecting, and meditating without prejudice,
I am like a spear rotating in the sky.
Having cleared all outer and inner doubts,
Though they say I don't know all the teachings, I'm at ease!

The Ati realization of this roaming yogi
Is like escaping prison without depending on others.
Being an expert in study, explanation, and meditation,
Though they say I have no skill in social affairs, I'm
    at ease!

Caring more for others than for oneself
Seems to be the life story of a bodhisattva's practice.
As I don't give instructions to please the crowd,
Though they say I don't satisfy people, I'm at ease!

Providing the three types of generosity,[12]
I am like a wish-fulfilling gem found by a beggar.
As I offer whatever I have to the guru,
Even if I starve or freeze to death, I'm at ease!

Accompanied by the guide of the three disciplines,[13]
I am like a road over a dangerous precipice.
As I respect good, bad, and average above myself,
Though they say I am insignificant and feeble, I'm
    at ease!

Wearing the armor of the three types of patience,
I am like a tortoise climbing up a royal castle.
As I let go of all worldly actions,
Though they say I am powerless, I'm at ease!

Galloping the horse of the three zeals,
I am like someone being blamed for hidden faults.
Going into exile without despair,
Though they say I had nowhere to go, I'm at ease!

Holding the citadel of the three concentrations,
I am like the sun shining in a cloudless sky.
Having totally resolved my mind to its depth,
Though they say my wrong views are irreligious,
    I'm at ease!

Supported by the confidence of the three trainings,
I am like someone observing the lower heights from the
    peak of Mount Meru.
I, the Ati Yoga practitioner, perfect the access to all vehicles,
    and
Though they say I am a non-Buddhist sorcerer, I'm at ease!

Then the Dharma College was established, and the wheel of the Dharma was turned extensively. When Master Vairo was teaching the Dharma, a lattice of rainbows and various lights radiated in the sky. Many gods appeared in the sky throwing different kinds of divine flowers, the earth shook, and many other wondrous miracles occurred. Everybody was amazed and regretted having previously banished Vairotsana. Some wept, some prostrated, some cried, and some rolled on the ground; and they all made confession to Vairotsana with different offerings of wealth.

They asked if the master had had trouble when he was banished to Tsawarong, whether he had converted the people from Tsawarong to the holy Dharma, and how it was possible that someone like the master had ever been banished, and they all wept. Then Master Vairotsana said, "Now that you have purified your obscurations, don't cry anymore," and told them:

> All you scholars, two types of Sangha, king, ministers,
>   and subjects, listen!
> I, the monk Vairotsana,
> Let the royal garuda of self-existing awareness fly
> In the pure skylike dharmata, immense space.
> I am free of any signs of injury, hope, fear, or effort
> And abide in great bliss without suffering.

And:

> By the light rays of the ever-perfect Vajrasattva's
>   heart
> And Vairotsana's residual karma and prayers,
> The sun of the doctrine rose in Tsawarong.
> Wisdom rays illuminated the darkness of ignorance,
> And destined great beings were introduced to true
>   enlightenment.
> I gradually matured faithful worthy students
> And planted virtuous seeds for those who lack merit,
> Turning the Tsawarong country into virtue.

Thus he spoke, and continued:

A blessed mind emanation of Manjushri,
The exalted Trisong Deutsen, the great king,
Who has been as kind to the people as a mother to her
    children,
Saw that no one but Lekdrub and I, Vairo, would be able
    to find
The effortless great bliss of primordial enlightenment,
Which utterly transcends the teachings of cause and
    effect.
So when the compassionate Lord Trisong
First planned to search for the pith instructions,
I made the difficult promise to go.

The king sent gold dust, the most precious wealth,
To please the Indian scholars,
And I journeyed the long distance, so difficult to travel.
I passed through dangerous passages that were hard to cross
And went to India, so troublesome to reach.
I deceived an old Brahmin woman, who was hard to fool,
And met Prahe, Manjushri, and many others,
Who are hard to meet even after eons of practice.

I pleased the Indian aryas, who are hard to please,
Found the supreme pith instructions, which are hard
    to find,
And realized my own mind as the Buddha, which is hard
    to realize.
My mind perfected the doctrine that is hard to perfect,
And I accomplished miraculous speed walking, which is
    hard to accomplish.
I analyzed dreams and experiences, which are hard to
    analyze,
And wore worn-out boots backward, which are hard
    to wear.

I escaped on long paths where it's hard to flee
And arrived in the presence of the king, who was
    impressed.

I fulfilled his wishes with the essence of the doctrine,
But the time to convert Tibet hadn't come.
Due to the slander of the Indian king and the Tibetan
    ministers,
As well as residual karma, prayers, and the compassion
    of the exalted ones,
I, Vairotsana, was banished to Tsawarong,
Where I spread the doctrine.

To pacify the pride, arrogance, and haughtiness
Of narrow-minded beings in this dark age,
Who boast about the minor troubles they endure for the
    sake of Dharma,
And to support faithful ones who practice in accord with
    the Dharma but
Feel discouraged and lose heart from unjust blame and
    undeserved misery,
I apparently experienced some difficulties.
For the sake of future yogis,
Out of compassion, I spread the doctrine.

Meanwhile Padmasambhava, who had been invited from Oddiyana, the abbot Shantarakshita from Zahor, the Kashmiri pandita Vimalamitra, and the 108 resident translators and scholars requested, "Since you promised to be our Dharma king, please translate the sacred teachings from India—the Buddha's words and the treatises, tantras, scriptures, and pith instructions—into Tibetan, without leaving any out!"

The Translators and Scholars Translate Many Tantra Sections and Instructions in the Translation Hall at Samye

Then the translators and scholars went to the Translation Hall.[14] First, they translated ten sutras regarding the expedient meaning of the shravakas and pratyekabuddhas: the *Sutra Showing Right and Wrong,* the *Sutra of One Hundred Karmas,* the *Sutra of Discerning Imputations,* the *Sutra on the Description of Karma, Hundred Stories of Purna,* the *Sutra of the Brahmin Master, Special Utterances,* the *Sutra on the Application of Mindfulness,* the *Sutra of* the *Wise and the Foolish*, the *Sutra on Refuting Bad Discipline*, and the *Sutra Repaid with Gratitude*.

Then they translated the Four Sets of Scriptures on Basic Vinaya: *Scripture on Discernment*, *Highest Scripture*, *Minor Scripture*, and *Twofold Pratimoksha Sutra*.

From the middle set of teachings on the Bodhisattva Collections, they translated the *Seventeen Paramitas of Mother and Son* and many sutras expounding the *prajnaparamita*[15] and emptiness.

From the final teachings on absolute truth, they translated the *Sutra of the Ten Wheels of Kshitigarbha*, the *Sutra of the Great Multitude*, *Jewel Mound Sutra*, the *Sutra of the Descent to Lanka*, the *White Lotus Sutra*, the *Parinirvana Sutra*, *Definite Commentary on Wisdom Mind*, the *Sutra of the Dense Array of Adornments*, the *Sacred Gold Light Sutra*, and many others.

From the treatises that clarify the intent of three cycles of the Buddha's teachings, they translated many major texts on Vinaya, many commentaries on the sutras, *Great Treasury of Detailed Exposition*, and the Seven Shastras on Abhidharma. They translated five of Vasubandhu's treatises on Svatantrika: *Treatise on the Five Aggregates*, *Twenty Verses*, *Thirty Verses*, *Verses on Accomplishing Activity*, and *Commentary on Reasoning*, and countless authoritative commentaries on the *Abhidharmakosha* and so forth.

Of the Bodhisattva Commentaries, they translated Nagarjuna's *Collections of Madhyamaka Reasoning*, *Collection of Hymns*, and *Collection of Messages*; Aryadeva's *Four Hundred Sections on Madhyamaka*; Bhavaviveka's *Blaze of Reasoning*; Buddhapalita's *Buddhapala*; Chandrakirti's *Madhyamakavatara*; Jnanagarbha's *Discernment of the Two Truths*; Shantarakshita's *Ornament of the Middle Way*; Kamalashila's *Presentation of Madhyamaka*; Ashvaghosha's *Jataka Tale Poetry*; Dharmatrata's *Special Utterances*; Dignaga's *One Hundred Eight Treatises*; Dharmakirti's Seven Treatises on Logic and *Discerning Logic*; Shantideva's *The Way of the Bodhisattva* and *Compendium of Instructions*; the Five Teachings of Lord Maitreya received by Asanga, as well as his Five Treatises on the Levels and *Treatise on the Three Sets of Precepts*, and many other commentaries.

From the commentaries on the sutras on absolute truth, they translated Vasubandhu's *Commentary on the Ten Stages*, Pundarika's *Root and Branches of the Stages*, *Explanation of the Intent*, and *Sixty Chapters of Instructions*, as well as countless other texts by many learned and accomplished Indians. This, however, is just a rough summary.

From the cycle of Vajrayana teachings, they translated the *Sutra Designed as a Jewel Chest, Wish-Fulfilling Jewel, Collection of Precious Pinnacles*, the *Five Sets of Great Dharanis*, and the *One Hundred Sixty Minor Dharanis*.

Of the Kriya cycle they translated the six root tantras: the *Body Tantra of the Immaculate Ushnisha*, the *Speech Tantra of the Meaningful Lasso*, the *Mind Tantra of Supreme Knowledge*, the *Exposition Tantra of Eminent Courage*, the *Sutikara Tantra*, and the two *Unshakable Tantras*.

Of the general Kriya tantras they translated the *Manjushri Root Tantra*, and of the detailed ones: *Detailed Description of Ritual Tantra*, the later *Long Dhyana Dharani*, the *Emanation of Light Rays Tantra*, the *Secret General Tantra*, the *King of Mastery Tantra*, the *Manjushri Root Tantra of the Three Families*, the *Secret Tantra of Manjushri*, the *Manjushri Six Realm Tantra*, and the later *Tantra of Manjushri's Secret Teaching*. From the exposition tantras arranged in writing they translated *Ocean of Single Daka Practices*, *Chanting the Names of Manjushri*, and so forth. They translated twenty-one sutras and tantras on Avalokiteshvara, *Lotus Net*, the *Skillful Lasso Tantra, Wish-Fulfilling Wheel, Thousand-Armed Thousand-Eyed Lion's Roar*, the *Lotus Crown Tantra, Meditation on Avalokiteshvara*, and so forth.

From the Vajrapani cycle they translated the *Root Tantra of the Ferocious One* and the subsequent and final tantras: *Underground Vajra, Vajra Subduing the Three Worlds, Indestructible Blissful Wrath*, the *Indestructible Confidence Tantra, Vajra Essence Shower*, the *Vajra Subjugator Root Tantra, Summit of the Indestructible Mount Meru Mansion*, and so forth.

They also translated the *Majestic Blazing Tara Tantra*, the *Tsundha Tantra*, the *Black Yamantaka Tantra*, and countless other dharani mantras.

From the Upa Tantra cycle they translated the *Enlightenment of Vairochana Root Tantra*, the exposition tantra *Brilliant Sun*, the root tantras and the final tantras, the *Tantra Manifesting as the Inner Son Victorious in the Three Worlds*, the ten thousand sections of *Chanting the Names of Manjushri (Arya-manjushri-nama-samgiti), Blazing Mass of Fire*, the *Tantra of Vajrapani's Empowerment Outlining the Three Precepts*, and so forth.

From the Yoga tantras they translated the *Tsatathasamgraha*, the exposition tantras *Vajra Peak, Consecration*, the *Tantra Purifying the Lower Realms*, the first supreme amendment of the *Tantra of Unexcelled*

Knowledge Vanquishing the Three Worlds, the *Tantra of the Magical Net of Manjushri*, the *Vajra Essence Ornament Tantras*, and their infinite commentaries, sadhanas, empowerments, instructions, and traditions.

From the Maha Yoga cycle they translated the Eighteen Root Tantras, *Fourfold Magical Net of Vairochana*, the *Secret Vajrasattva Tantra*, *Eightfold Magical Net*, *Eight Sadhana Teachings*, the general and special tantras, the *Manjushri Body Tantra of Secret Black Moon*, the *Padma Speech Tantra of Supreme Steed Display*, the *Vishuddha Mind Tantra of Heruka Galpo*, the *Nectar Quality Tantra of the Major and Minor Display*, the *Kilaya Activity Tantra of Bidyotamala*, the *Mamo Bumtig* and the Six Sadhana Sections, the *Tana Gana Amrita Torma Rakta Tantras*, and so forth.

From the cycle of inner Anu Yoga scriptures they translated the seven root scriptures: the *Wisdom Mudra Root Tantra*, *Scripture of Display*, *Six Abhisheka Vidyadharas*, *Supreme Samadhi*, *Secret Entrance Commentary*, *Nonstraying Vajra*, and the *Tarakuta Scripture*.

From the major scriptures they translated the Seven Inner Root Scriptures: the *Scripture of the Embodiment of Realization*, *Compendium of Knowledge*, *Great Mind Scripture*, *Awesome Wisdom Lightning*, *Play of the Cuckoo*, *Galpoche*, and *Supramundane Scripture*.

From the tantras they translated the *Supreme Body Tantra Blazing Like Cosmic Fire*, the *Melodious Speech Tantra of the Wrathful King*, *Embodiment of Great Power*, the *Supreme Pundarika Mind Tantra*, the *Spontaneously Perfect Quality Tantra of the Nonstraying Goddess*, the *Activity Tantra of the Sixfold Meditation Object*, the Collection of Anuttara Tantras, the General Tantras, and so forth.

From the Ati Yoga Great Perfection tantras they translated the Five Root Tantras, the Seven Branch Tantras, the Four Exposition Tantras with the appendixes, and the Eighteen Major Scriptures of the Mind Class; of the Space Class they translated the White Sections, the Black Sections, and the Variegated Sections of the Mother and Son Cycle; and of the Instruction Class they translated the canon,[16] the rediscovered texts,[17] and the oral lineage, with their related commentaries and sadhana manuals, as well as inconceivable corresponding treatises.

The masters miraculously took these texts from the abodes of the gods, nagas, yakshas, and dakinis, Oddiyana, Nalanda Monastic College, and so forth. These are the Indian books that now comprise part of the Samye treasury.

Vairotsana also translated mixed texts on astrology and medicine, as well as mixed sutras and tantras. He signed his sutra translations as Yeshe De, his tantra translations as Vairotsana, his Bon translations as Genjak Tangta, his astrological translations as Indra Vairo, and his medical translations as Chobar. He translated most of these teachings and sutras in Tibet. Having pronounced the auspiciousness of the Buddha's first teachings, he said:

> All the Buddha's teachings, from the first ones until his
>   nirvana,
> The Four Noble Truths, the vehicle of dialectics,
> And his final teachings on the definitive meaning,
> Were translated in their entirety by me, Yeshe De.
> Of the esoteric Secret Mantra I produced translator's
>   colophons
> For twenty-six hundred Secret Mantra deity sadhanas,
> Such as Samantabhadra, the five buddha families,
>   Vajradhara,
> The lords of the three families, the eight sadhana teachings,
>   Yamantaka,
> As well as six million two hundred thousand tantras.
> I relied on twenty-five scholars, who attained rainbow body,
> Such as Prahe, Manjushri, Shri Singha, Padmasambhava,
>   and so forth.
> For the sake of Tibet I translated a thousand Tantra Sections
> And ten million pith instructions and put them in order.
> The only spiritual teachers greater than me in the Jambu
>   continent
> Are Shri Singha in India and Padmasambhava in Tibet.
> I, Vairotsana, am incomparable;
> But instead of seeing my qualities, others perceive them
>   as faults.
> My body will vanish into the sky like a rainbow;
> Then the translators, siddhas, and great panditas,
> The king, ministers, and subjects, all of whom
> Understand but a drop of Vairotsana's talents, will claim to
>   be wise.

> I pray that they will attain enlightenment in this life
> And accomplish the rainbow body.

Upon saying this, he manifested in the form of Buddha Vairochana and dissolved into dharmata space. As his retinue wailed and supplicated, he appeared on the throne in front of them for a while. Then the great panditas who had come from India, the Tibetan translators, siddhas, king, ministers, and subjects all offered a ganachakra and a golden mandala and praised the master:

> In the past, present, and future
> There has never been a translator like you, Vairotsana,
> Nor will anyone like you ever appear again.
> You attained the supreme and common siddhis and the
>   vajra rainbow body;
> Such an accomplished vidyadhara will never appear again.
> Expert in all vehicles, from the Tripitaka up to the
>   great Ati,
> King of learned ones, such a sublime scholar
> Has never appeared before and will never appear again.
> In future, anyone who merely knows any colloquial Indian
>   language
> May be considered as a great translator,
> But they won't approach even a fraction of Vairotsana's
>   knowledge.
> Though Vairotsana is called a translator, in fact, he is a
>   supreme scholar.
> You Tibetans should know how much you owe him for
>   the Dharma!
> In the future, if wrong teachings spread,
> They should be judged against Vairotsana's translations.
> The light of his teachings, you Tibetans, can illuminate the
>   darkness of ignorance!

Thus praising, they did countless prostrations and circumambulations.

Then, as the teachings were finished, Master Vairo, Yudra, and some exceptional disciples stayed one year in the Chimphu Hermitage.

Vairotsana Goes Once More to Tsawarong, and After Predicting the Instruction Lineage of the Vidyadharas, He Departs for the Pure Land

Then Vairo returned to Gyalmo Tsawarong, where he met the king and ministers and discussed the Dharma. He remained there, teaching the pith instructions to worthy recipients. Meanwhile, people heard that Vairotsana was staying in Tsawarong and invited him to Kham; Master Vimala and two other panditas were also invited. At the Tungcham Chen Hermitage in Kham, Vairotsana translated the Sadhana Sections, such as the Interpretation of Mantra and so forth.

Then Vairo, Pam Sangye Gonpo, and Bes Dorje Gyaltsen meditated together. To his exceptional disciples Vairo taught many tantras and pith instructions concerning the Ati Mind Class and so forth. He also taught the Eighteen Major Scriptures of the Mind Class with the pointing out instructions and symbols.

Concerning this, the first lineage goes from Vairo to Trisong Deutsen, to whom he taught the Five Early Translations of the Mind Class, *Ocean Expanse Instructions*, and other tantras and pith instructions that are taught secretly. The middle lineage concerns the teachings he gave to Master Yudra Nyingpo, who gave them to Master Nyag Jnana and Ma Rinchen Chok. The final lineage goes through Prince Yudra Nyingpo, Pam Sangye Gonpo, Gya Lodro Shonnu, and Bes Dorje Gyaltsen; they are the teachings that the master taught them when they went to see him at the Tungcham Chenpo Hermitage in Kham and meditated there.

Then Vairo went back to Samye and stayed on top of Hepo Mountain, where to his common disciples he taught the commentaries on the expedient meaning, some teachings on cause and effect, and the conclusion of various teachings he had not completed before; to his exceptional disciples he taught some special Ati instructions.

In the presence of the great lord, headed by Yudra and the king, seven of his disciples who attained rainbow body celebrated the profound feast offering in an elaborate way. With Yudra leading, the disciples prayed:

> Regent of the Buddha, your body unites all the
>   victorious ones;
> Your speech contains the ocean of scriptures and tantras;
> Your mind is the expanse of the tathagatas, the Great Space.

Precious great light illuminating the darkness,
Though you look after us Tibetans,
So that your future followers may obtain confidence,
How many siddhas will there appear who will practice
This profound vajra path, the master's oral transmission?

The master looked pleased and said:

Listen carefully, king, subjects, and disciples! My mind is like a cloudless sky, fulfilling all hopes and wishes. Listen to me! My old son Mipham Gonpo will benefit beings for five hundred years; then he will pass away into the dharmadhatu, without remainder of aggregates. Yudra Nyingpo, you who are so learned now, will benefit the human realm for 370 years; then you will join me in the pure lands. Zangmo Rinchen Ying will appear and live 270 years; then she will pass away into the dharmadhatu without remainder of aggregates. Khug Gyur Sangwachok will appear and live 190 years; then he will pass away without remainder of aggregates.

The lineage holder of the teachings of these vidyadharas is Ngenlam Changchub Gyaltsen; he will live 178 years and will pass away without remainder of aggregates. His son Zang Rinchen Kyi will live 144 years and pass away without remainder. Khug Gyur Salwachok will live 177 years and will pass away without remainder. Then Nyang Changchub Lek and two disciples will live a hundred years; later, they will pass away without a trace while attending a feast ceremony. Nyang Sherab Jungney will appear and live 103 years; he and his disciple will pass away without remainder at the Rock of Chimphu. Nyang Changchub Trakpa will appear; he will live 107 years and join the family of the sugatas. Bha Yeshe Changchub will appear; he will live ninety-eight years and will proceed into the sky as a white ball, without remains. Dampa Sata will appear and live 113 years; then his body will turn into five-colored light.

Concerning the lineage holders of my oral transmission, there will be many siddhas who will complete their life span. In China, Tibet, Tsawarong, and other places, I will have 170 sons holding the oral lineage who will attain rainbow body, such as Dharma Singha, Lakna Dorje, Jnana, and others. There will be countless indescribably great yogis, who will perfect their life span and attain realization.

When he had said that, he transformed into a blue sphere with a white syllable A in the center and disappeared. As all his disciples lamented and fervently prayed, his voice came from the sky:

> OM! This unchanging, spontaneously present dharmadhatu
>   pure land
> Is free of high and low, good and bad, or acceptance and
>   rejection:
> How great the dharmadhatu wisdom experience is!

As he said that, he manifested Vairochana's dharmadhatu pure land with the revered one himself as Buddha Vairochana, surrounded by an inconceivable retinue of sugatas of the five families. His gathering of heart-sons could miraculously fly in the sky like birds. Then, as they prayed one-pointedly, the body of the exalted one, upright and dazzling, swirling in rainbow light, appeared in front of the disciples. Led by the king, the subjects offered the master an array of countless divine and human precious gems and prayed:

> Vairochana, embodiment of all the buddhas,
> You appeared as Vairo himself for the sake of sentient
>   beings
> And dispelled the dense darkness with the holy Dharma.
> Though you have always been very kind to us,
> In the future, as we Tibetans are cowards,
> Please think of us with great compassion and bear with us!

At that time, seated on the throne, the master sometimes appeared in radiant light, sometimes as Buddha Vairochana, sometimes as Buddha Shakyamuni, sometimes as Ananda, sometimes as a text, a vajra, a bell, a gem, a lotus, and so forth, manifesting countless transformations of the five elements. Gyalmo Yudra and six other heart-sons requested the great lord, "Please tell us how many of the master's emanations will appear in Tibet to dispel the ignorance of beings of the dark age, and what their names will be!" The venerable one, endowed with wisdom eyes, said:

Listen, king, ministers, patrons, and friends!
My awareness-wisdom
Knows everything with vivid clarity, unrestricted.

In the Zahor region I shall emanate
As a bodhisattva called Atisha, refuge and protector
    of beings,
Who will elucidate the doctrine in Tibet.
As my speech emanation, he will hold the Tripitaka and the
    tantras.
Assigned as a great pandita, his knowledge and compassion
    will fully develop,
And he will be a doctrine-holder here in Tibet.

My local emanation, Trakpa Ngonshe, will hold the sciences
And attain mastery of the hidden treasures.
My emanation Dorje Lingpa, holder of Padma's doctrine,
Will uphold the teachings of the hidden treasures.
My emanation Rechung Dortrak
Will move from India to Tibet like the wind
And preside over dakini feast offerings in the celestial
    realms.

My emanation the omniscient Taranatha,
The most learned and accomplished here in Tibet,
Will sustain the life of the doctrine and be holder of the
    sutras and tantras.
My emanation the monk Yak, king of learned ones,
Will beautify Tibet with his knowledge and wisdom.
My emanation Zangkar Lotsawa
Will turn the Dharma wheel and serve the doctrine
    in Lhasa.

Through my prayers a great magnetizing being,
The siddha Kharnak, will appear and spread the instruction
    lineage.
Through Vairo's blessings, the heart-son of Orgyen called
    Kunkyong

Will preserve the doctrine of the hidden treasures.
My activity emanation Phagmo Drupa
Will be king of the Tibetans in U, Tsang, and Kham.

My emanation Myogom Repa will fulfill the benefit
    of beings
In the Tsawarong and Do Kham regions and will travel to
    the celestial realms.
Besides these, I will have countless indescribable in-
    carnations.
In the six realms of the Saha world,
There will be innumerable emanations of the learned
    Vairotsana,
Benefiting beings according to their needs.

Each of my hair pores will emanate ten million light rays,
And each light ray will send forth an emanation—
Panditas, translators, *arhats*,
Treasure revealers, siddhas, yogis, monks,
Kings, ministers, subjects, queens, women,
Food, drink, clothes, wealth—
In brief, benefiting sentient beings in accordance with
    their needs,
Fulfilling their wishes.

That is how it will be, Tibetan followers.
I shall not stay here much longer now.
As a flock of birds flies from a tree,
I won't stay for an instant; I'm going to the dharmadhatu!
Like the sun and moon setting in the expanse of the sky,
I won't stay for an instant; I'm going to care for the welfare
    of beings!

Thus speaking, he suddenly gazed into the sky. Then his disciples offered an immeasurable thanksgiving feast.

Meanwhile, the nun Litsa Tsultrim Dron from the Brown Willow
Grove in Khotan had heard that Master Vairo had gone to Samye, so she
went to meet and invite him to Khotan. When she met the master, she

checked her meditation with him. As their realization was identical, the master was extremely pleased. The nun Litsa Tsultrim Dron, who was endowed with the outer, inner, and secret qualities, had unfolded the unconditioned bliss of the enlightened mind and realized the essential meaning of the natural state.

Then, Master Vairo meditated for a while and decided to pass away. He gave his disciples a testament, and as he prepared his passing, Master Yudra Nyingpo, Pam Sangye Gonpo, Gya Lodro Shonnu, Bes Dorje Gyaltsen, King Saynaleg Jingyon's son, the king, and many ministers and disciples requested Master Vairo to tell them how he had gone to search for the essence of the doctrine, how the doctrine originated in Tibet, how the doctrine spread in India, how the master had found it and brought it to Tibet, what the master had taught in Samye, how he had spread the doctrine in the Tsawa country, and the master's history up to now.

They also requested him to relate again in the right order all the stories he had told them, as well as give them a list of all the books he owned, and the master related all this in full detail. Pam, Yudra, Nyag Jnana, and other disciples wrote down whatever Master Vairo said and summarized the previous contents. Master Vairo said:

> These stories are the mind essence of the victorious ones and the experiences of the gurus; revealing the view in actuality, they are a universal treasury of wisdom. Clearly showing the history of the Buddha's doctrine and how it was transmitted, it is a true skillful method to relate the historical background. Encountering these stories is the same as actually meeting the five buddha families, the vidyadharas of the oral transmission, and Master Vairo: That is why it is called the *Great Image*. It is the ultimate way to explain the history of the Buddha's doctrine, the index of the effortless doctrine.

Then they again prostrated to Vairo, placed their heads at his feet, and requested, "Please look upon us with kindness! How should we practice the instructions?"

Master Vairo said, "Just as the sky is inseparably united with the sun, moon, stars, and planets, for those of you who adore me, our minds are beyond meeting and parting within the dharmadhatu. Pray to me to look upon you with compassion so we may never be separate." Again he said, "Don't try to accomplish any worldly affairs. Through great compassion, do not let your disciples dissipate. With great devotion, do not separate from your guru even for an instant. By great discrimination, never regard yourself as better than anyone else."

The great master himself, accompanied by seven heart-sons headed by Yudra, the twenty-five disciples headed by the king, and the nun Litsa Tsultrim Dron, suddenly appeared on top of Hepori like a flash of lightning in the sky. At that time the revered one, gazing into space, performed countless dance movements with his arms and legs, while from the four infinite cardinal and intermediate directions of space the five family sugatas, dakas, dakinis, gurus, yidams, buddhas, and bodhisattvas gathered in the sky like rain clouds, and five-colored rainbow light surrounded the revered one and his seven disciples. At that time the king, subjects, and disciples prepared a grand and vast feast offering with boundless outer, inner, and secret offerings. Headed by the venerable Yudra, the disciples, king, and subjects, of one mind and voice, entreated the master:

> OM, Buddha Vairochana, dharmadhatu wisdom,
> Embodiment of the sugatas, single son of the victorious
>   ones,
> King of learned ones, Dharma Lord Vairo,
> Do not abandon us in this fearful abyss.
> Do not be like a leader of the blind refusing to guide a
>   group of blind men;
> Do not deprive us of your great compassion!
>
> In this gloomy land of Tibet, without refuge or protector,
> If your great compassion does not dispel the darkness,
> Who will eliminate the sufferings of hunger, thirst, and
>   heat?
> To whom will unprotected beings direct their hope?
> Do not leave your Tibetan followers behind on the plains!
> As the pure river of the four empowerments does not flow
> If the master decides to go to the celestial realms,
> In whom should we place our trust as an object of refuge?
>
> Who will dispel the obstacles to our Dharma practice?
> Whom will the faithful ones serve?
> Who will be the king's court priest?

Who will bestow the supreme maturing and liberating empowerments?
Who will remove obstacles and unfavorable circumstances?

Gurus, yidams, and protectors
Amidst the clouds and rainbow lights in the sky,
Do not invite our guru!
Precious omniscient one,
If you really must leave,
Do not abandon your heart-like disciples!

Thus, they cried out and wailed a lot and did countless prostrations
and circumambulations. The king and all the subjects then gathered in
front of the master, and the noble Master Vairo said:

Listen, Tibetan king, ministers, and followers,
I, Vairo, have something to tell you!
From the age of eight until thirteen,
I learned 360 different languages.
At the age of fourteen I went to India
And relied on twenty-five siddhas who attained rainbow
body,
Such as Prahe, Manjushri, Shri Singha, and so forth.

I studied with seventy-two accomplished scholars,
Enduring various hardships that brought me near death.
I translated all the Indian Dharma teachings into Tibetan,
And during the reign of the late Tibetan king,
I, Vairo, extensively worked for the benefit of beings.

Now I am nearly three hundred years old;
From here I will go to Brown Willow Grove in Khotan,
Where I will benefit beings for twenty years.
After that I will always remain happy in the dharmadhatu.

Now please don't despair.
Going or staying is the same to me, Vairo;
I was just a material guide.

Now that I am going, remain in good health, all of you!
With faith and respect, imagine that you're never apart
    from me!

Saying this, his right hand playing a teak *damaru*, he was instantly lifted up by the dakas and dakinis, and poised before them in the sky in the midst of rainbow light, he said to his Tibetan followers:

To be clever in words doesn't mean you are competent;
If you can integrate word and meaning, come up here!

Being attached to meditation is not *shamatha*;[18]
If you have realized your awareness, come up here!

Though you might experience objects and mind as one,
If your energy and mind have mingled, come up here!

Though there are many accomplished ones,
If you have attained a rainbow body, come up here!

My lineage is one of rainbow body vidyadharas;
Leaving a corpse behind won't do!

There are many lineage holders in Tibet now;
If they are real, they should act like this.
Come up here, you fortunate ones!

As he said this, his damaru sounded and his Dharma robe flapped in the wind. Seven of his disciples, headed by Yudra and Tsultrim Dron, flashing in the sky like lightning, disappeared into the sky. The king, ministers, and everyone else cried out and wailed, doing many prostrations, and prayed:

Now that the master is gone, Tibet has become a land of
    darkness!
As the only thing to do is practice the Dharma,
We promise to follow the master's example.
We will not interrupt any of the monthly offerings

And will remember the lord on the eighth day of the
    month.
Now that the sun of Tibet has set, we even lack the water
    of meditation!

Then the king and ministers went to the temple. Practicing the master's instructions, seven of his disciples, headed by Changchub Gyaltsen, attained rainbow body, and many of them became accomplished masters and scholars. On the special offering days the revered one, surrounded by an infinite retinue, would actually appear and give many indications. Vairotsana thus completed his actions to benefit beings in Tibet.

 *This completes the last chapter,
about his going to the pure land.*

Aspiration and Summary

WRITTEN BY DHARMA SENGE

The Conclusion of Extolling His Greatness, with the Seven-Branch Offering and the Aspiration Verse

As this reveals the mind essence of the buddhas and vidyadharas, it is called *Great Treasury of Realization, the Heart Essence*. As it represents the history of the doctrine, it is also called the *True Historic Exposition*. Since it is like actually meeting the victorious ones, the vidyadharas, and Vairo, it is also called the *Great Image*. As it shows in detail how the doctrine becomes widespread, it is also called *Index of the Doctrine*. The master himself along with seven of his heart-sons, including Yudra, arranged the table of contents and completed it.

> This detailed explanation of the great qualities of [Buddha] Vairochana,
> The emanated *lotsawa*, is like meeting Vairo in person.
> This *Great Image* of [Buddha] Vairochana is like an adornment of the fortunate ones:
> May those who wear this ornament attain the level of omniscience.
>
> Vairochana, your youthful vase body, endowed with all supreme aspects, which pacifies mental constructs from the beginning,

Possesses the six special qualities of supreme immutable
    great bliss,
Glowing with love for all living beings;
Lord of the dharmadhatu wisdom, the animate and
    inanimate in Akanishta,
You are endowed with the five spontaneously present
    certainties.

That great Vairochana, most supreme among all families,
Primordially fulfilling the sixteen aspects of perfect
    abandonment and realization,
With loving kindness to living creatures, like the full moon
    always shining on beings,
For the sake of those to be tamed in the snowy land, this
    wondrous necklace of beneficial and comforting light,
Amongst auspicious signs took birth in the form of a
    beautiful deer, friend of noble beings.

When King Trisong, controlling religion and politics like
    the sun and moon,
Craved the taste of nectar of the two truths,
The Immortal Lord proclaimed the thunder of the
    scriptures.
Respecting the Dharma king, who had realized truth,
At the age of sixteen he left for the noble land,
Miraculously drifting through sixteen trials.

With the Buddha's Three Pitakas, the four tantra
    classes,
The *Sutra of Unraveling the Intent*, and the instructions
    explained in the tantras,
He charioteered this country—how marvelous!
Miraculously dominating the Buddha's realm of the three
    kayas, Oddiyana, and the abodes of the gods, nagas,
    and yakshas,
From there he brought the true secret tantras, like a
    treasure from the ocean, which is not the story of other
    leaders.

Incomparable guide, skilled in leading beings through
    the ocean of existence,
Which is stirred by the wind of the five poisons and the
    turbulent waves of overwhelming misery,
From the never-ending dreadful city of samsara to the
    treasure island of the three kayas,
You ferry the different beings to be tamed in the
    compassionate boat of the nine gradual vehicles.

As your secret qualities of body, speech and mind are
    inconceivable,
To expand upon them with words and syllables would
    cause nothing but fatigue.
Pursuing the example of the infinite sky doesn't approach
    even a fraction of them,
So how could our naive minds evaluate them even
    approximately?

I prostrate in the expanse free of elaborations, inner
    luminosity,
Which is the primordially pure face of the youthful vase
    body.
Please accept the offerings of whatever appears
Through the spontaneously present eight gates,
Outward clarity from basic space, samsara and nirvana
    without duality.
In the absolute expanse, I confess the stains of conceptual
    imputations
Formed in the originally pure sky by external influence.
I rejoice in the garland of water bubbles of compassion,
The cloud of loving kindness of the sugatas, free of grudge.
By turning the wheel of the true meaning, please transform
    into summer
The golden earth of the absolute truth, covered with the
    frost of the dark age.
May the vajra body, indestructible by birth, old age,
    sickness, and death,
Dwell within the supreme unchanging rainbow body.

I dedicate the flow of the two accumulations, conditioned
and unconditioned,
To attain the state of great bliss where samsara and nirvana
are equal.

By the power and blessing of this dedication,
May I and all beings, equal to space,
From now until enlightenment,
In the care of Buddha Vairochana,
Swiftly attain unsurpassed enlightenment!

Summary of the Biography

It is said that the life story of the great Master Vairotsana was hidden as
a treasure by Shang Nas Sarba and rediscovered by Jo-Men.[1] Another
version came to Drom Ben Tashi Jungney, who revised it at Sertreng
Monastery, merging the profound and correct points into one. In fact, it
was supplemented with passages from the *Crystal Cave Chronicles*.[2] The
revision caused disorder in the sequence of the story, such as repeating
verses of the Kahma and Terma versions, and many other flaws. The Terma
version itself is genuine, but even though it contains many profound instructions especially for Tibetans, it is a version that the common reader
would find difficult to believe. The Kahma version was therefore chosen
to be engraved. This version existed in three separate sections with titles,
such as the *Image from India*, up to and including the Tibetan history; the
Image from Tibet; and the *Image from Tsawarong*. These three have been
combined into one biography, and nothing was left out. When this was
compared with six other manuscript copies of the *Great Image*, they all
seemed more or less similar.

The present edition was based on an earlier xylographic edition, but
this old edition was not only written in bad script and lacking one or two
pages, it was also full of misspellings. Looking at many different editions,
I used the most authentic one. There are still some minor doubtful points,
like whether Yudra was a beggar girl who obtained the male sex, a prince,
or a beggar's son; whether later as a beggar girl he was made king; and various other points, which should be determined by those endowed with
eyes of wisdom. Also, in both this text and the *Chronicles of Padma*, it is

said that the king died three months after Vairo left for Tsawarong. It is also said that when Vimalamitra came, the king was still alive; so there are various versions of the history. According to most biographies, there is no need to check whether the beginning, middle, and end coincide; an instant can be an eon, and an eon can be an instant. Enlightened activity is not categorically fixed. As the glorious lord, Arya Nagarjuna said, "The qualities of the omniscient ones can only be known by the omniscient ones. The vast weight of the earth can only be known by itself."

For the sake of remembering the kindness of the great translators and scholars of the past, with deliberate unshakable faith the very ignorant Dharma Senge,[3] of inferior intellect, published this as an inexhaustible Dharma gift. The woodblocks were sponsored by the former Lhalung treasurer, Kyabdal, and in the dragon year Chagpa Ratna offered a roll of good quality silk; Dolma Tsering, a wise lady from Lhasa, offered four Chinese silver coins, as well as a new black-striped robe; and Nying Nying, who used to offer butter lamps in Samye, offered a maroon hat made out of good felt cloth. By the power of this, may all sentient beings as vast as space quickly attain the unsurpassed state of the great Vairochana.

 The vagabond Dharma Senge composed the conclusion of extolling the greatness, as well as the summary of the biography with the seven-branch offering and the aspiration verse. May it be virtuous!

APPENDIX
*The Nine Vehicles**

Hinayana
The Hinayana path is based on renunciation motivated by the individual's wish to be free of suffering. When considered as an independent system, it is known as the "Lesser Vehicle"; when viewed as a part of the integrated path of the three vehicles, it is regarded as the "Fundamental Vehicle."

SHRAVAKAS
A *shravaka* (Tib. *nyan thos*; literally, "listener") is someone who fears the sufferings of samsara. Concerned with his own liberation, he listens to the teachings of the Buddha, realizes the suffering inherent in all conditioned phenomena, and meditates on the Four Noble Truths—suffering, its cause (the obscuring emotions), its extinction, and the path to attain this extinction.

View: A shravaka understands that there is no truly existent "self" inherent in an individual but maintains that phenomena are composed of indivisible particles and moments of consciousness, which are held to be truly existent. Such views define the Vaibhashika school.

Meditation: On the basis of flawless ethical behavior and self-discipline, the practitioner listens to the teachings, ponders their meaning, and assimilates this meaning through meditation. Applying antidotes, such as

*Based on Matthieu Ricard's explanation of the Nine Vehicles in *The Life of Shabkar*.

considering the unpleasant aspects of objects of desire, a shravaka conquers the conflicting emotions and attains inner calm. By cultivating insight, the practitioner comes to understand that an individual possesses no truly existent, independent "self."

Conduct: A shravaka practices twelve ascetic virtues and acts chiefly to achieve personal liberation.

Fruit: Beginning with the stage of "stream-enterer" and continuing with the stages of "once-returner" (one who will be reborn only one more time) and "non-returner" (one who will no longer be reborn in samsara), a shravaka attains nirvana and eventually becomes an *arhat*, "one who has destroyed his adversary," which are the obscuring emotions.

PRATYEKABUDDHAS

A *pratyekabuddha* (Tib. *rang sangs rgyas*, "one who becomes awakened alone") can attain the level of an arhat without relying upon a teacher in this lifetime (although he has met teachers in former lifetimes). Without recourse to an uncreated god, a pratyekabuddha believes that all phenomena come into existence through the combination of causes and conditions. Becoming acquainted with the fact of death, the pratekyabuddha grows weary of samsara and, pondering the causes of suffering and death, investigates the twelve links of dependent origination to find that the misery of samsara originates from ignorance.

View: Pratyekabuddhas realize that individuals and indivisible particles of matter are devoid of true existence, yet they still believe that moments of consciousness constitute real entities. Thus, they fully realize the selflessness of the individual but have a limited understanding of the selflessness of phenomena. This view characterizes the Sautrantika school.

Meditation: Pratyekabuddhas contemplate the twelve interdependent links. For example, upon seeing bones in a cemetery, one reflects upon death and finds out that it follows old age, which itself is the outcome of birth. Birth is the result of the drive toward existence, which arises from grasping, which is the result of craving, which arises from feeling, which arises from contact, which arises from the six senses, which arise from name and form, which arise from consciousness, which arises from karmic dispositions, which arise from ignorance. Following the chain from ignorance to death, the pratyekabuddha understands that ignorance, the clinging to phenomena as real, is the source of all suffering.

Action: Practicing for their own limited deliverance, pratyekabuddhas do not teach others verbally but inspire faith through their behavior as well as by displaying miracles, such as flying through the sky and transforming the upper half of their body into fire and the lower half into water, etc.

Fruit: Like shravakas, a pratyekabuddha's primary concern is his own welfare, and so he cannot attain complete buddhahood, but only the liberation of an arhat.

Mahayana

The Mahayana surpasses the Hinayana in several important aspects. A Mahayana practitioner is motivated by the altruistic intention to liberate others from suffering and help them attain buddhahood.

BODHISATTVAS

A bodhisattva recognizes the lack of true existence both of the individual and of all phenomena. Vowing to attain enlightenment for the sake of others, bodhisattvas develop limitless compassion for all suffering beings; in addition, their compassion is united with wisdom, the perfect realization of emptiness.

Having recognized the empty nature of phenomena, bodhisattvas regard everything as being like a dream or an illusion. However, their understanding of absolute truth does not lead them to ignore relative truth: with loving kindness and compassion, they act in perfect accord with the karmic law of cause and effect and work tirelessly to benefit beings. Realizing the ultimate nature, which is free from clinging and from all limiting conditions, a bodhisattva rests in the great evenness, the nondual absolute truth.

View: The Mahayana view involves a correct understanding of the lack of reality of both the individual and all phenomena. Various levels of understanding this view and of defining both absolute and relative truth are found in the Mahayana schools of Chittamatra and Madhyamaka.

The Chittamatrin philosophy states that all phenomena are the products of mind and are, therefore, unreal but postulates that in terms of absolute truth, self-cognizant nondual awareness truly exists.

The Madhyamaka has two main schools, the Svatantrika and the Prasangika. The Svatantrika school considers that in terms of absolute truth, phenomena have no true existence whatsoever; but in terms of relative truth, phenomena appear through the combination of causes and conditions, perform their function, and have a verifiable conventional existence. The Prasangika school asserts that from both an absolute and a relative point of view, phenomena are totally devoid of true existence and cannot be characterized by any concept such as "existent," "nonexistent," "both existent and nonexistent," or "neither existent nor nonexistent." According to Prasangika philosophy, absolute truth is the nondual pristine wisdom of the buddhas, free from conceptual elaboration.

Meditation: On the four "paths of learning" one practices the thirty-seven branches of enlightenment. Having recognized that the potential for achieving buddhahood, the *tathagatagarbha*, is present within oneself, one aspires to reach enlightenment. Through inner calm meditation (*shamatha*) one pacifies all clinging to outer perceptions, and develops a serene samadhi. Through insight meditation (*vipashyana*) one ascertains that all outer phenomena are unreal, like illusions, and that all inner fixations and dualistic notions of subject-object are empty. According to the Madhyamaka, not taking things as real while resting in the evenness of the absolute nature, one unites inner calm meditation and insight meditation.

Action: Between meditation sessions, considering others to be dearer than oneself, one acts for their benefit by practicing the six *paramitas* of generosity, morality, patience, effort, concentration, and wisdom. By becoming permeated with wisdom, the paramitas are transformed from ordinary virtues into transcendent activities.

Fruit: Eventually, having attained the path of "beyond training" and the eleventh *bhumi*, a bodhisattva becomes a fully enlightened buddha. Having fulfilled their own aspirations by realizing the *dharmakaya* for the sake of others, bodhisattvas manifest the *rupakaya* and perform compassionate activity for sentient beings until the end of samsara.

Vajrayana

The Vajrayana path is based on pure perception; the practitioner is motivated by the aspiration to swiftly free both self and others from delusion by employing skillful means. The Mahayana asserts that buddha-nature is present in every sentient being as a seed or potentiality. The Vajrayana considers this nature to be fully present as wisdom, or pristine awareness, the undeluded aspect and fundamental nature of the mind. Therefore, while the former vehicles are known as "Causal Vehicles," the Vajrayana is known as the "Resultant Vehicle." As it is said, "In the Causal Vehicles one recognizes the nature of mind as the cause of buddhahood; in the Resultant Vehicle one regards the nature of mind as buddhahood itself." Since the "result" of the path, buddhahood, is primordially present, one only needs to actualize it or divest it of its veils. The Vajrayana is also said to be unobscured, to provide many skillful means, and to be without difficulty and is intended for beings with the highest faculties.

The various levels of the Madhyamaka philosophy consider relative truth as false, impure, and rejectable, or as simply nonexistent. The Vajrayana, on the other hand, is able to make use of relative truth as a path by seeing phenomena as the unlimited display of primordial purity. The six classes of Vajrayana tantras teach this in an increasingly direct and profound way.

The gateway to the Vajrayana is empowerment. Through this ritual one is empowered to practice the Vajrayana teachings and thus to achieve ordinary and supreme spiritual attainments. The tantras and their related vehicles are categorized into three outer and three inner tantras.

THE THREE OUTER TANTRAS
Kriya Tantra
In Kriya Tantra, the tantra of activity, although one has gained some understanding of absolute truth, in relative truth one still seeks accomplishment as something to be gained from outside. Kriya Tantra emphasizes ritual cleanliness: cleanliness of the mandala and the sacred substances, and physical cleanliness of the practitioner who practices ablutions, changes clothes three times a day, and eats the three white and three sweet foods.

View: The view is based on the two truths. Absolute truth is the wisdom of mind's ultimate nature, which is pure, luminous, and empty. It is free of the four limiting concepts of existence, nonexistence, appearance, and emptiness. Relative truth is seen as perfect, since phenomena are perceived as constituting the mandala of enlightened deities.

Meditation: The deity who is the object of one's meditation is considered as a lord whom the practitioner supplicates in order to be granted accomplishment just as a servant would supplicate their master. Contemplating absolute truth without any specific object of focus is also practiced.

Action: One's conduct is focused on cleanliness, concentration, fasting, and mantra recitation.

Fruit: Realization of the three *kaya*s and five wisdoms of perfect buddhahood is attained in seven human lifetimes.

Upa Tantra

Upa Tantra, or "practice tantra," is also known as Ubhaya Tantra, "dual tantra," because it combines the view of the following vehicle, Yoga Tantra, with the conduct of Kriya Tantra. The empowerment is that of the five buddha families. Realization can be gained in five lifetimes.

View: The view is the same as that of Yoga Tantra.

Conduct: The conduct is the same as that of Kriya Tantra.

Yoga Tantra

Yoga Tantra, or "tantra of union with the nature," emphasizes inner practice more than outer conduct. The empowerment adds the blessing of the vajra master to the empowerment of Upa Tantra.

View: In absolute truth one realizes the nonconceptual ultimate nature and its expression, cognizance. As a result of this realization, within the "perfect" relative truth, phenomena appear as the "mandala of adamantine space," the *vajradhatu* mandala.

Meditation: In formal meditation one visualizes oneself as a deity; then one visualizes a similar wisdom deity from a buddha-field who comes to rest in the sky before the practitioner. The relationship between the deity and the practitioner is that of equals or friends. In objectless meditation, the practitioner merges the perception of phenomena with the absolute nature beyond characteristics and rests in evenness. Thus, phenomena are seen as the play of wisdom manifesting as deities.

Action: One still strives toward accomplishment and attempts to achieve the "good" and eschew the "bad." Deity yoga is stressed, and one strives to benefit others.

Fruit: Realization is attained in three lifetimes.

THE THREE INNER TANTRAS

The inner tantras are Maha Yoga, Anu Yoga, and Ati Yoga. The view of these tantras is to see all phenomena as primordially perfect and thus to realize the "great purity" and "great evenness." Deities are visualized in union, symbolizing the indivisibility of emptiness and compassion, or wisdom and means. The wisdom nature of the deity is considered to be inseparable from one's own nature. Action transcends accepting and rejecting. The fruit is buddhahood in one lifetime. Anu Yoga is like the path; it allows one to realize that phenomena are the nondual manifestation of space and primordial wisdom. Ati Yoga is like the fruit and allows one to realize the natural presence of primordial wisdom, beyond beginning and ending.

Maha Yoga

Maha Yoga is like the ground, or basis. All phenomena are recognized as the magical display of mind-as-such, the union of emptiness and appearances. It is called the "great yoga" because it brings realization of nonduality. Its gateway consists of four main empowerments: vase, secret, wisdom, and symbolic (or word) empowerment. These purify the defilements of the body, speech, and mind as well as their subtle obscurations and enable one to realize the four kayas.

View: Awareness, free from all conceptual limitations, is considered as absolute truth and as inherently endowed with all enlightened qualities. All phenomena—the outer universe, the various psychophysical elements of the body, as well as thoughts—arise as a mandala that stands for relative truth. The two truths, emptiness and phenomena, are inseparable, like gold and its color.

Meditation: Maha Yoga emphasizes the development stage, which focuses on the process of visualization. One sees oneself as a deity, which is the manifestation of one's own wisdom nature. The outer world is seen as a buddha-field and the beings within it as male and female deities. These methods help one to recognize the primordial, unchanging purity of phenomena, which is the true condition of things. One also practices the completion stage related to the channels (*nadi*), energy (*prana*), and essence (*bindu*). Formless meditation consists of merging one's mind with the profound, absolute nature.

Action: In the path of action, through the confidence born from skillful means such as devotion and pure perception, without rejection or attachment, one uses samsaric experiences as catalysts to foster one's practice.

Fruit: Realization is attained within this lifetime or in the ensuing *bardo* (the transitional state between death and rebirth).

Anu Yoga

Anu Yoga emphasizes the practice of the completion stage as well as perceiving the mandala as contained within one's own vajra body. Having realized the nonduality of the expanse of emptiness and pristine wisdom, through "union" and "liberation," one attains accomplishment. Anu Yoga is called the "ensuing yoga" because it focuses on the path of wisdom-desire that follows the experience of bliss. Its gateway, the empowerment, comprises thirty-six sections.

View: All phenomena are seen as the play of one's own mind. The uncreated aspect of mind, transcending all conditions, is called the "immaculate expanse of the mother Samantabhadri." Its all-pervading and unobstructed manifestation, which is mind's self-display, is the "wisdom father Samantabhadra." These two aspects have the same nature, called the "child of great bliss," in which the absolute expanse and pristine wisdom are united.

Meditation: One practices the path of skillful means, which focuses on the channels, energies, and vital essences of one's vajra body. Practicing the yogas of the "upper door" and the "lower door," one swiftly realizes one's inherent wisdom. One also practices the path of liberation without elaboration. Having merged with the depth of nonconceptual simplicity, without intentional meditation, one lets everything remain in the absolute nature, just as it is. In formal, elaborate practice, by uttering a mantra once, the mandala with its deities arises with perfect clarity, instantly, like a fish leaping out of water.

Action: This primarily involves resting in evenness. One also speaks of three actions: the "skylike conduct," which is a result of realizing the nonduality of the absolute expanse of emptiness and pristine wisdom; the "kinglike action," also called the "action resembling wood burning in a bonfire," which is a result of mastering the five poisons as five wisdoms; and the "uninterrupted riverlike action," which is due to realizing the sameness of samsara and nirvana.

Fruit: Within one lifetime, one actualizes the body of great bliss, which embodies the four kayas.

Ati Yoga

The extraordinary feature of Ati Yoga is that one continuously maintains lucid recognition of the ultimate nature of mind: pure, vividly clear, perfect in itself. It is cognizance that is naturally present, self-existing primordial wisdom, without any alteration or fabrication, beyond taking or rejecting, hope and fear. This is the "ultimate yoga," far surpassing all the lower vehicles (all of which entail striving, fabrication, and effort). Ati Yoga is also known as Dzogchen, the Great Perfection, meaning that all phenomena are naturally perfect in their primordial purity.

The gateway to Ati Yoga is the empowerment of the "efflorescence of awareness." According to the *Secret Heart Essence,* one receives four empowerments: elaborate, unelaborated, very unelaborated, and utterly unelaborated.

View: All phenomena within both samsara and nirvana are perfect in primordial buddhahood, the great sphere of dharmakaya, the self-existing pristine wisdom beyond search and effort.

Ati Yoga has three classes:

According to the Mind Class, all perceived phenomena are merely the play of mind-as-such.

According to the Space Class, self-existing wisdom and all the phenomena that spring from its continuum never stray from the expanse of Samantabhadri: they have always been pure and liberated.

According to the most extraordinary of the three, the class of pith instructions or Instruction Class, in the true nature of samsara and nirvana there are no obscurations to be rid of and no enlightenment to be acquired. To realize this allows the self-existing wisdom beyond intellect to arise instantaneously.

The first class is meant for individuals who are concerned with the workings of mind, the second for individuals whose minds are like the sky, and the third for individuals who transcend all effort.

Meditation: In the Mind Class, having recognized that all phenomena are the indescribable dharmakaya, the self-existing wisdom, one rests in the continuum of the awareness-emptiness. The enlightened mind is like infinite space, its potential for manifestation is like a mirror, and the limitless illusory phenomena are like the countless reflections in the mirror. Since everything arises as the play of the enlightened mind, one does not need to obstruct the arising of thoughts; one simply remains in the natural condition of mind-as-such.

In the Space Class, having recognized that all phenomena never leave the expanse of Samantabhadri and are primordially pure and free, one abides in the continuum of the ultimate nature without targets, effort, or seeking. There is no need to use antidotes: being empty, thoughts and perceptions vanish by themselves. Phenomena are like stars naturally arrayed as ornaments in the firmament of the absolute nature. One does not need to consider, as one does in the Mind Class, that they arise as the play of awareness. Everything is the infinite expanse of primordial liberation.

In the Instruction Class, having recognized that mind-as-such is primordially pure emptiness, one practices *trekcho*, leaving mind and all phenomena in their natural state of pristine liberation. Then, having discovered the naturally present mandala of one's body, one practices *thogal* and sees the very face of the naturally present luminosity, the pristine wisdom that dwells within oneself. Without leaning either toward the "clarity" aspect of the Mind Class nor toward the "empty" aspect of the Space Class, without considering either the self-liberation of thoughts or the way of letting them be in emptiness, one simply rests in the confident realization of primordial purity, which is inexpressible, beyond intellect, and of which phenomena are the natural radiance.

Trekcho, "cutting through," refers to breaking through the solidity of mental clinging; thogal, "direct leap," refers to going directly to the highest point of realization. These two are related to primordial purity and spontaneous presence, respectively. These extraordinary practices are found only in the teachings of the Great Perfection. It is said that the first eight vehicles use mind as the path and that only Ati Yoga uses awareness as the path.

Action: Since everything that arises is the play of the absolute nature, one acts within the continuum of nondual evenness, without accepting or rejecting, free from clinging and fixation.

Fruit: One presently dwells on the level of Samantabhadra. Outer phenomena are realized to be infinite buddha-fields. Having mastered the inner aggregates of one's illusory body, this body can turn into radiant light. Having mastered the innermost expanse of awareness, one puts an end to delusion. One has neither hope of attaining buddhahood nor fear of falling into samsara.

NOTES

The Homage

1. *Kun tu bzang po*, the "Ever Perfect" primordial buddha. In the primordial universal ground, there are neither sentient beings nor buddhas; neither ignorance nor enlightenment. It is a state of natural unchanging perfection beyond conditions and concepts. When the first manifestation of phenomena arises from the primordial ground, recognizing that this arising is the display of one's own awareness leads instantaneously to the primordial buddhahood of Samantabhadra. Not recognizing this to be the case and taking phenomena and beings to be concrete entities distinct from oneself leads instantaneously to the ignorance of sentient beings.

Preface

1. *mkhyen pa gsum*. These three are basic knowledge, knowledge of the path, and omniscience.
2. *rgyu 'bras kyi theg pa brgyad*. Of the nine vehicles, these are the first eight, which depend on cause and effect. The nine vehicles comprise the three vehicles of the sutras—those of the shravakas, pratyekabuddhas, and bodhisattvas—and the six vehicles of the tantras of Kriya, Upa, Yoga, Maha Yoga, Anu Yoga, and Ati Yoga. They can also be grouped into three vehicles: the Hinayana, which includes the first two, the Mahayana, the third, and the Vajrayana, the last six. For a detailed explanation, see the appendix.
3. Ati Yoga (Skt. *mahasandhi*). Also known as Great Perfection or Dzogchen. Ati Yoga is the third of the three inner tantras and is the summit of the nine vehicles, the highest teaching of the Nyingma, or Early Translation, school. In this world Vajrasattva revealed the Ati Yoga teachings to Prahevajra (Garab Dorje). From Garab it was transmitted to Manjushrimitra, Shri Singha, Jnanasutra, Vimalamitra, Padmasambhava, and Vairotsana, who are the most well-known human lineage masters. Many Dzogchen termas were concealed by these masters and revealed throughout the following centuries. The Ati Yoga scriptures are contained in three classes of Dzogchen tantras: the Mind Class, the Space Class, and the Instruction Class, of which Vairotsana brought the first two to Tibet. Vimalamitra and Padmasambhava mainly transmitted the

Instruction Class. The lineage of teachings is embodied in the oral instructions that are personally received from a qualified Dzogchen master. Liberation through Ati Yoga is attained by becoming familiar with insight into the nature of primordial enlightenment, which is free from accepting and rejecting. For a detailed explanation, see the appendix.

4. *'og min.* Literally, "that which is not below"; the Unexcelled Buddha-field. In general, this is the highest of all buddha-fields, the place where, according to Vajrayana, bodhisattvas attain final buddhahood. There are, in fact, six levels of Akanishta, ranging from the highest heaven of the form realm up to the ultimate pure land of the dharmakaya.

Chapter 1

1. *chos kyi dbyings.* The absolute expanse; emptiness pervaded with awareness.
2. *de bzhin gshegs pa.* Literally, "one who has gone thus to nirvana"; a buddha.
3. *kun tu bzang mo.* The consort of the primordial buddha Samantabhadra, the Ever-Perfect (see note 1 for the Homage). Their union symbolizes the inseparability of the phenomenal world and emptiness.
4. *ngo bo nyid kyi sku.* Essence body, sometimes counted as the fourth kaya and constituting the unity of the three kayas. Jamgon Kongtrul defines it as the aspect of dharmakaya that is "the nature of all phenomena, emptiness devoid of all constructs and endowed with the characteristic of natural purity."
5. *chos kyi sku.* The three kayas (*sku gsum*) are the dharmakaya (*chos kyi sku*), or absolute body; the sambhogakaya (*longs spyod kyi sku*), or body of enjoyment; and the nirmanakaya (*sprul sku*), or manifested body. Respectively, they correspond to the empty, cognizant, and compassionate aspects of a buddha.
6. *gsang sngags.* The path of the Secret Mantra is based on pure perception and is motivated by the aspiration to swiftly free oneself and others from delusion through skillful means (see appendix). The gateway to the Secret Mantra is the empowerment, or *abhisheka*, which is given by the spiritual master. It empowers one to practice the Secret Mantra teachings and thus to achieve ordinary and supreme spiritual attainments, or *siddhis*. The tantras and their related vehicles are categorized into three outer and three inner tantras, according to the level of their view, meditation, action, and fruit.
7. Ati. See note 3 of the Preface; also, see the appendix.
8. *longs spyod rdzogs sku.* Body of enjoyment. See note 5 of chapter 1.
9. *gsangs ba'i sku.* Esoteric form.
10. *rig 'dzin.* Awareness-holder; "one who, through profound means, holds the deities, mantras, and the wisdom of great bliss." In the Nyingma tradition there are four levels of vidyadhara: (1) totally matured (*rnam smin*), (2) mastering the duration of life (*tshe dbang*), (3) mahamudra (*phyag chen*), and (4) spontaneously accomplished (*lhun grub*).
11. *'khor ba.* The three worlds of existence: the world of desire, the world of form, and the formless world.
12. *'das.* Passed beyond the three worlds of existence.
13. *rdo rje sems dpa'.* The buddha who embodies the hundred families. The prac-

tice of Vajrasattva and recitation of his hundred-syllable mantra are the most effective for purifying negative actions. In the Ati Yoga lineage he is the sambhogakaya buddha.

14. *bkyed rdzogs gsum.* The main Secret Mantra practice goes through the two stages of development (*bskyed rim*) and completion (*rdzogs rim*) to culminate in the Great Perfection (*rdzogs chen*). Development stage practice is meditation through which one purifies oneself of the habitual clinging to the four kinds of birth (womb, egg, moisture, and miraculous). One meditates on forms, sounds, and thoughts as having the nature of deities, mantras, and wisdom. Completion stage practice with characteristics (*mtshan bcas*) is meditation on the channels and energies of the body visualized as a vajra body. Completion stage practice without characteristics (*mtshan med*) is meditation during which the forms visualized in the development stage are dissolved and one remains in the state of emptiness. For Great Perfection, see note 2 of the Preface; also, see the appendix.

15. *bde ba chen.* Blissful realm, the pure land of the Buddha Amitabha.

16. *mtshan dang dpe byad.* The thirty-two major and eighty minor marks of the buddhas. The thirty-two major marks are: palms and soles marked with doctrinal wheels; feet firm like those of a tortoise; webbed fingers and toes; soft and supple hands and feet; a body with seven well-proportioned parts; long toes and fingers; broad arches; a tall and straight body; inconspicuous ankles; body hairs that curl upward; antelopelike calves; long and beautiful arms; a supremely contracted sexual organ; a golden complexion and delicate skin; well-grown body hairs distinctly growing to the right; a hair-ringlet between the eyebrows; a lionlike chest; well-rounded shoulders; a broad back; a supreme sense of taste; a symmetrical body like a banyan tree; a protuberance on the head; a long and beautiful tongue; a Brahma-like voice; lionlike jaws; pure white teeth equal in size, close-fitting, and forty in number; sapphire blue eyes; and bovine eyelashes.

17. *gsang ba'i bdag po.* A synonym for Vajrapani, the compiler of the tantric teachings.

18. *sngags phyi pa gsum.* Kriya, Upa, and Yoga. See note 2 of the Preface; also, see the appendix.

19. *gsang ba'i dbang.* The second empowerment, which purifies the defilements of speech, enables one to meditate on the channels and energies and to recite mantras, and plants the seed for achieving vajra speech and the sambhogakaya.

Chapter 2

1. *thub pa drug.* In each of the six realms of beings an emanation of the tathagatas acts on behalf of the beings of that realm. As it says in the *Superior Magical Net*:

In the realms of the gods he is Lord Shakra,
Among the asuras he is Vemachitra,

Among men he is the lord of the Shakyas who subdues Mara,
In the domain of the hungry ghosts he is Jvalamukha,
To animals he is Simha,
And in the hells he is Yama, lord of deeds.

2. *sde snod gsum.* Three baskets, so-called because the palm-leaf folios on which the scriptures were originally written were collected and stored in baskets. It is the collection of Buddha Shakyamuni's teachings on Vinaya, Sutra, and Abhidharma.

3. *mi mjed 'jig rten.* Sahalokadhatu, the World of Endurance, our known world system. It is called the "world of endurance" because the beings endure unbearable suffering in it. *Saha* can also mean "undivided" because the karmas and disturbing emotions, cause and effect, are not separately divided or differentiated. The World of Endurance is the thirteenth among twenty-five world systems said to be resting one above the other on the palms of Buddha Vairochana.

4. *ston pa shakya thub pa.* The sage of the Shakyas. The Buddha of our time who lived around the fifth century B.C.

5. *rgyu mtshan nyid kyi bstan pa.* The teachings of Hinayana and Mahayana that regard the practices of the path as the causes for attaining the fruition of liberation and enlightenment.

6. *'bras bu gsang sngags kyi bstan pa.* The Secret Mantra Vajrayana system of taking the fruition as the path by regarding buddhahood as inherently present and the path as the act of uncovering one's basic state. This is different from the causal philosophical vehicles of Mahayana and Hinayana (see previous note). Ultimately, however, these two approaches are not in conflict.

7. Benares, India. At nearby Sarnath Buddha Shakyamuni turned the first wheel of the Dharma with his teachings on the Four Noble Truths.

8. Vajra seat. Located in Bihar, India. This is where the Buddha attained enlightenment.

9. A place near Rajgir, Bihar, where the Buddha taught.

10. *'dzam bu gling.* Our known world; the southern of four continents. It is called "Jambu" because it is adorned with the Jambubriksha (rose apple) tree, which is unique to this continent according to all major Indian religious traditions.

11. *dga' ldan.* "The Joyous"; the pure land of the thousand buddhas of this eon, which is inhabited only by bodhisattvas and buddhas. Also, the heavenly realm in which Lord Maitreya resides awaiting his appearance in this world as the next Buddha.

12. *thugs rje chen po, 'jam pal, phyag na rdo rje.* The lords of the three families.

13. *bden pa bzhi.* The truths of suffering, of the origin of suffering, of the cessation of suffering, and of the path. Buddha Shakyamuni taught these in Sarnath during the first turning of the Dharma wheel.

14. *nyan thos.* Literally, "listener"; someone who fears the sufferings of samsara. Concerned with his own liberation, he listens to the teachings of the Bud-

dha, realizes the suffering inherent in all conditioned phenomena, and meditates upon the Four Noble Truths. For a detailed explanation, see the appendix.

15. *'dul ba.* One of the three parts of the Tripitaka, these are the Buddha's teachings showing ethics, the discipline and moral conduct that is the foundation for all Dharma practice, for both lay and ordained people.

16. *pha rol tu phyin pa.* Literally, "reaching the other shore." The six paramitas, or perfections, are generosity, discipline, patience, ethics, concentration, and wisdom. Specifically, *paramita* means transcending concepts of subject, object, and action.

17. *mngon pa.* Metaphysics, which were taught by the Buddha during the second turning of the Dharma wheel.

18. *kun dga' bo.* The son of Buddha Shakyamuni's uncle, who became the Buddha's personal attendant. He could remember every word the Buddha spoke and compiled the Dharma teachings.

19. *bya rgyud.* The first outer tantra, the tantra of activity, which emphasizes ritual cleanliness: cleanliness of the mandala and sacred substances, as well as the physical cleanliness of the practitioner. See the appendix.

20. *spyod rgyud.* The second of the three outer tantras. It is called Upa Tantra, "practice tantra," or Ubhaya Tantra (*gnyis ka'i rgyud*), "dual tantra," because it practices the view of the subsequent vehicle, Yoga Tantra, along with the action, or conduct, of the former vehicle, Kriya Tantra. See the appendix.

21. *rnal 'byor rgyud.* The third of the three outer tantras. It is called "the tantra of union with the nature" because it emphasizes inner practice more than outer conduct. See the appendix.

22. *bsil ba'i tshal.* Cool Grove, a sacred charnel ground to the northeast of Bodhgaya, which is inhabited by many dakinis and savage beings. It has a great stupa, which contains many special tantras in caskets that were hidden by the dakinis. Padmasambhava did ascetic practices there for many years. Garab Dorje also spent many years there teaching the dakinis.

23. *lcang lo can.* The pure land of the Lord of Secrets, Vajrapani. Also, a place in ancient India.

24. *rgya byin.* The chief god in the realm of desire. He resides on the summit of Mount Sumeru in the Palace of Complete Victory and is also known as Shakra, the ruler of the devas.

25. *ri rab.* This is the mythological mountain at the center of our world system; it is surrounded by the four continents and is where the two lowest classes of gods of the desire realm live. Encircled by chains of lesser mountains, lakes, continents, and oceans, it is said to rise to a height of eighty-four thousand leagues above sea level.

26. *nye ba'i sras brgyad.* The bodhisattvas Manjushri, Vajrapani, Avalokiteshvara, Kshitigarbha, Sarvanavaranivishkambin, Akashagarbha, Maitreya, and Samantabhadra.

27. *rgyal po dza.* The first human recipient of the Maha Yoga teachings and an important figure in the transmission of Anu Yoga. It is said that King Ja was

either King Indrabhuti, who was empowered by the Buddha himself, or Indrabhuti's son.

28. *rnal 'byor chen po.* Maha Yoga is called the "great yoga" because it brings realization of nonduality. Its gateway consists of four main empowerments: the vase, secret, wisdom, and symbolic (or word) empowerments. These purify the defilements of body, speech, and mind as well as their subtle obscurations and enable one to realize the four kayas. See the appendix.

29. *ri ma la ya.* The place where Vajrapani taught the Secret Mantra to the five noble beings, which is situated on the island of Lanka (present-day Sri Lanka). It is now known as Adam's Peak.

30. A solitary bird that always dwells apart from others.

31. *gnod sbyin.* A class of semi-divine beings, generally benevolent but sometimes wicked. Many are powerful local divinities; others live on Mount Sumeru, guarding the realm of the gods.

32. *rdo rje 'chang.* Vajra-holder. An emanation of Samantabhadra. The dharmakaya buddha of the Sarma, or New Translation, schools. Can also refer to one's personal teacher of Vajrayana or to the all-embracing buddha-nature.

33. Learned masters, scholars, or professors of Buddhist philosophy.

34. *dngos grub.* The attainment resulting from Dharma practice, usually referring to the supreme accomplishment of complete enlightenment. It can also refer to the eight mundane accomplishments such as clairvoyance, flying in the sky, becoming invisible, and so forth. However, the most eminent attainments on the path are renunciation, compassion, unshakable faith, and realization of the correct view.

35. *dam pa'i rigs can lnga.* The five eminent beings were a god called Renowned Chief Protector (Skt. Yasasvi Varapala), a naga called Naga King Takshaka, a yaksha called Meteor Face (Skt. Ulkamukha), an ogre called Skillful Intellect (Skt. Matyaupayika), and a human being called Stainless Reputation (Skt. Vimalakirti). Some sources mention the god Indra in place of Vimalakirti. These five noble beings, having learnt through their supernatural cognitive powers that the Buddha had passed away, miraculously gathered at Mount Malaya.

36. *dpa' bo.* Tantric equivalent of a bodhisattva and the male equivalent of a dakini.

37. *rgyal rigs.* Members of the warrior or royal caste in Indian society.

38. *bde gshegs snying po.* Buddha-nature, the essence of enlightenment present in all sentient beings.

39. *mDo dgongs 'dus.* Although it is called a sutra, this text is one of the four root tantras of Anu Yoga.

40. Treasury of Wealth. An island in Oddiyana, in western India. As it is encircled by many sublime kinds of trees, this is why it is called Treasury of Wealth.

41. *o rgyan gyi yul.* The land in west India where the Buddha taught the tantras to King Indrabhuti. The king had the tantras written down and then taught them to the people. All the inhabitants of the land became accomplished and attained rainbow body, so it became a desolate place, which the nagas

transformed into a lake. Vajrapani revealed the tantras to the nagas and matured them. As a result, they gradually changed into men, practiced, and became accomplished. Their sons and daughters became dakas and dakinis, so it became known as the land of the dakinis. The lake eventually dried up and a self-created Heruka palace appeared, where the tantras were preserved. Accomplished masters such as Nagarjuna, Kukkuripa, etc., took most of the tantras from there.

42. *dPal gsang ba' rgyud*. The *Guhyagarbha Tantra* (*rgyud gsang ba'i snying po*), the main tantra of Maha Yoga.

43. *dga' rab*. Prahe, the first human teacher of the Dzogchen lineage. See note 4 of chapter 3.

Chapter 3

1. *rgyal ba dgongs rgyud*. The mind lineage of the conquerors originated from the primordial Buddha Samantabhadra and was transmitted from mind to mind up to and including Prahevajra.

2. *rig 'dzin rig pas rgyud*. This lineage was transmitted by the awareness-holders through symbols and extends from Manjushrimitra up to and including Vimalamitra.

3. *gang zag snyan rgyud*. The hearing lineage was transmitted orally through superior individuals starting from the lineages of Shri Singha up to the present.

4. *dga' rab rdo rje*. Indestructible Joy (Skt. Surati Vajra, Prahevajra, Pramoda Vajra). The incarnation of Sem Lhagchen (Adhichitta), a god who earlier had been empowered by the buddhas. Immaculately conceived, his mother was a nun, the daughter of King Uparaja (Dhahena Talo or Indrabhuti) of Oddiyana. Garab Dorje received all the tantras, scriptures, and oral instructions of Dzogchen from Vajrasattva and Vajrapani in person and became the first human vidyadhara in the Dzogchen lineage. Having reached the state of complete enlightenment through the effortless Great Perfection, he transmitted the teachings to his retinue of exceptional beings. Manjushrimitra is regarded as his chief disciple. Padmasambhava is also known to have received the transmission of the Dzogchen tantras directly from Garab Dorje's wisdom form. Garab Dorje passed away 540 years after the Buddha's nirvana.

5. *bstan gnyis*. The Hinayana and Mahayana doctrines.

6. *sum cu tsa gsum lha'i gnas*. A god realm in the world of desire and the abode of the celestial King Indra.

7. *kun dga' snying po*. Also known as Adhichitta, he was the son of the god Bhadrapala in the Heaven of the Thirty-three.

8. *tshangs pa, khyab 'jug, gu lang*. The three principal Hindu gods, the deities of the Vedas.

9. *sems dpa'i rdo rje*. Another name for Vajrapani.

10. *rigs lnga*. The five buddha families of Tathagata, Vajra, Ratna, Padma, and Karma. They represent the innate qualities of our enlightened essence.

11. *rgyal thabs spyi lugs*. The act of bestowing the four empowerments condensed into one, transferring the totality of blessings without any ritual or visual process. It like a king conferring sovereignty on his heir, instantaneously transferring enlightened realization from mind to mind.

12. *phyag rgya chen po*. The Great Seal. It refers to the seal of the absolute nature of all phenomena. The term is used for the teaching, the practice, and the supreme accomplishment.

Chapter 4

1. *rDo rje sems dpa' nam kha che*. The thirtieth chapter of the *All-Creating Monarch Tantra*, which is the fundamental tantra of the Dzogchen Mind Class scriptures. It is said that Garab Dorje recited this after he was born.

2. Spirits dwelling in charnel grounds.

3. *kLong dgu bam po nyi khri*. A series of Dzogchen scriptures of the Space Class. According to the *Longchen Chojung*, the *ninefold expanse* refers to the unborn expanse, the expanse of the fundamental essence, the expanse unborn from the origin, the expanse that transcends words, the expanse beyond concepts, the ineffable expanse, the expanse of the essential condition, the expanse that transcends all limits, and the expanse of nonduality.

4. *dam can*. The guardians and protectors of the Dharma.

5. *'jam dpal bshes gnyan*. Manjushrimitra had a vision of his yidam Manjushri who told him to go to the Sitavana charnel ground to attain enlightenment in one lifetime. He went there and met Prahevajra with whom he studied the doctrine for seventy-five years. After that, Prahevajra passed away into light; at Manjushrimitra's lamenting, he reappeared once more and dropped a gold casket the size of a fingernail into Manjushrimitra's hand. This contained his last testament called *The Three Words Striking the Vital Point*. Based on this testament of Prahevajra, Manjushrimitra later divided the six million four hundred thousand Ati Yoga verses into the Mind Class, the Space Class, and the Instruction Class.

6. *gshin rje gshed*. A wrathful form of Manjushri and the *yidam* of one of the eight sadhanas of Maha Yoga.

7. *Byang sems rdo la gser zhun*. A text written by Manjushrimitra as a confession to Prahevajra, which is one of the five major scriptures of the Mind Class that were translated by Vairotsana.

8. *khyi'i rgyal po*. King of Dogs. He is so called because in the daytime he taught a thousand warriors and yoginis in the guise of a dog; at night, they would perform feast offerings and other practices in the charnel grounds. He was an adept in the *Buddhasamayoga Tantra* and wrote many treatises.

Chapter 5

1. *klu*. Powerful long-living serpentlike beings dwelling in water domains and often guarding great treasures. Nagas belong half to the animal realm and half to the god realm. They generally live in the form of snakes, but many can change into human form.

2. *drang srong*. A rishi can be an inspired Vedic sage, a Brahminical ascetic with magical powers, or someone who has attained the power of truthful speech so that whatever he says comes true.

3. *bdag nyi ma*. She has sometimes been designated as a prostitute and sometimes as a nun; "prostitute" may describe the original subcaste of this teacher.

4. *tshogs 'khor* (Skt. *ganachakra*). Feast offering. A ritual for confession where food and drink are blessed, offered, and consumed as wisdom nectar.

5. The three categories of the Mind Class tantras.

6. Three dakinis residing in the cemeteries.

7. *sems sde*. According to the Mind Class, all perceived phenomena are none other than the play of the nature of mind, the inexpressible, self-existing wisdom (see appendix).

8. *klong sde*. According to the Space Class, self-existing wisdom and all phenomena emerging from its continuum never stray from the expanse of Samantabhadri: they are always pure and liberated (see appendix).

9. *man ngag gi sde*. According to the Instruction Class, in the true nature of samsara and nirvana there are no obscurations to be rid of and no enlightenment to be acquired (see appendix).

10. A class of semi-divine beings who sometimes act as protectors of the Dharma.

11. *kha sar pa ni'i lo*. Possibly a period of six months.

12. *bha ga la'i lo*. A period of six months.

13. *o rgyan gyi lo*. Possibly a period of six months.

14. *gsal byed rin po che 'bar ba'i dkyil 'khor*. The mandala through which direct pointing out of the nature of mind takes place.

Chapter 6

1. *lha tho tho ri snyan shal*. Usually called Lha Thothori Nyentsen, he was the first Dharma king of Tibet and the twenty-eighth hereditary king. He was considered to be an emanation of the bodhisattva Samantabhadra. While residing in the Yumbu Lhakhang Palace, a casket fell upon the palace roof. It contained the sealed stupa, the *Sutra Designed as a Jewel Chest*, and the *Sutra of a Hundredfold Homage for Amendment of Breaches*. The king didn't know what they were, but considering them to be auspicious, he called them the Awesome Secret. By the blessings received from venerating them, he was rejuvenated and changed from an old man of sixty-one years into a sixteen-year-old youth. (According to Dudjom Rinpoche's *The Nyingma School of Tibetan Buddhism*, this occurred in 433 A.D.) He then lived another sixty years and obtained the prediction that the Awesome Secret would be understood after five generations.

2. *srong btsan sgam po*. The second Dharma king of Tibet and the fifth hereditary king after Lha Thothori Nyentsen. He was considered to be an emanation of Avalokiteshvara. He started to rule the kingdom at the age of thirteen. At the age of fifteen he ordered his religious minister Gar, an emanation of Vajrapani, to invite the Nepalese Princess Bhrikuti, and the Chinese Princess Wencheng to be his consorts. As a dowry these princesses each brought an

image of Buddha Shakyamuni; these images were, respectively, the sizes of an eight-year-old and a twelve-year-old. While constructing the Jokhang Temple, the building work was disrupted by nonhuman beings. The king and his two consorts then went into retreat in the Maru Palace in the valley of Kyichu and attained accomplishment by practicing their meditative deity, on whose advice the king built the Border Taming, the Further Taming, and the District Controlling Temples. By doing so he subdued the malignant earth spirits and was able successfully to erect the Jokhang and Ramoche Temples, where the Shakyamuni images were housed.

3. *khri srong lde'u btsan.* (790–844). Trisong Deutsen was the third Dharma king of Tibet and an emanation of Manjushri. He appeared in the fifth reign after Songtsen Gampo and was thirteen years old when he started ruling the kingdom. At the age of twenty he invited Shantarakshita from Zahor to Tibet in order to propagate the true doctrine. Shantarakshita was unable to subdue the evil spirits to build Samye, and at his advice the king invited Padmasambhava, who subdued all the evil forces so that Samye could be completed. Wanting to introduce the true foundations of the sutra and mantra teachings by translating the true doctrine from Sanskrit to Tibetan, Trisong Deutsen invited many scholars from India to train intelligent Tibetan youths in the art of translation, such as Master Jinamitra, Sarvajnaveda, and Danashila. He also invited the great masters Vimalamitra and Shantigarbha and twelve monks of the Sarvastivadin order. According to the *'Dra 'bag*, he had passed away by the time Vimalamitra reached Tibet, three months after Vairotsana was banished to Tsawarong. Some sources say that he was born in 790 and passed away in 858.

4. *mchod rten phyag rgyas btab pa.* A stupa from the casket that fell on the roof of the Yumbu Lhakhang during the time of Lha Thothori Nyentsen.

5. *mDo sde za ma tog bkod pa* (Skt. *Karandavyuha-sutra*). A scripture on Avalokiteshvara found in the Mani Kahbum of Songtsen Gampo.

6. *dPang skong phyag brgya pa'i mdo* (Skt. *Sakshipuranasudraka-sutra*).

7. Up to this point all the Tibetan kings are said to have been divine beings who ascended to the heavens after fulfilling their reigns.

8. *thon mi sam bho tra.* An emanation of Manjushri who was a minister of King Songtsen Gampo. Sent to India by Songtsen Gampo to study grammar and writing, he created the forms of the Tibetan letters on the basis of the Indian scripts and composed eight treatises on Tibetan letters.

9. *mtha' 'dul.* The four Border Taming Temples built by Songtsen Gampo. See note 2 of chapter 6.

10. *yang 'dul.* The four Further Taming Temples built by Songtsen Gampo. See note 2 of chapter 6.

11. *ru 'dul.* The four District Controlling Temples built by Songtsen Gampo. See note 2 of chapter 6.

12. *lha sa'i gtsug lag khang gnyis.* The Jokhang and Ramoche Temples in Lhasa; these temples housed the two Shakyamuni images that were brought to Tibet by Songtsen Gampo's consorts.

13. The two Shakyamuni statues brought by Songten Gampo's consorts. See note 2 of chapter 6.

14. An abbot from Zahor, India, who was invited by King Trisong Deutsen to bring the true doctrine to Tibet. When he taught the doctrine of the ten virtues and the eighteen psychophysical bases there, the savage demons and deities of Tibet became angry; they caused lightning to strike Marpori, site of the present Potala Palace, a flood to sweep away the palace at Phangthang, the harvest to be destroyed, and many other calamities. So the evil ministers suggested the master go back where he came from. King Trisong made offerings and explained the situation to Shantarakshita, who said he would go to Nepal for the time being. He said that he would invite Padmasambhava to come to subdue the malignant spirits and told the king to invite him as well. Messengers were sent, and Padmasambhava, who already knew about the delegation, instantly traveled to Nepal to meet them. Shantarakshita ordained the first monks in Tibet and remained there until he passed away.

15. *has po ri*. A small mountain near Samye.

16. *pad ma 'byung gnas*. The Lotus-Born Guru, also known as Guru Rinpoche, the master considered to be the "second buddha," who established Buddhism in Tibet. He was an emanation of Amitabha and, according to the revealed treasures, was miraculously born from a lotus in a lake in Oddiyana. He was then adopted by King Indrabhuti but gave up the kingdom to practice asceticism in charnel grounds. He was blessed by the dakinis and followed countless masters in India. He attained long-life accomplishment in the Maratika Cave in Nepal and the attainments of Vajra Kilaya and Shri Heruka in Yangleshod in Nepal. Invited to Tibet, he subdued all the evil spirits; he traveled all over Tibet, blessing every single place and hiding treasures for future fortunate ones. He is said to have stayed in Tibet from when Trisong Deutsen was twenty-one years old until five years and six months after the king passed away, when he left for the Glorious Copper-Colored Mountain, the terrestrial pure land of Guru Rinpoche situated on the subcontinent Chamara to the southeast of the Jambu continent. Chamara is the central island of a configuration of nine islands inhabited by savage *rakshasas*. In the middle of Chamara rises into the skies the majestic red-colored mountain. On its summit lies the magical Lotus Light Palace, which is manifested from the natural expression of primordial wakefulness. Here resides Padmasambhava, transcending birth and death for as long as samsara continues in an indestructible bodily form through which he incessantly brings benefit to beings through magical emanations of his body, speech, and mind.

17. *bsam yas*. Literally, "inconceivable." The first monastery built in Tibet by King Trisong Deutsen.

18. Short for Kawa Paltsek, who was one of the Tibetan translators that was predicted by Padmasambhava at the time of Trisong Deutsen. While Vairotsana and Namkhai Nyingpo were sent to India, he stayed at Samye and translated the sutras and mantra teachings. Later, he went to India to invite Vimalami-

tra. He is considered the second greatest Tibetan translator and was one of the twenty-five close disciples of Padmasambhava.

19. Short for Chokro Lui Gyaltsen, who was predicted by Padmasambhava and trained as a translator during the time of Trisong Deutsen. Along with Kawa he translated the sutras and tantras while Vairo went to India. Later, he and Kawa went to India to invite Vimalamitra. He is considered the third greatest Tibetan translator and was also one of Padmasambhava's twenty-five close disciples.

20. Shantigarbha was one of the eight accomplished masters that gathered at the Sitavana charnel ground where each received a casket containing the transmitted precepts of Maha Yoga from the dakini Mahakarmendrani (Leskyi Wangmo). Shantigarbha received the casket containing the Malign Mantra (Mospa Dragngag) and attained accomplishment. He was invited to Tibet by Trisong Deutsen and propagated the Yamari (Shinje) cycle of teachings.

21. Buddhaguhya was born in central India and ordained at Nalanda. He was a disciple of Buddhajnanapada and attained accomplishment by practicing Manjushri. He then went to Oddiyana where he studied Yoga Tantra and the *Five Inner Unsurpassed Tantrapitaka* with Master Lilavajra. He became an adept in the *Magical Net Tantra* and went to visit Avalokiteshvara on Mount Potala. There he also met Arya Tara, who advised him to go to Mount Kailash to practice the means for attainment there. For many years he taught the doctrine near Varanasi and then was reminded by Manjushri of Arya Tara's prediction, so he went to Mount Kailash where he attained accomplishment. He was then able to speak with Manjushri and have nonhuman beings act as his servants. He composed many great works and at Mount Kailash gave instructions on the Secret Essence cycle to such disciples as Drenkha Murtri and Jampal Gocha.

22. *gang ri ti se.* A sacred mountain in western Tibet.

23. Master Humkara was born in a Brahmin family in Nepal and was an expert in the Vedas. Later, he became a Buddhist and was ordained at Nalanda. He became an expert in the teachings of the prajnaparamita and the Secret Mantra. In the Sitavana charnel ground he was given the casket containing the transmitted precepts of Vishuddha (Yangdag) through which he attained accomplishment. He benefited beings through his teachings on the development and completion stages, on which he wrote many treatises. He passed away by flying to the pure land of Akshobhya. His main disciples were Avadhuti and Buddhashrisanti of Oddiyana.

24. *nub nam mkha'i snying po.* One of the translators sent to India by King Trisong Deutsen in order to search for the teachings. Along with his companions, four other translators, he studied the Yangdag Heruka doctrine with Master Humkara. Upon his return to Tibet, he gave the teachings to King Trisong Deutsen, but due to the influence of Queen Margyen and the evil ministers, he was banished to Lhodrag Kharchu in southern Tibet, where he attained accomplishment through Yangdag. He was able to emanate fire from his body, leave his body prints in rocks, ascend the rays of the sun, and stab his *phurba*

into rock. His four companions also attained accomplishment, even though all of them were also banished to different areas in Tibet.

25. A place in the Nyemo district near Uyuk.

26. Alternate name for Vairotsana's mother.

27. By "gone to fetch eyes" Vairo means getting oil for the lamp; by "in search of gossip" he means finding alcohol, which makes one's tongue wag. See the introduction by Thinley Norbu Rinpoche.

28. *dkar gsum mngar gsum*. The three whites are curd, milk, and butter, and the three sweets are sugar, honey, and molasses.

29. *sad mi mi bdun*. The seven men to be tested were the first seven fully ordained monks in Tibet, who were ordained by Shantarakshita. They were the minister Ba Trhizi, Ba Selnang, Pagor Vairotsana, Ngenlam Gyalwa Chokyang, Ma Rinchen Chok, Khon Lui Wangpo, and Lasum Gyalwa Changchub. Later, when the king was satisified with how they had turned out, he had Shantarakshita ordain another 300 people.

30. *rab byung*. Fully ordained monks.

31. *tsha ba rong*. A river valley in the far east of Kham.

32. *tshal bu bya gdong*. King Trisong Deutsen's horse that he sent with Vairotsana and Tsang Lekdrub when they set out for India.

Chapter 7

1. According to some sources, Hedo was Vairotsana's uncle, who had adopted him when his father died.

2. *'dod khams*. One of the three worlds of existence, which contains the six realms of beings.

3. *dug lnga*. The five conflicting emotions of anger, desire, ignorance, jealousy, and pride.

4. *gzugs khams*. The second world of existence, which consists of seventeen regions.

5. *gzugs med khams*. The third of the three worlds of samsara, which consists of four spheres.

6. *bden pa bzhi*. (1) The truth of suffering, (2) the truth of the origin of suffering, (3) the truth of the cessation of suffering, and (4) the truth of the path.

7. *lam lnga*. The paths of accumulation, joining, seeing, meditation, and beyond training. These five paths cover the entire process from sincerely beginning Dharma practice to complete enlightenment.

8. *skyes bu zung bzhi ya brgyad*. The four pairs of noble beings that are the eight results of the shravaka path. These are: stream-enterers, the pair that enters and becomes established in the stream to nirvana; once-returners, the pair that enters and becomes established in a single rebirth; non-returners, the pair that enters and becomes established in not returning to samsara; and the pair that enters and becomes established as arhats. See the appendix.

9. *rang rgyal*. "Solitary enlightened ones." Arhats who attain nirvana by contemplation on the twelve links of dependent origination in reverse order, without needing to receive teachings from a teacher in that lifetime. They

       lack the complete realization of a buddha and thus cannot benefit beings in the same way as a buddha. See the appendix.

10. *rten 'brel bcu gnyis*. The twelve links of dependent origination are: ignorance; habitual tendencies; consciousness; name and form; the six activity fields of eye, ear, nose, tongue, body and intellect; contact; feeling; craving; aggregates; birth; old age; and death.

11. *bse ru lta bu*. The first of the two stages of the pratyekabuddha. See the appendix.

12. *bden gnyis*. Relative and absolute truth. Relative truth describes the seeming, superficial, and apparent mode of all things. Absolute truth describes the real, true, and unmistaken mode. These two aspects of reality are defined in different ways by the four philosophical schools as well as by the tantras of the Vajrayana, each definition progressively deeper and closer to describing things as they are.

13. *sa bcu*. The ten levels of a noble bodhisattva's development into a fully enlightened buddha: the Joyous, the Stainless, the Radiant, the Brilliant, the Hard to Conquer, the Realized, the Reaching Far, the Unshakable, the Good Intelligence, and the Cloud of Dharma. On each stage subtler defilements are purified and ever more enlightened qualities become manifest.

14. *dag pa rnam gsum*. The three purities in Kriya Tantra are: the purity of deity and mantra, the purity of substance and rapture, and the purity of mantra and contemplation. See the appendix.

15. *sems dpa'i rnal 'byor*. Sattvayoga encompasses the contents of the three outer tantras, in particular Yoga Tantra. See the appendix.

16. *ting 'dzin rnam gsum*. The three samadhis in Maha Yoga are: the samadhi of suchness, the all-illuminating samadhi, and the samadhi of the seed syllable.

17. *'khor lo tshogs chen*. Name for the thirteenth level of realization.

18. The present district of Bihar in central India.

19. Shri Singha was the chief disciple and successor of Manjushrimitra in the lineage of the Dzogchen teachings. He was born in the city of Shokyam in China and studied the common sciences under Master Haribhala. He had a vision of Avalokiteshvara, who told him to go to the Sosadvipa charnel ground in India to realize the result of enlightenment. To be able to understand the result, he first went to Wutaishan to study the other Secret Mantra tantras with Master Bhelakirti. He thoroughly mastered them, became a monk, and kept the Vinaya vows for thirty years. Avalokiteshvara again told him to go to Sosadvipa, so he spent three years practicing the means for attaining miraculous power so he could travel to India without hardship. Traveling to Sosadvipa eighteen inches above the earth, he met Manjushrimitra and prayed to be accepted as his disciple. Manjushrimitra was delighted and gave him instructions for twenty-five years, after which Manjushrimitra's body vanished into light. As Shri Singha cried out in anguish, Manjushrimitra appeared once more and dropped a jeweled casket the size of a fingernail into Shri Singha's hand. It contained his testament called *Six Experiences of Meditation*, through which Shri Singha understood the profound truth. Shri Singha extracted the

tantras that had been concealed in Bodhgaya and went to China, where he classified the Ati Yoga Instruction Class into four cycles: outer, inner, secret, and innermost secret. Collecting the first three cycles for those requiring elaboration, he concealed them in the balcony of the Bodhi Tree Temple. According to the dakinis' prediction, he concealed the innermost secret cycle in a pillar of the Myriad Gate Temple and then remained in the Siljin charnel ground. His main disciples were Jnanasutra, Vimalamitra, Padmasambhava, and Vairotsana.

20. The place where Shri Singha lived when he imparted the teachings to Vairotsana. It had several congregation halls and, according to this text, is near Kutra Lake. Other sources have placed Shri Singha's residence in Oddiyana. This text, however, never mentions where Dhahena is located, and as the scholars keep going back and forth from Nalanda to Bodhgaya, one would think it more likely to be in central India, since no places leading toward Oddiyana in the west are mentioned in the *Great Image* during Vairotsana's travels. The *Golden Garland Chronicles* mentions that after leaving Shri Singha, Vairotsana returned from Bodhgaya to Tibet in two days. According to Hanson-Barber's dissertation on Vairotsana, Dhahena is situated in southern India at a place called Shri Dhayakataka, which is located on the Krishna River not far from Shriparvata and Mount Potala.

21. *thig le nyag gcig.* Another name for dharmakaya.

22. *dkon mchog gsum.* The Buddha, the Dharma, and the Sangha, also called the Three Jewels.

23. *seng ge rab brtan.* Steadfast Lion. Among the six emanations of the Buddha in the six realms of beings, this is the Muni of the animal realm.

Chapter 8

1. *rig pa'i khu byug.* This and the following seventeen titles are the Eighteen Major Dzogchen Tantras of the Mind Class taught by Shri Singha to Vairotsana and Tsang Lekdrub.

2. *che ba lnga.* According to the Nyingma Gyudbum these are: the greatness of direct manifestation of enlightenment, the greatness of enlightenment in the ultimate dimension of phenomena, the greatness of enlightenment in the dharmakaya, the greatness of enlightenment that proves its own nature, and the greatness of the absolute nonexistence of enlightenment.

Chapter 9

1. *lcags kyi drel rta.* A practice to accomplish speed walking.

2. *rnam par snang mdzad.* The buddha Vairochana, chief buddha of the Tathagata family.

3. *ston pa gnyis.* It is unclear who these two teachers are, and after checking with many learned masters, nobody could make sense out of it. The text here may be a misspelling and is more likely to be *stong pa nyid,* which is the subject of the question. But since the spelling is the same in various editions of the *Great Image,* I have left it as it is.

Chapter 10

1. *ni gu.* A female soothsayer.
2. *pra se na.* A way of doing divination by looking at images in a mirror.
3. This refers to how Shri Singha hid when teaching Vairo and Lekdrub. To prevent the scholars from finding out through divination, he placed a pot on top of three rocks, covered the pot with a net, and placed a pan of water on top of the pot; Shri Singha sat inside the pot and taught Vairo and Lekdrub through a tube.
4. Queen Tsepongza Margyen was the senior consort of Trisong Deutsen and bore him three sons. She was in favor of the Bon tradition and became openly hostile to Buddhist teachers.

Chapter 11

1. Nyoshul Khen Rinpoche explained these metaphors in this way. A similar explanation is also found in the *Golden Garland Chronicles*. These are the first five teachings of the Mind Class translated by Vairotsana on his return to Tibet. *Entering into All Objects* is another name for *Soaring Garuda*.
2. *mDo bcu.* An exposition tantra of the *All-Creating Monarch Tantra* in ten chapters. Along with the *mDo rtsa* and the *mDo 'grel* these comprise the thirteen sutras of the Mind Class. See note 6 in chapter 13.
3. *rigs gsum mgon.* The three main bodhisattvas: Manjushri, Avalokiteshvara, and Vajrapani.
4. *dur khrod brgyad.* (1) Cool Grove, Sitavana, in the east; (2) Perfected in Body to the south; (3) Lotus Mound to the west; (4) Lanka Mound to the north; (5) Spontaneous Mound to the southeast; (6) Display of Great Secret to the southwest; (7) Pervasive Great Joy to the northwest; and (8) World Mound to the northeast.
5. *rgyan drug.* The six great Indian masters Nagarjuna, Asanga, Dignaga, Aryadeva, Vasubandhu, and Dharmakirti.
6. *mi 'am ci.* Mythical beings with horse heads and human bodies (or vice versa). Along with the *gandharvas* they are celebrated as celestial musicians.
7. The text here suddenly changes into first person.
8. Ngam Tara Lugong was one of the most influential Bon ministers at the time.
9. As explained in the *Crystal Cave Chronicles*, Queen Margyen was in love with Vairotsana and wanted a relationship with him. Because he refused to have an affair with her, she exposed him to the Bon ministers
10. *bdud rigs.* A category of demons.
11. *yar lha sham po.* A Dharma protector who rides a white yak.
12. *tshogs.* A feast assembly performed by Vajrayana practitioners to accumulate merit and purify the sacred commitments.
13. Vimalamitra was born in western India and had a vision of Vajrasattva, who told him that he had been born as a scholar five hundred times but that to attain enlightenment he had to go to the Bodhi Tree Temple in China. He went there, met Master Shri Singha, and received all the instructions of the

oral lineage but was not given the books. Upon a prediction from the dakinis, he went to the Bhasing charnel ground in India and prayed to receive
the most profound instructions. Master Jnanasutra gave him the elaborate
and unelaborated empowerments, and after practicing the "separation of
samsara and nirvana" and receiving the very unelaborated empowerment, he
attained an extraordinary understanding and a white syllable A appeared at
the tip of his nose. He then received the extremely unelaborated empowerment through which he perceived the naked mind essence. Jnanasutra gave
him all the instructions and texts related to these empowerments, and for
ten years Vimalamitra practiced them to refine his understanding. When he
vanished into light, Jnanasutra left Vimalamitra a testament called the *Four
Meditation Methods*, through which he acquired an undeluded understanding. Later, Vimalamitra lived in the Prabhaskara charnel ground where he
turned the wheel of the Dharma and attained the rainbow body of supreme
transformation. He copied the most secret books three times and hid them
in Oddiyana, Kashmir, and the Prabhaskara cemetery. He was nearly two
hundred years old when King Trisong Deutsen sent the translators Kawa
Paltsek and Chokro Lui Gyaltsen to invite him to Tibet; seeing that Tibet
was ripe for conversion, he went there with them. Because of dissension created by jealous Indians, he had to display his miraculous powers to induce
faith in the Tibetans. He translated texts on the general vehicles of cause and
effect, and with Yudra Nyingpo he translated the Later Translations, the thirteen texts of the Ati Yoga Mind Class. In secret he gave the most profound
esoteric instructions to King Trisong Deutsen and Nyang Tingdzin Zangpo,
but because there were no other suitable students, he translated and concealed the books in Chimphu. He spent thirteen years in Tibet and then
went to Wutaishan in China, Five-Peaked Mountain, which was sacred to
Manjushri, where he promised to remain alive for the remaining time of the
Buddha's doctrine and to send an emanation to Tibet every hundred years to
explain the Nyingthig teachings.

14. *dge 'dun sde gnyis*. These are (1) ordained renunciates who shave their heads
and wear red and yellow robes, and (2) Vajrayana practitioners, known as
tantrikas, who are not celibate, wear white robes, and grow their hair long.

15. *ri bo rtse nga* (Chinese: Wutaishan). A place in eastern China sacred to Manjushri, where Vimalamitra is supposed to reside and from where he is said to
send an emanation to Tibet once every century.

16. *lha bu'i bdud*. The demon of the devaputras. According to the Chod teachings there are four *maras*: the demon of the aggregates, the demon of the
emotional disturbances, the demon of the Lord of Death, and the demon of
the child of gods. "Godly son demon" is defined as "distraction in the meditation state and the tendency to postpone practice, creating obstacles for
samadhi."

17. *dri za'i grong khyer*. One of the eight traditional analogies of illusion.

18. *rgyal 'gong*. A type of mischievous spirit.

Chapter 12

1. *rgyal mo mdo zhen phan bus*. Comparing the incomprehensible text here with the same passage in the *Golden Garland Chronicles*: It seems that the people from Gyalmo headed by the king's son Palshe threw Vairo in the pit, and later it was again Palshe who approached the entrance of the hole.

2. *pu rgyal*. A form of address for the Tibetan King. *Pu* is a misspelling of *sPur*, an ancient name for Tibet; *rgyal* means king.

3. *nyon mongs*. The five conflicting emotions of ignorance, desire, anger, jealousy, and pride.

4. *srin po*. One of the eight classes of gods and demons. Also, the cannibal savages inhabiting the southwestern continent of Chamara. At times *raksha* refers to the unruly and untamed expression of ignorance and disturbing emotions.

5. *ba shi*. Unable to find out the meaning of this word after consulting with various lamas, I compared it with the text in the *Golden Garland Chronicles*, where the word is *sgyu ma*, implying that the king considered Vairo to be a magician of some sort.

6. *theg dman*. The Hinayana. See the appendix.

Chapter 13

1. Khon Lui Wangpo was one the seven men to be tested, that is, the first seven monks ordained by Shantarakshita in Tibet. He was also one of the twenty-five close disciples of Padmasambhava According to the *Chronicles* it was Kawa Paltsek and Chokro Lui Gyaltsen that were sent to invite Vimamalitra.

2. KA and KHA are the first two letters of the Tibetan alphabet. A is the last one.

3. *phyi 'gyur bcu gsum*. The thirteen scriptures of the Eighteen Major Scriptures of the Mind Class, which were translated by Vimalamitra and Yudra Nyingpo.

4. *sgyu 'phrul 'drwa ba* (Skt. *Mayajala*). The *Guhyagarbha Tantra*, which is the main Maha Yoga tantra and is the same as the *Essence of Secrets*.

5. *mDo rtsa, mDo lung*, and *mDo 'grel*. These are thirteen scriptures that belong to the Mind Class and are commonly known as the Thirteen Sutras. The Five Early Translations and the Thirteen Later Translations, along with the *All-Creating Monarch*, the *Marvelous*, and the Thirteen Sutras, are the twenty-one major scriptures of the Mind Class, which were brought to Tibet by Vairotsana and Vimalamitra.

6. According to the *Chronicles*, it was Queen Margyen who poisoned him out of jealousy.

7. Gold, silver, turquoise, coral, and pearl.

8. *zhabs tog rnam gsum*. The best service to one's guru is the offering of one's practice, mediocre service is to serve one's guru with body and speech, and inferior service is the offering of material things.

9. *shes rab rnam gsum*. Discriminative awareness resulting from study, reflection, and meditation practice.

10. *bslab pa gsum*. The three trainings of discipline, samadhi, and discriminating knowledge.

11. *sde snod gsum*. The Tripitaka. The three collections of the teachings of Buddha Shakyamuni: Vinaya, Sutra, and Abhidharma. Their purpose is the development of the three trainings of discipline, concentration, and discriminating knowledge while their function is to remedy the three poisons of desire, anger, and delusion. The Tibetan version of the Tripitaka fills more than one hundred large volumes, each with more than six hundred large pages. In a wider sense, all of the Dharma, both sutra and tantra, is contained within the three collections and the three trainings.

12. *sbyin pa gsum*. Generosity of material things, generosity of protection from fear, and generosity of the Dharma teachings.

13. *tshul khrims gsum*. The three kinds of discipline according to the Bodhisattva Vehicle are practicing virtue, acting for the sake of others, and refraining from misdeeds.

14. *sgra 'gyur gling*. One of the temples at Samye that was specifically used for translation. Samye was constructed according to the Buddhist view of the universe, with the main temple as Mount Meru and the surrounding temples as the four main continents, the eight subcontinents, and the sun and moon.

15. *sher phyin*. The perfection of wisdom.

16. *bka' ma*. The canonical lineage of the Nyingma school, the teachings translated chiefly during the period of Padmasambhava's stay in Tibet and transmitted from master to student until the present day.

17. *gterma*. The lineage of the rediscovered treasures, which refers to the transmission through treasures hidden mainly by Padmasambhava and Yeshe Tsogyal, to be discovered at the proper time by a *terton*, a treasure revealer, for the benefit of future disciples. The Terma tradition is one of the two chief traditions of the Nyingma school, the other being the Kahma tradition. See the previous note.

18. *zhi gnas*. Calm abiding, tranquility meditation.

Aspiration and Summary

1. *jo mo sman mo*. A female treasure revealer who lived 1248–83. She was an emanation of Yeshe Tsogyal and one of the wives of the great terton Guru Chowang. She rediscovered one version of the *Great Image*. Her main treasure was the *Gathering of All Secrets of the Dakinis*. After she passed away by flying off into space, this treasure remained in the possession of the dakinis until Jamyang Khyentse Wangpo rediscovered it.

2. *bKa' thang shal brag ma*, also called *Pad ma'i bka' thang*. A treasure about the life of Guru Padmasambhava that was revealed by Orgyen Lingpa.

3. Dharma Senge lived in the nineteenth century. He was a student of the first Dodupchen Rinpoche and one of the teachers of Shukseb Jetsun. Having compiled this biography, he was aware of the defects and contradictions in the text; not satisfied with his editorial work, he pleads for future readers to examine it carefully.

GLOSSARY

abbot (Tib. *mkhan po*) In general, the transmitter of the monastic vows. This title is also given to a person who has attained a high degree of knowledge of Dharma and is authorized to teach it.

Abbot Rabnang (Tib. *mkhan po rab snang*) One of the Indian Dzogchen lineage masters, who was a disciple of the prostitute Barani and the teacher of abbot Maharaja.

Abhidharma (Skt.; Tib. *mngon pa*) The third section of the Tripitaka (the other two sections are Vinaya and Sutra). Systematic teachings on metaphysics, focusing on the training of discriminating knowledge by analyzing elements of experience and investigating the nature of existing things.

absolute truth (Tib. *don dam*) The ultimate nature of the mind and the true status of all phenomena; the state beyond all conceptual constructs, which can be known only by primordial wisdom and in a manner that transcends duality.

accomplishment (Skt. *siddhi*; Tib. *dngos grub*) Accomplishment is described as either supreme or common. Supreme accomplishment is the attainment of buddhahood. Common accomplishments are the miraculous powers acquired in the course of spiritual training. The attainment of these powers, which are similar in kind to those acquired by the practitioners of some non-Buddhist traditions, are not regarded as ends in themselves. When they arise, however, they are taken as signs of progress on the path and are employed for the benefit of the teachings and disciples.

Adhichitta (Skt.; Tib. *sems lhag can*) Prahevajra's previous incarnation in the celestial realms.

aggregates (Skt. *skandha*; Tib. *phung po*) The five aggregates are the basic component elements of form, feeling, perception, conditioning factors, and consciousness. When they appear together, the illusion of a self is produced in the ignorant mind.

Akanishta (Skt.; Tib. *'og min*) Literally, "which is not below"; the Unexcelled Buddha-field. In general, the highest of all buddha-fields. According to the Vajrayana, the place where bodhisattvas attain final buddhahood. There are, in fact, six levels of Akanishta, ranging from the highest heaven of the form realm up to the ultimate pure land of the dharmakaya.

Ala Zenkar Rinpoche (Tib. *alak gzan dkar rin po che*) Great Nyingma scholar from eastern Tibet who is said to be an emanation of Do Khyentse and who at present lives in New York.

all-ground consciousness (Skt. *alaya-vijnana*; Tib. *kun gzhi'i rnam shes*) Consciousness as the ground of all experience. According to the Mahayana, the all-ground is the fundamental and indeterminate level of the mind in which karmic imprints are stored.

Ananda (Skt.; Tib. *kun dga' bo*) The son of Buddha Shakyamuni's uncle who became the Buddha's personal attendant. Ananda was able to remember every word the Buddha spoke; he compiled the Buddha's teachings and served as the second patriarch in the oral transmission of the Dharma.

Anandagarbha (Skt.; Tib. *kun dga' snying po*) See **Adhichitta**.

Anu Yoga (Skt.; Tib. *rjes su rnal 'byor*) The second of the inner tantras, according to the system of nine vehicles used in the Nyingma tradition. Anu Yoga emphasizes the perfection stage of tantric practice, which consists of meditation on emptiness as well as on the subtle channels, energies, and essences of the physical body.

appearances (Tib. *snang ba*) See **perceptions**.

arhat (Skt.; Tib. *dgra bcom pa*) Literally, "foe-destroyer," one who has vanquished the enemies of conflicting emotion and realized the nonexistence of the personal self, thus being forever free from the sufferings of samsara. Arhatship is the goal of the teachings of the Fundamental Vehicle, or Hinayana.

arya (Skt.; Tib. *'phags pa*) Sublime or noble one, one who has transcended samsaric existence. There are four classes of sublime beings: arhats, pratyekabuddhas, bodhisattvas, and buddhas.

asura (Skt.; Tib. *lha min*) Demi-god, one of the six classes of beings in samsara. The asuras are usually considered to be similar to the gods with whom they are sometimes classified. Their dominant emotional characteristic is envy, and they are constantly at war with the gods, of whom they are jealous.

Ati, Ati Yoga (Skt.; Tib. *rdzogs chen*) The last and highest of the inner tantras; the summit of the system of nine vehicles according to the Nyingma classification; a synonym of Dzogchen, the Great Perfection.

Atsantra Aloke (Skt.; Tib. *a tsan tra a lo ke*) One of the Indian Dzogchen lineage masters who was a disciple of Princess Gomadevi and the teacher of Kukkuraja the Elder.

Avalokiteshvara (Skt.; Tib. *spyan ras gzigs*) The "Lord Who Sees"; name of the bodhisattva who embodies the speech and compassion of all the buddhas and who is sometimes referred to as *Lokeshvara*, the Lord of the World. The sambhogakaya emanation of Buddha Amitabha.

awareness (Skt. *vidya*; Tib. *rig pa*) When referring to the view of the Great Perfection, awareness means consciousness devoid of ignorance and dualistic fixation.

Bengali year (Tib. *bha ga li'i lo*) A period of six months.

Bes Dorje Gyaltsen (Tib. *sbas rdo rje rgyal mtshan*) A disciple of Yudra Nyingpo and one of the lineage masters of Vairotsana's teachings.

Bhagavan (Skt.; Tib. *bcom ldan 'das*) An epithet of the Buddha, sometimes translated as "the Blessed One" or "the Blessed Lord." The title can be analyzed etymologically as "the one who has vanquished (*bcom*) the four demons, who possesses (*ldan*) all qualities, and who is beyond ('*das*) samsara and nirvana."

Bhashita (Skt.; Tib. *drang srong bha shi ta*) One of the Indian Dzogchen lineage masters, a disciple of Kukkuraja and the teacher of Dagnyima.

bhikshu (Skt.; Tib. *dge slong*) A fully ordained Buddhist monk.

bhumi (Skt.; Tib. *sa*) The levels or stages of the bodhisattvas.

Bodhgaya (Skt. *vajrasana*; Tib. *rdo rje gdan*) Vajra seat. The place in Bihar, India, where all the buddhas of this eon have attained and will attain enlightenment.

bodhi (Skt.; Tib. *byang chub*) Enlightenment, awakening, a state of realization.

Bodhichitta Written in Pure Gold on Stone (Tib. *Byang sems rdo la gser zhun*) A text written by Manjushrimitra as a confession to Prahevajra; one of the five major scriptures of the Mind Class that were translated by Vairotsana.

bodhichitta (Skt.; Tib. *byang chub, byang chub kyi sems*) Awakened state of mind. Can refer to the aspiration to attain enlightenment for the sake of all beings or, in the context of Dzogchen, the innate awareness of awakened mind.

bodhisattva (Skt.; Tib. *byang chub sems dpa'*) One who, through compassion, strives to attain the full enlightenment of buddhahood for the sake of all beings. Bodhisattvas may be "ordinary" or "noble" depending on whether or not they have attained the path of seeing and are residing on one of the ten bhumis.

Bonpo (Tib. *bon po*) The religion prevalent in Tibet before the establishment of Buddhism in the ninth century.

Brahma (Skt.; Tib. *tshangs pa*) In the Buddhist tradition, this name refers to the ruler of the gods in the form realm.

Brahmin (Skt.; Tib. *bram ze*) Member of the priestly caste of ancient India. This term often indicates hermits and spiritual practitioners. It should be noted that the Buddha rejected the caste system and proclaimed on several occasions that the true Brahmin is not someone so designated through an accident of birth, but one who has thoroughly overcome defilement and attained freedom. See *caste*.

Buddha Shakyamuni (Skt.; Tib. *sangs rgyas sha kya thub pa*) The sage of the Shakyas; the Buddha of our time who lived around the fifth century B.C.

Buddha (Skt.; Tib. *sangs rgyas*) The Fully Awakened One, a being who has removed the emotional and cognitive veils and is endowed with all enlightened qualities of realization.

buddha-field (Tib. *zhing khams*) A sphere or dimension manifested by a buddha or great bodhisattva in which beings may abide and progress toward enlightenment without ever falling back into lower states of existence. Also, any place seen as the pure manifestation of spontaneous wisdom is a buddha-field.

Buddhaguhya (Skt.; Tib. *sangs rgyas gsang ba*) A master of Maha Yoga and a teacher of both Guru Padmasambhava and Vimalamitra.

Buddhagupta (Skt.; Tib. *bhu ta kug ta*) One of the Indian lineage masters of Dzogchen; a disciple of Devaraja and the teacher of Shri Singha.

caste (Tib. *rigs*) The traditional class distinction of Indian society associated with different psychological types and the kind of work or social function deemed appropriate to each. In the course of time, the caste system became extremely complex. Buddhist texts refer only to the original fourfold system and repudiate it in the sense of rejecting the idea, still current in Indian society, that such distinctions are immutably dictated by the circumstances of birth. These four classes are the royal or ruling class (*kshatriya, rgyal rigs*), the priestly class (*brahmin, bram bze rigs*), the merchant class (*vaishya, rje'u rigs*), and the menial class (*shudra, dmangs rigs*).

causal philosophical teachings (Tib. *rgyu mtshan nyid kyi bstan pa*) The teachings of Hinayana and Mahayana that regard the practices of the path as the causes for attaining the fruition of liberation and enlightenment.

Changlochen (Tib. *lcang lo can*) The pure land of the Lord of Secrets, Vajrapani.

Chimphu (Tib. *chims phu*) The hermitage of caves above Samye where Padmasambhava and many other great masters spent years in retreat.

Chokro Lui Gyaltsen (Tib. *lcog ro klu'i rgyal mtshan*) Predicted by Padmasambhava and trained as a translator during the time of Trisong Deutsen, along with Kawa Paltsek he translated the sutras and tantras while Vairo went to India. Later, he and Kawa went to India to invite Vimalamitra to Tibet. He is considered the third greatest Tibetan translator and was also one of Padmasambhava's twenty-five disciples. Also referred to as Chok.

Chronicles of Padma (Tib. *Pad ma'i bka' thang*) See *Crystal Cave Chronicles*.

Cloud Mass Wheel (Tib. *'khor lo tshogs chen*) Name for the thirteenth level of realization.

Conqueror (Skt. *jina*; Tib. *rgyal ba*) An epithet of the Buddha.

Crystal Cave Chronicles (Tib. *bKa' thang shel brag ma*) Treasure text on the life of Padmasambhava revealed by Orgyen Lingpa (1323–74). It was revealed at the Crystal Cave of Yarlung, thus its title.

Cuckoo of Awareness (Tib. *Rig pa'i khu byug*) The first of the Eighteen Major Scriptures of the Mind Class taught by Shri Singha to Vairotsana and Tsang Lekdrub.

Cycle of Instructions Directly Showing Self-Liberation (Tib. *Rang grol mngon sum du ston pa man ngag gi skor*) The last of the three categories of the Mind Class tantras.

Dagnyima (Tib. *bdag nyi ma*) One of the Dzogchen lineage masters who is sometimes designated as a prostitute and sometimes as a nun; prostitute may describe the sub-caste of the origin of this teacher. She received the transmission of the mind essence from Rishi Bhashita and became a teacher of Nagarjuna.

daka (Skt.; Tib. *dpa' bo*) Literally, "hero." Tantric equivalent of a bodhisattva; the male equivalent of a dakini.

dakini (Skt.; Tib. *mkha' 'gro ma*) Literally, "moving through space." The representation of wisdom in female form. There are several levels of dakinis: wisdom dakinis who have complete realization and worldly dakinis who possess various spiritual powers. The word is also used as a title for great women teachers and as a respectful form of addressing the wives of spiritual masters.

damaru (Tib. *da ma ru*) A small hand drum made from human skulls used in tantric rituals.

demon (Skt. *mara*; Tib. *bdud*) This term is used to designate either a malevolent spirit or, symbolically, a negative force or obstacle on the path. The four demons (*bdud bzhi*), or maras, are of the latter kind. The demon of the aggregates refers to the five *skandhas* (body, feeling, perception, conditioning factors, and consciousness) as described in Buddhist teachings, which form the basis of suffering in samsara. The demon of the emotions refers to the conflicting emotions, which provoke suffering. The demon of death refers not only to death itself but also to the momentary transience of all phenomena, the nature of which is suffering. The demon child of the gods refers to mental wandering and the attachment to phenomena apprehended as truly existent.

deva (Skt.; Tib. *lha*) Gods, the highest of the six classes of samsaric beings, who enjoy the temporal bliss of the heavenly state.

Devaraja (Skt.; Tib. *bde wa ra dza*) One of the Indian lineage masters of the Dzogchen teachings, who was a disciple of Manjushri Bhadra and the teacher of Buddhagupta.

development and completion (Tib. *bskyed rdzogs*) The two principal phases of tantric practice. The development stage (*bskyed rim*) involves meditation on sights, sounds, and thoughts as deities, mantras, and wisdom, respectively. The completion stage (*rdzogs rim*) refers to the dissolution of visualized forms into and the experience of emptiness. It also indicates meditation on the subtle channels, energies, and essential substances of the body. Development and completion may also refer to the first two inner tantras, Maha and Anu.

Dhahena Talo (Skt.; Tib. *dha he na ta lo*) A king of Oddiyana who was a direct disciple of Prahevajra and Manjushrimitra. He was the father of Princess Parani and Prince Rajahasti, and the teacher of Rajahasti.

Dhahena (Skt.; Tib. *dha he na*) The place where Shri Singha lived when he taught Vairotsana and Lekdrub. It has not been determined whether this is situated in Oddiyana or in central India.

Dhanakosha (Skt.; Tib. *dha na ko sha*) Treasury of Wealth. An island in Oddiyana, or present-day western India, encircled by many sublime kinds of trees, which is why it is called Treasury of Wealth.

dharani (Skt.; Tib. *gzungs*) A verbal formula, often quite long, blessed by a buddha or a bodhisattva, similar to the mantras of the Vajrayana but found in the sutra tradition. The term is also used to refer to the siddhi of unfailing memory.

Dharma protector (Skt. *dharmapala*; Tib. *chos skyong*) The Dharma protectors guard the teachings from being diluted and their transmission from being disturbed or distorted. Protectors are sometimes emanations of buddhas or bodhisattvas and sometimes spirits, gods, or demons that have been subjugated by a great spiritual master and bound under oath.

Dharma Senge (Tib. *dha rma seng ge*) A master who lived in the nineteenth century and was a teacher of Shukseb Jetsun and a student of the first Dodupchen Rinpoche.

Dharma (Skt.; Tib. *chos*) The common term for the Buddhist doctrine. In its widest sense it means all that can be known. In this text, the term is used exclusively to indicate the teaching of the Buddha. It has two aspects: the Dharma of transmission (*lung gi chos*), namely, the teachings that are actually given, and the Dharma of realization (*rtogs pa'i chos*), or the states of wisdom, etc., that are attained through the application of the teachings. *Dharma* can also simply mean "phenomena."

dharmadhatu (Skt.; Tib. *chos dbyings*) The absolute expanse; emptiness pervaded with awareness.

dharmakaya (Skt.; Tib. *chos sku*) The first of the three kayas, which is devoid of constructs, like space. The body of enlightened qualities. See *three kayas*.

dharmapalas (Skt.; Tib. *chos skyong*) Protectors of the teachings. These are either enlightened beings or spirits and gods who have been subjugated by great masters and bound under oath to guard the teachings. Their task is to protect the doctrine, its upholders, and practitioners. See **Dharma protector**.

dharmata (Skt.; Tib. *chos nyid*) The innate nature of phenomena and mind; emptiness.

Dilgo Khyentse Rinpoche (Tib. *ldil mgo mkhyen brtse rin po che*) (1910–91) Treasure revealer who was regarded by followers of all the four schools as one of the greatest Tibetan masters of the last century.

distinguishing, resolving, and self-liberation (Tib. *shan 'byed, la bzla, rang grol*) The three essential points in *trekcho* meditation, corresponding to the three categories of the Mind Class scriptures.

duality (Tib. *gnyis 'dzin, gzung 'dzin*) The ordinary perception of unenlightened beings. The apprehension of phenomena in terms of subject and object and the belief in their true existence.

Dusong Mangpoje (Tib. *'dus srong mang po rje*) King Mangsong Mangtsen's son, who ruled Tibet 676–704.

Dzogchen (Tib. *rdzogs chen*) The highest teaching of the Nyingma. See **Ati**.

Dzongsar Khyentse Rinpoche (Tib. *rdzongs gsar mkhyen brtse rin po che*) Reincarnation of Jamyang Chokyi Lodro, who was regarded as the greatest Tibetan master of the last century.

Early and Later Translation (Tib. *sNga 'gyur phyi 'gyur*) In this text this refers to the Eighteen Major Scriptures of the Mind Class.

Early Translation (Tib. *snga 'gyur*) Refers to the Nyingma school.

eight charnel grounds (Tib. *dur khrod brgyad*) Frightening places where dakas and dakinis meet, which internally correspond to the eight consciousnesses.

eight classes of gods and demons (Tib. *lha srin sde brgyad*) According to the sutras, these are the devas, nagas, yakshas, gandharvas, asuras, garudas, kinnaras, and mahoragas, all of whom were able to receive and practice the Buddha's teachings. These eight classes can also refer to eight types of mundane spirits that can help or harm but are invisible to human beings: *ging, mara, tsen, yaksha, rakshasa, mamo, rahula,* and *naga*.

Eight Sadhana Teachings (Tib. *sGrub pa bka' brgyad*) Eight chief yidam deities of Maha Yoga and their corresponding tantras and sadhanas: Manjushri Body, Lotus Speech, Vishuddha Mind, Nectar Quality, Kilaya Activity, Liberating Sorcery of Mother Deities, Maledictory Fierce Mantra, and Mundane Worship.

eight vehicles (Tib. *theg pa brgyad*) Of the nine vehicles these are the first eight, which depend on cause and effect. The nine vehicles comprise the three vehicles of the sutras—those of the shravakas, pratyekabuddhas, and bodhisattvas—and the six vehicles of Kriya, Upa, Yoga, Maha Yoga, Anu Yoga, and Ati Yoga tantras.

They can also be grouped into three vehicles: Hinayana, which includes the first two; Mahayana, the third one; and Vajrayana, the last six.

Eighteen Major Scriptures of the Mind Class (Tib. *Sems sde bco brgyad*) A set of Dzogchen tantras taught by Shri Singha to Vairotsana and Tsang Lekdrub, of which the first five were translated by Vairotsana before his exile to Tsawarong and the remaining thirteen were later translated by Vimalamitra and Yudra Nyingpo.

Eighteen Root Tantras of Maha Yoga (Tib. *Ma ha yo ga'i rgyud sde bco brgyad*) Five root tantras of body, speech, mind, quality, and activity: *Sarvabuddha Samayoga, Secret Moon Essence, Gathering of Secrets, Glorious Supreme Primal Tantra,* and *Activity Garland.* Five display tantras related to sadhana practice: *Heruka Display Tantra, Supreme Steed Display Tantra, Compassion Display Tantra, Nectar Display Tantra,* and *Twelvefold Kilaya Tantra.* Five tantras related to conduct: *Mountain Pile, Awesome Wisdom Lightning, Arrangement of Precepts, One-Pointed Samadhi,* and *Rampant Elephant Tantra.* Two subsequent tantras for amending incompleteness: *Magical Net of Vairochana* and *Skillful Lasso.* The one outstanding tantra that epitomizes them all is the *Essence of Secrets, the Tantra of the Magical Net of Vajrasattva,* known as the *Guhyagarbha.*

Eighteen Tantras of the Mind Class (Tib. *Sems sde bco brgyad*) See *Eighteen Major Scriptures of the Mind Class.*

Embodiment of Realization (Tib. *dGongs 'dus*) Abbreviation of the *Scripture of the Embodiment of the Realization of All Buddhas;* the most important Anu Yoga scripture.

empowerment (Skt. *abhisheka*; Tib. *dbang*) The authorization to practice the Vajrayana teachings, which is the indispensable entrance to tantric practice. It enables one to master one's innate vajra body, speech, and mind and regard forms as deities, sound as mantras, and thought as wisdom.

empowerment of direct anointment (Tib. *rgyal thabs spyi blugs*) Empowerment without any ritual or visual process; the complete and instantaneous transfer of enlightened realization from mind to mind. *rgyal thabs* refers to the means of the conqueror, and *spyi lugs* to the pouring of the transmission, like a king pouring sovereignty to his heir.

emptiness (Skt. *shunyata*; Tib. *stong pa nyid*) The ultimate nature of phenomena.

enlightenment (Skt. *bodhi*; Tib. *byang chub*) Generally means the state of buddhahood, characterized by the perfection of the accumulations of merit and wisdom and by the removal of the two obscurations. It can also refer to the lower stages of enlightenment of an arhat or pratyekabuddha.

eon (Skt. *kalpa*; Tib. *bskal pa*) World age; cosmic cycle. A great kalpa corresponds to a cycle of formation and destruction of a universe and is divided into eighty intermediate kalpas. An intermediate kalpa is composed of one small kalpa during which life span, etc., increase and one small kalpa during which they decrease.

equality, evenness (Skt. *samata*; Tib. *mnyam pa nyid*) The fact that all things have the nature of emptiness.

Essence of Secrets (Skt. *Guhyagarbha*; Tib. *gSang ba'i snying po*) The widely renowned tantra of the Early Translation, which is the chief of the Eighteen Maha Yoga Tantras.

expedient and definitive meanings (Skt. *neyartha, nitharta*; Tib. *drang don dang nges don*)The expedient meaning refers to conventional teachings on the Four Noble Truths, karma, path, and result, which are designed to lead the practitioner to the definitive meaning, the insight into emptiness, suchness, and buddha-nature.

feast offering (Skt. *ganachakra*; Tib. *tshogs 'khor*)A ritual offering in tantric Buddhism in which oblations of food and drink are blessed as the elixir of wisdom and offered to the yidam deity as well as to the mandala of one's own body in order to purify breaches of one's sacred commitments.

fierce mantras (Tib. *drag ngags*) A type of mantra belonging to the wrathful deities that is used to dispel demonic forces that obstruct the Buddhist doctrine or the welfare of beings.

five conflicting emotions (Tib. *nyon mongs lnga*) Ignorance, desire, anger, jealousy, and pride.

Five Early Translations (Tib. *sNga 'gyur lnga*) The Dzogchen Mind Class scriptures that were translated by Vairotsana.

five elements (Tib. *'byung ba lnga*) Earth, water, fire, and wind or air, as principles of solidity, liquidity, heat, movement, and space.

five eminent beings (Tib. *dra ma lnga*) The five eminent beings were a god called Renowned Chief Protector (Skt. *Yasasvi Varapala*), a naga called Naga King Takshaka, a yaksha called Meteor Face (Skt. *Ulkamukha*), an ogre called Skillful Intellect (Skt. *Matyaupayika*), and a human being called Stainless Reputation (Skt. *Vimalakirti*). Some sources mention the god Indra in place of Vimalakirti. Through their supernatural cognitive powers these five noble beings knew that the Buddha had passed away and then miraculously gathered at Mount Malaya.

five families (Skt. *panchakula*; Tib. *rigs lnga*) The five buddha families: Tathagata, Vajra, Ratna, Padma, and Karma. They represent five aspects of the innate qualities of our enlightened essence. Each of them is presided over by a buddha: respectively, Vairochana, Akshobhya, Ratnasambhava, Amitabha, and Amoghasiddhi.

five greatnesses (Tib. *che ba lnga*) The greatness of direct manifestation of enlightenment; the greatness of enlightenment in the ultimate dimension of phenomena; the greatness of enlightenment in the dharmakaya; the greatness of enlightenment that proves its own nature; and the greatness of the absolute nonexistence of enlightenment.

five kayas (Skt. *panchakaya*; Tib. *sku lnga*) In the Mahayana, the transcendent reality of perfect buddhahood is described in terms of two, three, four, or five bodies, or *kayas*. The two bodies, in the first case, are the dharmakaya, the Body of Truth, and the rupakaya, the Body of Form. The dharmakaya is the absolute or "emptiness" aspect of buddhahood. The rupakaya is subdivided into the sambhogakaya, the Body of Perfect Enjoyment, and the nirmanakaya, the Body of Manifestation. The sambhogakaya, or the spontaneous clarity aspect of buddhahood, is perceptible only to beings of extremely high realization. The nirmanakaya, the compassionate aspect, is perceptible to ordinary beings and appears in the world most often in human form. The system of four bodies consists of the three just referred to together with the svabhavikakaya, or Body of Suchness, which refers to the union of the previous three.

five paths (Skt. *panchamarga*; Tib. *lam lnga*) The paths of accumulation, joining, seeing, meditation, and beyond training. These five paths cover the entire path from sincerely beginning Dharma practice to complete enlightenment.

five poisons (Tib. *nyon mongs lnga*) The five conflicting emotions of anger, desire, ignorance, jealousy, and pride.

five precious things (Tib. *rin chen lnga*) Gold, silver, turquoise, coral, and pearl.

five sciences (Tib. *rig pa'i gnas lnga*) The five disciplines of grammar, dialectics, healing, philosophy, and "arts and crafts."

five wisdoms (Skt. *panchajnana*; Tib. *ye shes lnga*) The five wisdoms of buddhahood corresponding to the five buddha families: mirror-like wisdom (Vajra family), wisdom of equality (Ratna, or Jewel family), all-discerning wisdom (Padma, or Lotus family), all-accomplishing wisdom (Karma, or Action family) and wisdom of dharmadhatu (Tathagata family). They represent five distinctive functions of our enlightened essence.

Five-Peaked Mountain (Tib. *ri bo rtse lnga*) In Chinese, Wutaishan. A place in eastern China sacred to Manjushri, where Vimalamitra is supposed to reside.

formless realm (Tib. *gzugs med khams*) The four highest states of samsaric existence.

four continents (Tib. *gling bzhi*) The four continents located in the four directions around Mount Meru, constituting a universe. They are the semi-circular Sublime Body in the east; the trapezoidal Land of Rose Apples in the south; the circular Bountiful Cow in the west; and the square Unpleasant Sound in the north.

four empowerments (Skt. *abhisheka*; Tib. *dbang*)The transference of wisdom power from the master to disciples that authorizes and enables them to engage in a practice and reap its fruit. There are four levels of tantric empowerment. The first is the vase empowerment, which purifies the defilements and obscurations associated with the body, grants the blessings of the vajra body, authorizes the disciples to practice the yogas of the development stage, and enables them to attain the nirmanakaya. The second is the secret empowerment. This purifies the defilements and obscurations of the speech faculty, grants the blessings of vajra speech, authorizes disciples to practice the yogas of the perfection stage, and enables them to attain the sambhogakaya. The third is the wisdom empowerment, which purifies the defilements and obscurations associated with the mind, grants the blessings of the vajra mind, authorizes disciples to practice the yogas of the skillful path, and enables them to attain the dharmakaya. The final empowerment, which is often simply referred to as the fourth initiation, is the word empowerment. This purifies the defilements of body, speech, and mind and all karmic and cognitive obscurations; it grants the blessings of primordial wisdom, authorizes disciples to engage in the practice of Dzogchen, and enables them to attain the svabhavikakaya.

four kayas (Tib. *sku bzhi*) The dharmakaya, sambhogakaya, and nirmanakaya as well as the svabhavikakaya, the kaya of the nature as it is, which represents the inseparability of the first three.

Four Truths (Tib. *bden pa bzhi*) The truths of suffering, origin, cessation, and path expounded by the Buddha Shakyamuni in his first teaching. These teachings, referred to as the first turning of the Dharma wheel, are the foundation of the Hinayana and Mahayana teachings.

fruition (Skt. *phala*; Tib. *'bras bu*) The result of the path; the state of perfect enlightenment.

gandharva (Skt.; Tib. *dri za*) Literally, "scent eater," a member of a class of nonhumans who are said to be nourished on smells. They are also a type of celestial musician living on the rim of Mount Meru in cloudlike castles. The metaphor "city of gandharvas" is used to point out the illusoriness of phenomena.

Garab Dorje (Skt. *Prahevajra*; Tib. *dga' rab rdo rje*) The first human vidyadhara in the Dzogchen lineage.

garuda (Tib. *khyung*) A kind of bird, in both the Indian and Tibetan traditions. A creature of great size, immediately upon hatching it is able to fly. A symbol of primordial wisdom.

gods (Skt. *deva*; Tib. *lha*) According to the Buddhist tradition, a class of beings that is superior to humans, which although not immortal enjoy immense power, bliss, and longevity. The term is also used to refer to powerful spirits as well as to the deities visualized in tantric meditation, which are not to be understood as "gods" in the ordinary sense of the word.

Gomadevi (Skt.; Tib. *go ma de byi*) A princess who was one of the Indian lineage masters of the Dzogchen teachings. She was a disciple of the scholar Maharaja and the teacher of Atsantra Aloke.

Great Perfection (Skt. *mahasandhi*; Tib. *rdzogs pa chen po*) The ultimate view of the Nyingma school. See *Ati, Ati Yoga*.

Great Space Vajrasattva (Tib. *rDo rje sems dpa' namkha' che*) The thirtieth chapter (volume *ka*) of the *All-Creating Monarch Tantra*, which is the fundamental tantra of the Dzogchen Mind Class scriptures. It is said that Prahevajra recited this after he was born. Also called *Vajrasattva, Great Space Tantra*.

Great Vehicle (Skt. *mahayana*; Tib. *theg pa chen po*) See **Mahayana**.

Guhyagarbha (Skt.; Tib. *gSang ba'i snying po*) *Essence of Secrets*. The chief Maha Yoga tantra of the Nyingma school.

guhyakaya (Skt.; Tib. *gsangs ba'i sku*) Esoteric form.

Gungsong Gungtsen (Tib. *gung srong gung btsan*) King Songtsen Gampo's son, who ruled Tibet for a few years but died at the age of nineteen.

Gya Lodro Shonnu (Tib. *rgya blo gros gzhon nu*) One of Yudra Nyingpo's main disciples who became a lineage holder.

Gyalmo Tsawarong (Tib. *rgyal mo tsha ba rong*) District between eastern Tibet and China.

habitual tendencies (Skt. *vasana*; Tib. *bag chags*) Habitual patterns of thought, speech, or action.

Hashang (Tib. *ha shang*) A Chinese Buddhist master who was invited to Tibet by King Songtsen Gampo. Also mentioned as one of the Chinese yogis that Vairotsana received teachings from in China.

hearing lineage of individuals (Tib. *gang zag snyan rgyud*) The orally transmitted lineage through individuals in which it is necessary for the teacher to use words for the disciple to hear, rather than transmitting them mind-to-mind or through symbols.

Heaven of the Thirty-three (Tib. *sum cu tsa gsum lha'i gnas*) See **Thirty-three**.

hell (Skt. *naraka*; Tib. *dmyal ba*) One of the six realms where beings experience intense suffering as a result of past actions, especially those actions related to anger, such as killing. There are eighteen different hells, eight hot and eight cold as well as neighboring hells and ephemeral hells.

Hepori (Tib. *has po ri*) A small mountain near Samye that is considered to be one of the four sacred mountains in Tibet.

heretic (Tib. *mu stegs pa*) Non-Buddhist. Refers to teachers of non-Buddhist philosophies who adhere to the extreme views of eternalism or nihilism.

Heruka (Skt.; Tib. *khrag 'thung*) Literally, "blood drinker." A wrathful deity, drinker of the blood of ego-clinging.

Hinayana (Skt.; Tib. *theg dman*)The fundamental system of Buddhist thought and practice deriving from the first turning of the wheel of Dharma and centering around the teachings on the Four Noble Truths and the twelvefold chain of dependent arising.

Humkara (Skt.; Tib. *hung ka ra*) He was born in a Brahmin family in Nepal and was an expert in the Vedas. He later became a Buddhist and got ordained at Nalanda. He became an expert in the teachings of the prajnaparamita and the Secret Mantra. In the Sitavana charnel ground he was given the casket containing the transmitted precepts of Vishuddha, through which he attained accomplishment. He benefited beings through his teachings on the development and perfection stages, on which he wrote many treatises. He passed away by flying to the pure land of Akshobhya and his main disciples were Avadhuti and Buddhashrisanti of Oddiyana.

ignorance (Skt. *avidya*; Tib. *ma rig pa*) In a Buddhist context, ignorance is not mere nescience; it is mistaken apprehension. It is the incorrect understanding of, or failure to recognize, the ultimate nature of beings and phenomena and falsely ascribing true existence to them.

Illuminating Blazing Gem (Tib. *gsal byed rin po che 'bar ba'i dkyil 'khor*) Name of the mandala through which direct pointing out of the mind essence is given.

Indra (Skt.; Tib. *dbang po*) The supreme god and king of the Heaven of the Thirty-three. Indra is regarded as a protector of the Buddhist doctrine. He resides on the summit of Mount Sumeru in the Palace of Complete Victory and is also known as Shakra (*brgya byin*), the ruler of the devas.

Indrabhuti (Skt.; Tib. *indra bhu ti*) King of Oddiyana who found, fostered, and for a time protected Padmasambhava.

innate nature (Skt. *dharmata*; Tib. *chos nyid*) The true nature of phenomena.

Instruction Class (Tib. *man ngag gi sde*) The third division of Ati Yoga, as arranged by Manjushrimitra.

Iron Mule (Tib. *lcags drel*) A practice to accomplish speed walking.

Jambu continent (Skt. *Jampudvipa*; Tib. *'dzam bu gling*) The world in which we live. Literally, "the Land of Rose Apples," the continent south of Mount Meru.

Jnanagarbha (Skt.; Tib. *ye shes snying po*) A master of Nalanda University and the ordaining abbot of Shantarakshita. He was an exponent of the "upper school" of Svatantrika Madhyamaka and the author of the celebrated *Two Truths of the Middle Way*.

Jokhang (Tib. *jo khang*) The main temple in Lhasa that was built by Songtsen Gampo and that housed the Shakyamuni image brought to Tibet by his wife.

Jomo Menmo (1248–83) (Tib. *jo mo sman mo*) Female treasure revealer. She was an emanation of Yeshe Tsogyal, the main consort of Padmasambhava, and was one of the wives of the great *terton* Guru Chowang (1212–70). She rediscovered one version of the *Great Image*.

Kahma (Tib. *bka' ma*) The oral lineage of the Nyingma school, the teachings translated chiefly during the period of Padmasambhava's stay in Tibet and transmitted from master to student until the present day.

Kailash (Tib. *ti se*) Sacred mountain in western Tibet, also known as Mount Tisey.

kalantaka (Tib. *ka lan ta ka*) A solitary bird that always dwells apart from others.

karma (Skt.; Tib. *las*) Action, the unerring law of cause and effect according to which all experiences are the result of previous actions and all actions are the seeds of future existential situations. Actions resulting in the experience of happiness are defined as virtuous; actions that give rise to suffering are described as nonvirtuous.

Kawa Paltsek (Tib. *ska ba dpal brtsegs*) One of the Tibetan translators who were predicted by Padmasambhava at the time of Trisong Deutsen. While Vairotsana and Namkhai Nyingpo were sent to India, Kawa Paltsek stayed at Samye and translated the sutras and mantra teachings. Later, he went to India to invite Vimalamitra to Tibet. He is considered the second greatest translator and was one of the twenty-five close disciples of Padmasambhava.

Khasarpani year (Tib. *kha sar pa ni'i lo*) Possibly a period of six months.

Khon Lui Wangpo (Tib. *'khon klu'i dbang po*) One the seven men to be tested, the first seven monks ordained by Shantarakshita. Another of the twenty-five close disciples of Padmasambhava. According to the *Chronicles*, Kawa Paltsek was sent to India with Chokro Lui Gyaltsen, not Khon Lui Wangpo, to invite Vimalamitra to Tibet.

Khotan (Tib. *li yul*) Located in Chinese Turkestan, Khotan was one of the greatest Buddhist centers during the first millennium A.D.

Kilaya (Skt.; Tib. *phurba*) The activity aspect of all the buddhas, a wrathful manifestation of Vajrasattva. The practice of this deity is related to the four aspects of the Kila: the ritual object, compassion, bodhichitta, and awareness-wisdom.

King Ja (Tib. *rgyal po dza*) The first human recipient of the Maha Yoga tantras and an important figure in the transmission of Anu Yoga. Some sources say he is the same as King Indrabhuti, also known as Indrabodhi.

kinnara (Skt.; Tib. *mi 'am ci*) A mythical creature that is half man and half animal. Along with the gandharvas, the kinnaras are celebrated as celestial musicians.

klesha (Skt.; Tib. *nyon mongs pa*) Conflicting emotions. Mental factors that produce states of mental torment both immediately and in the long term. See *five poisons*.

Kriya (Skt.; Tib. *bya ba*) The tantra of activity, which is the first of the three outer tantras. Kriya Tantra emphasizes ritual cleanliness—cleanliness of the mandala and the sacred substances—and physical cleanliness of the practitioner, who practices ablutions, changes clothes three times a day, and eats specific foods.

kshatriya (Skt.; Tib. *rgyal rigs*) One of the four classes of the ancient Indian social system, the warrior or royal caste.

Kukkuraja (Skt.; Tib. *khyi 'i rgyal po*) King of Dogs. He is so called because in the daytime he taught a thousand warriors and yoginis in the guise of a dog, and at night they would perform feast offerings and other practices in the charnel grounds. There were two Kukkurajas, the Elder and the Younger; the Younger is also called Dhahuna.

Kumara (Skt.; Tib. *ku ma ra*) One of the swift-footed border guards in India who became Vairotsana's friend.

Kungamo (Tib. *kun dga' mo*) One of the Indian Dzogchen lineage masters, a disciple of Shri Singha.

lama (Skt. *guru*; Tib. *bla ma*) Tibetan term for a highly realized spiritual teacher. In colloquial language it is sometimes used as a polite way of addressing a monk.

Lekdrub of Tsang (Tib. *gtsang legs grub*) Vairotsana's companion on the journey to India. After receiving transmission from Shri Singha, he decided to return to Tibet but was killed by border guards. He reincarnated as Yudra Nyingpo in Tsawarong.

level (Skt. *bhumi*; Tib. *sa*) The levels or stages of a bodhisattva on the way to perfect enlightenment.

Lhasa (Tib. *lha sa*) Literally means "abode of the gods." The capital of Tibet.

Lha Thothori Nyenshel (Tib. *lha tho tho ri snyan shal*) Born in 374 C.E., he was the first Dharma king of Tibet and the twenty-eighth hereditary king. He was also an emanation of the bodhisattva Samantabhadra. Also known as Lha Thothori Nyentsen.

Lord of Secrets (Tib. *gsang ba'i bdag po*) Synonym for Vajrapani, an emanation of Vajrasattva and the compiler of the tantric teachings.

lotsawa (Skt. *locchava*; Tib. *lo tsa ba*) Tibetan translators of the canonical texts who usually worked closely with Indian panditas. The title literally means "bilingual."

lower realms (Tib. *ngan song*) The hell, hungry ghost, and animal realms.

luminosity (Skt. *prabhasvara*; Tib. *'od gsal*) The clarity or knowing aspect of the mind. Refers to being free from the darkness of unknowing and endowed with the ability to cognize.

Magadha (Skt.; Tib. *ma ga dha*) Present-day Bihar, in central India.

Mahamudra (Skt.; Tib. *phyag rgya chen po*) Literally, "Great Seal." This refers to the seal of the absolute nature of all phenomena. The term is used for the teaching, the practice, and the supreme accomplishment.

Maharaja (Skt.; Tib. *ma ha ra dza*) An abbot from Oddiyana who was one of the Dzogchen lineage masters. He was a disciple of Rabnang and the teacher of Princess Gomadevi.

Mahayana (Skt.; Tib. *theg pa chen po*) The Great Vehicle. The characteristic of Mahayana is the profound view of the emptiness of the ego and of all phenomena coupled with universal compassion and the desire to deliver all beings from suffering and its causes.

Maha Yoga (Skt.; Tib. *rnal 'byor chen po*) The first of the three inner tantras. Maha Yoga scripture is divided into the Tantra Section and the Sadhana Section. The Tantra Section consists of the Eighteen Maha Yoga Tantras, and the Sadhana Section of the *Eight Sadhana Teachings*. The Maha Yoga scriptures emphasize the means of the development stage and the view that liberation is attained by growing accustomed to insight into the nature of the indivisibility of the two truths.

major and minor marks of a Buddha (Tib. *mtshan dang dpe byad*) Thirty-two major physical signs of realization (e.g., the *ushnisha*, or crown protuberance) and eighty minor characteristics (e.g., copper-colored fingernails) that are typical of a buddha.

mamo (Skt.; Tib. *ma mo*) A class of semi-divine beings who sometimes act as protectors of the Dharma.

mandala (Skt.; Tib. *dkyil 'khor*) Literally, "center and surrounding." A mandala is a symbolic graphic representation of a deity's realm of existence.

Mangsong Mangtsen (Tib. *mang srong mang btsan*) Songtsen Gampo's nephew, who ruled Tibet after Songtsen Gampo until his son Dusong Mangpoje took over.

Manjushri (Skt.; Tib. *'jam dpal dyangs*) One of the eight main bodhisattvas who personifies the perfection of transcendent knowledge.

Manjushrimitra (Skt.; Tib. *'jam dpal gshad snyan*) Second human master in the lineage of the Great Perfection and the chief disciple of Prahevajra. He divided the Dzogchen teachings into the Mind Class, the Space Class, and the Instruction Class.

mantra (Skt.; Tib. *sngags*) Syllables or formulas that, when recited with appropriate visualizations, etc., protect the mind of the practitioner from ordinary perceptions. They are invocations and manifestations of the yidam deity in the form of sound.

Mantrayana (Skt.; Tib. *gsang sngags*) See **Vajrayana**.

mara (Skt.; Tib. *bdud*) See **demon**.

Margyen (Tib. *mar rgyan*) Red Ornament. This queen was the senior consort of Trisong Deutsen and bore him three sons. According to some sources, she poisoned her son Mune Tsenpo when he came to power because he married his father's younger consort Phoyongza. She was in favor of the Bon tradition and openly hostile to Buddhist teachers.

meditate, meditation (Tib. *sgom pa*) To let the mind rest on an object of contemplation. Alternatively, to maintain the flow of the view.

Mind Class (Tib. *sems sde,*) The first of the three divisions of Ati Yoga.

mind essence (Tib. *sems nyid, dgongs pa'i bcud*) The nature of one's mind, which is taught to be identical to the essence of all enlightened beings. It should be distinguished from "mind" (*sems*), which refers to ordinary discursive thinking based on ignorance of the nature of thought.

mind lineage through the Conquerors (Tib. *rig 'dzin brda brgyud*) The transmission of the teachings from mind to mind, according to this text, from Samantabhadra up to and including Prahevajra.

Mount Malaya (Skt. *Malayagiri;* Tib. *ri ma la ya*) The place where the Lord of Secrets taught the Secret Mantra to the five noble beings, situated on present-day Sri Lanka. It is now known as Adam's Peak.

Mount Meru (Tib. *ri rab*) The mythological mountain at the center of our world-system surrounded by the four continents where the two lowest classes of gods of the world of desire live. It is encircled by chains of lesser mountains, lakes, continents, and oceans and is said to have an altitude of eighty-four thousand leagues above sea level.

mudra (Skt.; Tib. *phyag rgya*) Can refer to a gesture, a spiritual consort, or the bodily form of a deity.

Naga King Nanda (Tib. *klu'i rgyal po 'dga' bo*) One of the Indian Dzogchen lineage masters, a disciple of Prahevajra, Prince Rajahasti, and Princess Parani, and the teacher of Yakshini Changchubma.

naga (Skt.; Tib. *klu*) Powerful, long-living serpent-like beings dwelling in water domains and often guarding great treasures. Nagas belong half to the animal realm and half to the god realm. They generally live in the form of snakes, but many can change into human form.

Nagarjuna (Skt.; Tib. *klu grub*) Great Indian master of philosophy and a tantric siddha. He received the Lotus Speech tantras, which he accomplished and transmitted to Padmasambhava. He recovered the Prajnaparamita sutras from the land of the nagas and was the founder of the Madhyamaka philosophy. According to this text, he is a disciple of Dagnyima and the teacher of Kukkuraja.

Nalanda (Skt.; Tib. *na lan dra*) The famous monastic university built at the birthplace of Shariputra some distance north of Bodhgaya in Bihar. Nalanda had a long and illustrious history, and many of the greatest masters of the Mahayana lived, studied, and taught there. It was destroyed in 1200 C.E.

nectar (Skt. *amrita*; Tib. *bdud rtsi*) The ambrosia of the gods that confers immortality or other powers.

Ngam Tara Lugong (Tib. *ngam ta ra klu gong*) One of the most influential Bon ministers during the reign of King Trisong Deutsen.

nigu (Tib. *ni gu*) A female soothsayer.

nine vehicles (Tib. *theg pa dgu*) The traditional classification of the Dharma according to the Nyingma school. The first three vehicles are known as the three causal vehicles of the shravakas, pratyekabuddhas, and bodhisattvas. Following these are the three vehicles of the outer tantras, namely, Kriya Yoga, Upa Yoga, and Yoga Tantras. Finally, there are the three vehicles of the inner tantras: Maha Yoga, Anu Yoga, and Ati Yoga Tantras.

Ninefold Expanse (Tib. *klong dgu*) Nine subdivisions of the Space Class teachings of the Great Perfection.

nirmanakaya (Skt.; Tib. *sprul sku*) Manifested body. The third of the three kayas. The aspect of enlightenment that can be perceived by ordinary beings.

nirvana (Skt.; Tib. *myang ngan 'das*) Literally, "the state beyond suffering." This term indicates the various levels of enlightenment attainable in both the Hinayana and Mahayana.

nonarising (Tib. *skye ba med pa*) In the aspect of ultimate truth, all phenomena are devoid of an independent, concrete identity, and therefore, they ultimately do not come into being, abide in time and place, or cease to exist.

nonconceptual (Tib. *mi dmigs*) Thought-free, not held in mind, free of all discursive activity.

Nub Namkhai Nyingpo (Tib. *snub nam mka'i snying po*) One of the translators who were sent to India by King Trisong Deutsen in order to search for the teachings. Along with his companions he studied the Yangdag Heruka doctrine with Master Humkara.

Nyag Jnana Kumara (Tib. *nyag ye shes gzhon nu*) Expert translator and disciple of Padmasambhava, Vimalamitra, Vairotsana, and Yudra Nyingpo. He worked closely with Vimalamitra in translating the Maha Yoga and Ati Yoga tantras.

Nyemo Chekar (Tib. *snye mo bye dkar*) Vairotsana's birthplace near Uyuk in the Nyemo area.

obscurations (Skt. *avarana*; Tib. *sgrib pa*) Mental factors that veil the true nature of the mind. In the general Buddhist teachings, several types are mentioned: the obscuration of karma preventing one from entering the path of enlightenment; the obscuration of disturbing emotions preventing progress along the path; the obscuration of habitual tendencies preventing the vanishing of confusion; and the final obscuration of dualistic knowledge preventing the full attainment of buddhahood.

Oddiyana year (Tib. *o rgyan gyi lo*) According to this text, a period of six months.

Oddiyana (Skt.; Tib. *o rgyan*) Also called Orgyen or Urgyen, a region in ancient India corresponding, according to some authorities, to the valley of Swat between Afghanistan and Kashmir. Oddiyana was the birthplace of Padmasambhava and Garab Dorje.

ogre (Skt. *raksha*; Tib. *srin po*) One of the eight classes of gods and demons. Also refers to the cannibal savages inhabiting the southwestern continent of Chamara. At times *raksha* refers to the unruly and untamed expression of ignorance and disturbing emotions.

oracular mirror (Tib. *pra se na*) A way of doing divination by looking at images in a mirror.

outer tantras (Tib. *phyi rgyud*) The tantras belonging to the three vehicles of Kriya, Upa, and Yoga.

Padmasambhava (Tib. *pad ma 'byung gnas*) Literally, "lotus born." Padmasambhava was predicted by the Buddha Shakyamuni as the one who would propagate the teachings of the Vajrayana. Invited to Tibet by King Trisong Deutsen in the ninth century, he subjugated the evil forces hostile to the propagation of the Buddhist doctrine there, spread the Secret Mantra teachings, and hid innumerable spiritual treasures for the sake of future generations.

Pagor Hedo (Tib. *pa gor he 'dod*) Vairotsana's father, though some sources claim he was Vairotsana's uncle who adopted his nephew after the father died.

Pam Mipham Gonpo (Tib. *spam mi pham mgon po*) A disciple of Vairotsana. He was one hundred years old when he met Vairotsana. After receiving the instructions from Vairotsana, he attained instant realization and became one of the lineage masters. It is said that all his disciples attained rainbow body.

Pam Sangye Gonpo (Tib. *spam sangs rgyas mgon po*) A disciple of Yudra Nyingpo who became one of the lineage holders.

pandita (Skt.; Tib. *pan di ta*) A learned master, scholar, or professor of Buddhist philosophy.

paramita (Skt.; Tib. *pha rol tu phyin pa*) A transcendent perfection or virtue, the practice of which leads to buddhahood and, therefore, forms the practice of bodhisattvas. There are six paramitas: generosity, ethical discipline, patience, diligence, concentration, and wisdom.

path (Skt. *marga*; Tib. *lam*) Progress toward enlightenment is described, in both the Mahayana and Hinayana, in terms of the five paths of accumulation, joining, seeing, meditation, and no more learning. The first four constitute the path of learning, whereas the path of no more learning is buddhahood.

perceptions (Tib. *snang ba*) That which appears to the eyes of each individual according to one's tendencies or spiritual development. There are three types of perception: (1) The deluded perceptions that arise in the consciousness of beings of the six realms due to misunderstanding are called the impure deluded perceptions of the universe and beings. (2) The perceptions of interdependence, magical illusions, corresponding to the eight similes of illusion that one does not apprehend as real; these are the perceptions of the bodhisattvas of the ten levels in their post-meditation state. (3) The authentic, perfect perceptions of wisdom; when one has realized the natural state of everything, beings and the universe appear as the display of the kayas and wisdoms.

pitaka(Skt.; Tib. *snod*) Literally, "basket." A collection of scriptures.

pith instructions (Skt. *upadesha*; Tib. *man ngag*) Instructions explaining the most profound points of practice in a condensed and direct way.

pointing-out instruction (Tib. *ngo sprod*) The direct introduction to the nature of mind that is given by the root guru and leads to the recognition of mind nature.

Prahevajra (Skt.; Tib. *dga' rabs rdo rje*) Commonly known as Garab Dorje. The name literally means "indestructible joy." He received all the tantras, scriptures, and oral instructions of Dzogchen from Vajrasattva and Vajrapani in person and became the first human vidyadhara in the Dzogchen lineage. Manjushrimitra is regarded as his chief disciple. He passed away 540 years after the Buddha's nirvana.

prajnaparamita (Skt.; Tib. *shes rab kyi pha rol tu phyin pa*) Either the paramita of transcendent wisdom, the knowledge of emptiness, or the collection of sutras belonging to the second turning of the Dharma wheel that expounds the doctrine of emptiness.

pratyekabuddha (Skt.; Tib. *rang sangs rgyas*) Literally, "solitary buddha." One who attains the cessation of suffering without relying on a teacher by meditating on the twelve links of dependent arising. Though realizing the emptiness of perceived phenomena, they lack the complete realization of a buddha and so cannot benefit limitless beings.

preta (Skt.; Tib. *yi dvags*) Famished spirits or hungry ghosts, one of the six classes of beings in samsara.

primordial purity (Tib. *ka dag*) The basic nature of sentient beings, which is originally untainted by defilement and beyond confusion and liberation.

Princess Parani (Tib. *sras mo pa ra ni*) King Dhahena Talo's daughter, who was one of the Indian Dzogchen lineage masters. She was a direct disciple of Prahevajra and Rajahasti and was the teacher of Naga King Nanda.

prostitute Barani (Tib. *smad 'tshong ma ba ra ni*) One of the Indian Dzogchen lineage masters; a disciple of Yakshini Changchubma and the teacher of the abbot Rabnang.

Pure Gold on Stone (Tib. *rDo la gser zhun*) A text written by Manjushrimitra as a confession to Prahevajra, which is one of the Eighteen Major Scriptures of the Mind Class.

pure land (Tib. *zhing khams*) A place or world manifested by a buddha or great bodhisattva through the spontaneous qualities of his realization. A place where beings can progress toward enlightenment without falling back into the lower realms of samsara. Also, any place whatsoever when it is perceived as a pure manifestation of spontaneous wisdom.

pure perception (Tib. *dag snang*) The perception of the world and its contents as a pure buddha-field or as the display of kayas and wisdoms.

putra (Skt.; Tib. *pu tra*) Spirits dwelling in charnel grounds.

Rajahasti the Elder (Tib. *thu bo ra dza ha ti*) Son of King Dhahena Talo, who was a direct disciple of Prahevajra and Manjushrimitra and the teacher of Princess Parani.

Resolving King's Cycle (Tib. *La bzla rgyal po'i skor*) The second of the three categories of Mind Class tantras.

Resultant Vehicle (Tib. *'bras bu'i theg pa*) Resultant Vehicle of the Secret Mantra. The Secret Mantra system of taking the fruition as the path by regarding buddhahood as inherently present and the path as the act of uncovering one's basic state. This is different from the "causal philosophical vehicles" of Mahayana and Hinayana that regard the path as that which leads to and produces the state of buddhahood. Ultimately, these two approaches are not in conflict.

rishi (Skt.; Tib. *drang srong*) Name given to the great sages of Indian mythology, who were endowed with great longevity and magical powers and were instrumental in the creation, or reception, of the Vedas. In the Buddhist context, this word is usually translated as sage, hermit, or saint.

sacred commitment (Skt. *samaya*; Tib. *dam tshig*) See ***samaya***.

sadhana (Skt.; Tib. *sgrub thabs*) Method of accomplishment. A tantric meditative practice involving visualization of deities and the recitation of mantra.

Saha (Skt.; Tib. *mi mjed*) The name of our present world system. *Saha* means "enduring" because sentient beings endure unbearable suffering here.

samadhi (Skt.; Tib. *bsam gtan*) Meditative absorption of different degrees.

Samantabhadra (Skt.; Tib. *kun tu bzang po*) Literally, "Ever-Excellent One." (1) Bodhisattva Samantabhadra, one of the eight close sons of the Buddha, renowned for his offerings emanated through the power of his concentration; (2) the primordial buddha who has never fallen into delusion and who is the symbol of awareness, the ever-present pure and luminous nature of the mind.

Samantabhadri (Skt.; Tib. *kun tu bzang mo*) The consort of the primordial Buddha Samantabhadra. Their union symbolizes the inseparability of the phenomenal world and emptiness.

samaya (Skt.; Tib. *dam tshig*) The commitment established between the master and disciples on whom empowerment is conferred.

sambhogakaya (Skt.; Tib. *longs spyod rdzogs pa'i sku*) Body of enjoyment.

samsara (Skt.; Tib. *'khor ba*) The wheel, or round, of existence; the state of being unenlightened in which the mind, enslaved by the three poisons of desire, anger, and ignorance, evolves uncontrolled from one state to another, passing through an endless stream of psychophysical experiences, all of which are characterized by suffering.

Samye (Tib. *bsam yas*) Literally "inconceivable." The first monastery in Tibet, it is located in the Tsangpo Valley southeast of Lhasa; built by King Trisong Deutsen, it was consecrated by Padmasambhava.

Sangha (Skt.; Tib. *dge 'dun*) The community of Buddhist practitioners, whether monastic or lay. The term *noble Sangha* refers to those members of the Buddhist community who have attained the path of seeing and beyond.

Sattvavajra (Skt.; Tib. *sems dpa rdo rje*) Another name for Vajrapani.

sattvayoga (Skt.; Tib. *sems dpa'i rnal 'byor*) Encompasses the contents of the three outer tantras, in particular Yoga Tantra.

scripture (Tib. *mdo, lung*) In this text, this refers to scriptures belonging to either Anu or Ati Yoga.

Scripture of the Embodiment of Realization (Tib. *mDo dgongs 'dus*) One of the four root tantras of Anu Yoga.

secret empowerment (Tib. *gsang ba'i dbang*) The second empowerment, which purifies the defilements of speech, enables one to meditate on the channels and energies and to recite mantras and plants the seed for obtaining the vajra speech and the sambhogakaya.

Secret Mantra (Tib. *gsang ngags*) A branch of the Great Vehicle that uses the special techniques of the tantras to traverse the path of enlightenment more rapidly for all beings.

self-existing wisdom (Tib. *rang byung ye shes*) Basic wakefulness that is independent of intellectual constructs.

sentient being (Tib. *sems can*) Any living being in the six realms who has not attained liberation.

seven men to be tested (Tib. *sad mi mi bdun*) The first seven fully ordained monks in Tibet, who were ordained by the abbot Shantarakshita. They were the minister

Ba Trhizi, Ba Selnang, Pagor Vairotsana, Ngenlam Gyalwa Chokyang, Ma Rinchen Chok, Khon Lui Wangpo, and Lasum Gyalwa Changchub. When the king decided they turned out well, he had Shantarakshita ordain another three hundred people.

shamatha (Skt.; Tib. *zhi gnas*) Essentially a concentration in which the mind remains focused on an object of concentration. It is a state of calm abiding, which, though of great importance, is incapable unto itself of overcoming ignorance and the conception of a self.

Shantarakshita (Skt.; Tib. *zhi ba mtsho*) Also known as Khenpo Bodhisattva. An emanation of the bodhisattva Vajrapani, he was the abbot of Vikramashila and Samye. He ordained the first monks in Tibet and was the founder of a philosophical school combining Madhyamaka and Yogachara.

Shantigarbha (Skt.; Tib. *zhi ba'i snying po*) One of the eight accomplished masters that gathered at the Sitavana charnel ground and received from the dakini Mahakarmendrani a casket containing the transmitted precepts of Maha Yoga. Shantigarbha received the casket containing the Malign Mantra and attained the accomplishment. He was invited to Tibet by Trisong Deutsen and propagated the Yamari cycle of teachings.

shastra (Skt.; Tib. *bstan bcos*) A commentary on the words of the Buddha.

shravaka (Skt.; Tib. *nyan thos*) A follower of Hinayana, whose goal is to be free of the sufferings of samsara. Unlike the followers of the Great Vehicle, shravakas do not aspire to full enlightenment for the sake of all beings.

Shravasimha. See Shravasinha.

Shravasinha (Skt.; Tib. *seng ge rab rten*) Steadfast Lion, the Muni of the animal realm. Also called Shravasimha.

Shri Singha (Skt.; Tib. *shri sing ha*) The chief disciple and successor of Manjushrimitra in the lineage of the Dzogchen teachings. He extracted the tantras that had been concealed in Bodhgaya and went to China, where he classified the Ati Yoga Instruction Class into four cycles: outer, inner, secret, and innermost secret. His main disciples were Jnanasutra, Vimalamitra, Padmasambhava, and Vairotsana.

siddha (Skt.; Tib. *grub thob*) One who has gained accomplishment through the practice of the Vajrayana.

siddhi (Skt.; Tib. *dngos grub*) See *accomplishment*.

single sphere (Tib. *thig le nyag gcig*) A symbolic description of dharmakaya being like a single sphere because it is devoid of duality and limitation and defies all conceptual constructs that could be formed about it.

Sitavana (Skt.; Tib. *sil bai' tshal*) Cool Grove, a sacred charnel ground to the northeast of Bodhgaya, which is inhabited by many dakinis and savage beings.

It has a great stupa, which contains many special tantras in caskets that were hidden by the dakinis. Padmasambhava practiced ascetics there for many years. Garab Dorje also spent many years there teaching the dakinis, and it was there that Manjushrimitra met him.

Six Munis (Tib. *thub pa drug*) In each of the six realms of beings, an emanation of the tathagatas acts on behalf of the beings of that realm.

Six Ornaments (Tib. *rgyan drug*) The six great Indian masters Nagarjuna, Asanga, Dignaga, Aryadeva, Vasubandhu, and Dharmakirti.

six realms (Tib. *rigs drug*) Six modes of existence caused and dominated by a particular mental poison: the realms of the hells (anger), pretas (miserliness), animals (ignorance), humans (desire), demigods (jealousy), and gods (pride). They correspond to deluded perceptions produced by karma and apprehended as real.

skillful means (Tib. *thabs*, Skt. *upaya*) This refers to compassion, the counterpart of the wisdom of emptiness. By extension, it refers to all kinds of action and training performed with the attitude of bodhichitta.

Songtsen Gampo (Tib. *srong btsan sgam po*) (609–49) An emanation of Avalokiteshvara who was the second Dharma king of Tibet and the fifth hereditary king after Lha Thothori Nyenshel. He married two Buddhist princesses, Bhrikuti of Nepal and Wen Cheng of China. He built the first Buddhist temples, established a code of laws based on Dharma principles, developed the Tibetan script with the help of his minister Thonmi Sambhota, and began the translation of Buddhist texts into Tibetan.

Space Class (Tib. *klong sde*) The second division of the Mind Class, which emphasizes emptiness.

speed walking, swift-footed (Tib. *rkang mgyogs*) The yogic art of being able to walk extremely fast, covering a huge distance in a short time through control of the inner currents of energy.

Spirit King (Tib. *rgyal 'gong*) A mischievous male spirit of a class of spirits born of the union of the *rgyal po* and *'gong po*.

spontaneous presence (Tib. *lhun grub*) One of the two main aspects of the Dzogchen teaching, the other being "primordial purity."

stupa (Skt.; Tib. *mchod rten*) Literally, "support of offering." Monuments often containing relics of Buddhist saints. Stupas are built according to universal principles of harmony and order. Often quite large, they focus and radiate healing energy throughout the six realms of existence.

suchness (Skt. *tathata*; Tib. *de bzhin nyid*) Synonym for emptiness or the nature of things, dharmata. It is also used to describe the unity of dependent origination and emptiness.

sugata (Skt.; Tib. *bde bar gshegs pa*) Literally, "one who has gone to and proceeds in bliss," an epithet of the buddhas.

sugatagarbha (Skt.; Tib. *bde gshegs snying po*) The potential for buddhahood, the luminous and empty nature of the mind.

Sukhavati (Skt.; Tib. *bde ba can*) Literally, "the Blissful,"; the name of the Western Paradise, the pure land of Buddha Amitabha.

Sutra Designed Like a Jewel Chest (Skt. *Karandavyuha-sutra*; Tib. *mDo sde za ma tog bkod pa*) A scripture on Avalokiteshvara that comes in the Mani Kahbum of King Songtsen Gampo.

Sutra of a Hundredfold Homage for Amendment of Breaches (Skt. *Sakshipuranasu-draka-sutra*; Tib. *dpang skong phyag brgya pa'i mdo*) The first Buddhist text that appeared in Tibet, which fell on to the roof of King Lha Thothori Nyenshel's palace during the fifth century and was translated by Thonmi Sambhota.

sutra (Skt.; Tib. *mdo*) A discourse or teaching by the Buddha. Also refers to all the causal teachings that regard the path as the cause of enlightenment.

svabhavikakaya (Skt.; Tib. *ngo bo nyid kyi sku*) Essence body, sometimes counted as the fourth kaya, and constituting the unity of the three kayas. Jamgon Kongtrul defines it as the aspect of dharmakaya that is "the nature of all phenomena, emptiness devoid of all constructs and endowed with the characteristic of natural purity."

symbol lineage through the vidyadharas (Tib. *rig 'dzin brda rgyud*) This lineage is transmitted through the awareness-holders by means of symbols or gestures; according to this text it goes from Manjushrimitra up to and including Vimalamitra.

Tantra Section (Tib. *rgyud sde*) One of the two divisions of Maha Yoga. The Maha Yoga tantras appeared in this world when revealed to King Ja by Vajrasattva and the Lord of Secrets.

tantra (Skt.; Tib. *rgyud*) Literally, "continuity." The Vajrayana teachings given by the Buddha in his sambhogakaya form. Tantra can also refer to all the resultant teachings of Vajrayana as a whole.

tantras, scriptures, and instructions (Tib. *rgyud lung man ngag*) Refers to the teachings of Maha Yoga, Anu Yoga, and Ati Yoga, respectively. Can also refer to the three categories of the fundamental scriptures of Dzogchen.

tathagata (Skt.; Tib. *de bzhin gshegs pa*) Literally, "one who has gone thus"; a synonym for fully enlightened buddha.

tathagatagarbha (Skt.; Tib. *de gshegs snying po*) Buddha-nature; the essence of enlightenment present in all sentient beings.

ten directions (Tib. *phyogs bcu*) The four cardinal and intermediary directions, together with the zenith and nadir.

ten levels (Tib. *sa bcu*) This refers to the ten stages of a noble bodhisattva's development into a fully enlightened buddha. On each stage more subtle defilements are purified and a further degree of enlightened qualities is manifested.

Ten Sutras (Tib. *mDo bcu*) An exposition tantra of the *All-Creating Monarch Tantra*.

terma (Tib. *gter ma*) Literally, "treasures." The transmission through concealed treasures hidden by Guru Rinpoche and Yeshe Tsogyal that are to be revealed at the proper time by a treasure revealer for the benefit of future disciples. It is one of the two chief traditions of the Nyingma school, the other being the Kahma tradition. This tradition is said to continue even long after the Vinaya of the Buddha will have disappeared.

terton (Tib. *gter ston*) A revealer of hidden treasures. Tertons are said to be reincarnations of Padmasambhava's close disciples who made the aspiration to benefit beings in the future.

Thinley Norbu Rinpoche (Tib. *phrin las nor bu rin po che*) A highly learned and realized being, he is one of the late Kyabje Dudjom Rinpoche's sons and holder of the Dudjom Tersar lineage. He lives in the United States and has published some of the most amazing books on Dharma written in English.

Thirteen Sutras (Tib. *mDo bcu gsum*) A set of scriptures belonging to the Mind Class.

Thirty-three (Skt. *Trayastrimsha*; Tib. *sum bcu rtsa gsum*) The second divine sphere of the desire realm, situated on the summit of Mount Meru and presided over by thirty-three gods of whom Indra is the chief.

Thonmi Sambhota (Tib. *thon mi sam bho tra*) An emanation of Manjushri who was a minister of King Songtsen Gampo. Sent to India by Songtsen Gampo to study grammar and writing, on the basis of the Indian scripts he created the forms of the Tibetan letters and composed eight treatises on the Tibetan alphabet.

Three Classes of Dzogchen (Tib. *rdzogs chen sde gsum*) After Garab Dorje established the six million four hundred thousand Dzogchen tantras in the human world, Manjushrimitra divided them into three categories: the Mind Class emphasizing luminosity; the Space Class emphasizing emptiness; and the Instruction Class emphasizing their inseparability.

three families (Tib. *rigs gsum*) The three main bodhisattvas: Samantabhadra, Avalokiteshvara, and Manjushri.

three inner tantras (Tib. *nang rgyud gsum*) Maha, Anu, and Ati. These three tantra classes are the special characteristics of the Nyingma school of the early translation. They are also known as "development, completion, and Great Perfection," or as "tantras, scriptures, and instructions."

three kayas (Tib. *sku gsum*) Dharmakaya, sambhogakaya, and nirmanakaya. The three kayas as ground are "essence, nature, and expression," as path they are "bliss, clarity, and nonthought," and as fruition they are the "three kayas of buddhahood." See *five kayas.*

three kinds of discipline (Tib. *tshul khrims gsum*) According to the Bodhisattva Vehicle these are gathering virtues, benefiting sentient beings, and refraining from misdeeds.

three kinds of wisdom (Tib. *shes rab gsum*) The discriminating wisdoms resulting from hearing, contemplating, and practicing the teachings.

three knowledges (Tib. *mkhyen pa gsum*) Basic knowledge, knowledge of the path, and omniscience.

three poisons (Tib. *dug gsum*) The three main afflictions of attachment, hatred, and ignorance.

three purities (Tib. *dag pa gsum*) In Kriya Tantra, the purity of deity and mantra, the purity of substance and rapture, and the purity of mantra and contemplation.

three samadhis (Tib. *ting nge 'dzin gsum*) In Maha Yoga, the samadhi of suchness, the all-illuminating samadhi, and the samadhi of the seed syllable.

three services (Tib. *zhabs tog gsum*) The best service to one's guru is the offering of one's practice, mediocre service is to serve one's guru with body and speech, and inferior service is the offering of material things.

three sweets (Tib. *mngar gsum*) Sugar, honey, and molasses.

three trainings (Skt. *trishika*; Tib. *bslabs pa gsum*) Trainings in ethical discipline, concentration, and discriminating knowledge. The three trainings form the basis of the Buddhist path.

three types of generosity (Tib. *sbyin pa gsum*) Generosity of material things, of protection from fear, and of the Dharma teachings.

three whites (Tib. *dkar gsum*) Curd, milk, and butter.

three worlds (Tib. *khams gsum*) The world of desire, the world of form, and the world of formlessness.

three-thousandfold world (Tib. *stong gsum*) A billionfold cosmic system of worlds, each of which comprises a Mount Meru and four cosmic continents.

Translation Hall (Tib. *sgra 'gyur gling*) One of the temples at Samye that was specifically used for translation. Samye was constructed according to the Buddhist view of the universe, with the main temple as Mount Meru and the surrounding temples like the four main continents, the eight subcontinents, and the sun and moon.

Tripitaka (Skt.; Tib. *sde snod gsum*) The three collections of the words of the Buddha (Vinaya, Sutra, and Abhidharma). Their purpose is the development of the three trainings of discipline, concentration, and discriminating knowledge, while their function is to remedy the three poisons of desire, anger, and ignorance.

Trisong Deutsen (Tib. *khri srong de'u btsan*) The third Dharma king of Tibet and an emanation of Manjushri. He appeared in the fifth reign after Songtsen Gampo and was thirteen years old when he started ruling the kingdom. He invited many masters to Tibet to propagate the true doctrine, built Samye, and established Buddhism as the state religion of Tibet. There are many different opinions about his birth and death dates.

Tsamunshri, Tsamuntri, Namdruma (Skt.; Tib. *tsa mun shri, tsa mun tri, nam gru ma*) Names of dakinis residing in the cemeteries.

Tsangpo (Skt. *Brahmaputra*; Tib. *gtsang po*) The river flowing past Samye.

Tsawarong (Tib. *tsha ba rong*)The river valley of Gyalmo Tsawarong in the far east of Kham.

Tsultrim Dron (Tib. *tshul khrims sgron*) A nun from Khotan who became Vairotsana's foremost female disciple.

Tushita (Skt.; Tib. *dga' ldan*) Literally, "the Joyous." The name of the pure land of the thousand buddhas of this eon, inhabited only by bodhisattvas and buddhas. The heavenly realm in which Lord Maitreya resides awaiting his appearance in this world as the next Buddha.

twelve links of dependent origination (Tib. *rten 'brel bcu gnyis*) These are: ignorance; habitual tendencies; consciousness; name and form; the six activity fields of eye, ear, nose, tongue, body, and intellect; contact; feeling; craving; aggregates; birth; old age; and death.

Twenty Thousand Sections of the Ninefold Expanse (Tib. *kLong dgu bam po nyi khri*) Important teachings of the Space Class.

two accumulations (Skt. *sambharadvaya*; Tib. *tshogs gnyis*) The accumulations of merit and wisdom.

two doctrines (Tib. *bstan gnyis*) The Hinayana and Mahayana doctrines.

two truths (Tib. *bden gnyis*) Relative truth and absolute truth. Relative truth describes the seeming, superficial, and apparent mode of all things. Absolute truth describes the real, true, and unmistaken mode.

two types of Sangha (Tib. *dge bdun sde gnyis*) Twofold division of the religious community: ordained renunciates who shave their head and wear red and yellow robes, and Vajrayana practitioners who are not celibate, wear white robes, and grow their hair long.

Upa Tantra (Skt.; Tib. *spyod rgyud*) The second of the three outer tantras.

Vairochana (Skt.; Tib. *rnam par snang mdzad*) The main buddha of the Tathagata family, which corresponds to the aggregate of form.

vajra (Skt.; Tib. *rdo rje*) Diamond or vajra weapon; a symbol of indestructibility. Also represents skillful means or compassion. The vajra is frequently employed in tantric rituals in conjunction with the bell, which in turn symbolizes the wisdom of emptiness.

Vajradhara (Skt.; Tib. *rdo rje 'dzin pa*) Vajra-holder. Emanation of Samantabhadra. The dharmakaya buddha of the New Schools. Can also refer to one's personal teacher of Vajrayana or to the all-embracing buddha-nature.

Vajrapani (Skt.; Tib. *phyag na rdo rje*) A great bodhisattva, one of the eight close sons. He personifies the power and mind of all buddhas.

Vajrasattva (Skt.; Tib. *rdo rje sems dpa'*) The buddha who embodies the hundred families. The practice of Vajrasattva and recitation of his hundred-syllable mantra are the most effective methods for purifying negative actions. In the Ati Yoga lineage he is the sambhogakaya buddha.

Vajrasattva, Great Space Tantra. See Great Space Vajrasattva.

Vajrayana (Skt.; Tib. *rdo rje theg pa*) The corpus of teachings and practices based on the tantras, scriptures that discourse upon the primordial purity of the mind. See *Secret Mantra*.

Varanasi (Tib. *wa ra na si*) A city in India on the Ganges, a main place of pilgrimage for Hindus. At nearby Sarnath, the Buddha Shakyamuni turned the first wheel of the Dharma with his teachings on the Four Noble Truths.

vehicle (Skt. *yana*; Tib. *thegpa*) The means for traveling the path to enlightenment.

vidyadhara (Skt.; Tib. *rig 'dzin*) Literally, "awareness-holder." Someone of high attainment in the Vajrayana. According to the Nyingma tradition, there are four levels of vidyadhara corresponding to the ten (sometimes eleven) levels of realization of the Sutrayana. They are: (1) the vidyadhara with corporal residue, (2) the vidyadhara with power over life, (3) the Mahamudra vidyadhara, and (4) the vidyadhara of spontaneous presence.

view (Skt. *dristi*; Tib. *lta ba*) The authentic point of view, the actual knowledge and experience of the natural state.

Vimalamitra (Skt.; Tib. *dri med bshes gnyen*) One of the greatest masters and scholars of Indian Buddhism. He went to Tibet in the ninth century where he taught and translated numerous Sanskrit texts. He was one of the principal sources, together with Guru Padmasambhava, of the Dzogchen teachings in Tibet.

Vinaya (Skt.; Tib. *'dul ba*) The name of the Buddhist ethical teachings in general and of the code of monastic discipline in particular.

Vishuddha (Skt.; Tib. *yang dag*) The heruka of the Vajra family; alternatively, the tantric teachings connected to that wrathful deity. Also, one of the Eight Sadhana Teachings of the Nyingma school.

vow-holder (Tib. *dam can*) Oath-bound guardians and dharmapalas.

Vulture Peak (Tib. *bya rgod phung po'i ri*) Place near Rajgir in Bihar, central India, where the Buddha taught.

wisdom (1) (Skt. *prajna*; Tib. *shes rab*) The ability to discern correctly, the understanding of emptiness.

wisdom (2) (Skt. *jnana*; Tib. *ye shes*) The primordial and nondual knowing aspect of the nature of the mind.

wish-fulfilling gem (Skt. *chintamani*; Tib. *yid bzhin nor bu*) A fabulous jewel that fulfills all wishes that is found in the realms of the gods or nagas. The Buddha, one's master, and the nature of mind are often referred to as wish-fulfilling gems.

wish-fulfilling tree (Tib. *dpag bsam gyi shing*) A magical tree that has its roots in the asura, or demi-god, realm but bears its fruit in the divine sphere of the Thirty-three.

world of desire (Tib. *'dod khams*) A general term referring to the six samsaric realms; the first of the three worlds of existence.

yaksha (Skt.; Tib. *gnod sbyin*) A class of semi-divine beings, generally benevolent but sometimes wicked. Many are powerful local divinities; others live on Mount Sumeru, guarding the realm of the gods.

Yakshini Changchubma (Skt.; Tib. *gnod sbyin mo byang chub ma*) One of the Indian Dzogchen lineage masters, who was a direct disciple of Prahevajra and Naga King Nanda. She was the teacher of the prostitute Barani.

Yamantaka (Skt.; Tib. *gshin rje gshed*) A wrathful form of Manjushri, yidam of one of the Eight Sadhana Teachings of Maha Yoga.

Yangleshod (Tib. *yang le shod*) A cave in the southern part of the Kathmandu Valley in Nepal, where Padmasambhava attained accomplishment of Mahamudra through the practice of Vishuddha and Kilaya.

Yarlha Shampo (Tib. *yar lha sham po*) Deity riding a white yak, oath-bound by Padmasambhava. Also refers to a mountain in the Yarlung Valley of central Tibet, where the first king of Tibet is said to have descended from the sky.

yidam (Tib. *yid dam*) Tantric deities that represent different aspects of enlightenment. Yidams may be peaceful or wrathful, male or female, and are meditated upon according to the nature and needs of the individual practitioner.

Yoga Tantra (Skt.; Tib. *rnal 'byor rgyud*) The third of the three outer tantras, which emphasizes the view rather than the conduct and regards the deity as being at the same level as oneself.

yoga (Skt.; Tib. *rnal 'byor*) Literally, "joining" or "union" with the natural state of the mind. A term commonly used to refer to spiritual practice.

yogi (Skt.; Tib. *rnal 'byor pa*) Tantric practitioner. In this text it refers to someone who has already attained stability in the natural state of mind.

Yudra Nyingpo (Tib. *g.yu sgra snying po*) The main disciple and lineage holder of Vairotsana. He was the reincarnation of Tsang Lekdrub.

BIBLIOGRAPHY

Primary Text Translated

Great Image: The Life of Vairotsana, The – *bai ro'i 'dra 'bag chen mo (rje bstun thams cad mkhyen pa bai ro tsa na'i rnam thar 'dra 'bag chen mo)*. Compiled by Yudra Nyingpo and other disciples. Xylographic edition, Lhasa. Sichuan, China: People's Publishing House, 1995.

Works Cited in the Text

Abhidharma Sutras – *mdo sde mngon pa*.

Abhidharmakosha – *chos mngon mdzod*.

Activity Tantra of the Sixfold Meditation Object – *phrin las sgom don drug pa*.

All-Creating Monarch Tantra – *kun byed rgyal po*, one of the Major Scriptures of the Mind Class.

All-Embodying Jewel – *rin chen kun 'dus*, one of the Eighteen Major Scriptures of the Mind Class.

Assembly of Secrets – Guhyasamaja, *gSang ba 'dus pa*.

Avadhara Tantras – *a ba dha ra'i rgyud*.

Awesome Wisdom Lightning – *ye shes rngam glog*.

Basis of Minor Scriptures – Vinaya-ksudraka-vastu, *lung phran tshegs kyi gzhi*.

Black Yamantaka Tantra – Krsnayamari-tantra, *gshin rje nag po'i rgyud*.

Blaze of Reasoning – Bidyotamala, *rtog ge 'bar ba*, by Bhavaviveka.

Blazing Like Kalpa-Fire Tantra – *bskal pa me ltar 'bar ba'i rgyud*.

Blazing Mass of Fire Tantra – *me dpung 'bar ba*.

Bodhisattva Tantras – *byang chub sems dpa'i tan tra*.

Body Tantra of the Immaculate Ushnisha – *sku rgyud gtsug tor*.

Brilliant Sun Tantra – *nyi ma gzi brjid*, an Upa Yoga exposition tantra.

Buddhapala – *bu dha pa li*, by Buddhapalita.

Canon – *bka' ma* [of the Instruction Class].

Chanting the Names of Manjushri – Arya-manjushri-nama-samgiti, *bstod pa glur blang*.

Collection of Anuttara Tantras– bla med 'dus rgyud.

Collection of Hymns – bstod tshogs, by Nagarjuna.

Collection of Messages – gtam tshogs, by Nagarjuna.

Collection of Precious Pinnacles – Mahasannipata-ratnaketu, 'dus pa rin chen tog.

Collections of Madhyamaka Reasoning – dbu ma rig pa'i tshogs, by Nagarjuna.

Commentary on Mind – sems kyi ti ka, one of the Eighteen Major Scriptures of the Mind Class.

Commentary on Reasoning – Vyakhyayukti, rnam bshad rigs pa, by Vasubandhu.

Commentary on the Ten Stages – sa bcu'i 'grel ba, by Vasubandhu.

Compendium of Instructions – Shikshasamuccaya, bslab btus, by Shantideva.

Compendium of Knowledge – kun 'dus rig pa, a major Anu Yoga tantra.

Concealed Cycle – *gab pa'i skor.*

Condition of Mindfulness, Instructions on the – dran pa rkyen gyi man ngag.

Consecration Tantra – byin gyis brlab pa.

Crystal Cave Chronicles – bka' thang shel brag.

Cuckoo of Awareness – rig pa'i khu byug, one of the Eighteen Major Scriptures of the Mind Class.

Cycle of Instructions Directly Showing Self-Liberation – *rang grol mngon sum du ston pa man ngag gi skor.*

Definite Commentary on Wisdom Mind – Samdhinirmochana-sutra, dgongs pa nges 'grel.

Detailed Description of Ritual Tantra – bye brag cho ga zhib mor ston pa'i rgyud.

Discerning Logic – dbang sde rab 'byed gtan tshig, by Dharmakirti.

Discernment of the Two Truths – Satyadvaya-vibhanga, gden gnyis rnam 'byed, by Jnanagarbha.

Distinguishing Brahmin's Cycle – *shan 'byed bram ze'i skor.*

Eight Chapters of the Prakarana – pra ka ra na sde brgyad, a text on Abhidharma by Vasubandhu.

Eight Sadhana Teachings – sgrub pa bka' brgyad.

Eighteen Maha Yoga Root Tantras – *rtsa ba'i tan tra sde bco brgyad.*

Eighteen Major Scriptures of the Mind Class – *sems sde bco brgyad.* Taught by Shri Singha to Vairotsana and Tsang Lekdrub. According to this text they are: *Cuckoo of Awareness, Shaking of Great Power, Sixfold Sphere, Soaring Garuda, Never-Waning Banner, Wish-Fulfilling Gem, Supreme Lord, King of Assumption, All-Embodying Jewel, Infinite Bliss, Wheel of Life, Commentary of Mind, King of Space, Jewel-Studded Bliss, Universal Bondage, Pure Gold on Stone, Spontaneous Summit,* and *Marvelous.*

Eighteen Tantras – *tan tra sde bco bgryad.*

Eightfold Magical Net – sgyu 'phrul sde brgyad.

Emanation of Light Rays Tantra – *'od zer 'phro rgyud.*

Enlightenment of Vairochana Root Tantra – *Vairocanabhisambodhi-tantra, rnam par snag mdzad mngon par rdzogs par byang chub pa'i rgyud.*

Entering into All Objects – *yul ni kun la 'jug pa,* one of the Major Scriptures of the Mind Class.

Entering the Middle Way – *Madhyamakavatara, dbu ma 'jug pa,* by Chandrakirti.

Essence of Secrets, the Tantra of the Magical Net of Vajrasattva – *Guhyagarbha-tantra, rgyud gsang ba snying po,* the main Maha Yoga tantra.

Explanation of the Intent – *dgongs 'grel,* by Pundarika.

Fierce Mantras, drag sngags.

Five Earlier Translations – *snga sgrur lnga.*

Five Root Tantras – *rtsa rgyud sde lnga,* of Ati Yoga.

Five Sets of Great Dharanis – *gzungs gra lnga.*

Five Sutra Collections – *'bum sde lnga.*

Five Teachings of Lord Maitreya – *byams chos sde lnga,* taught by Buddha Maitreya to Asanga in Tushita Heaven: *Abhisamayalamkara, mngon rtogs rgyan; Mahayana-sutra-alamkara, mdo sde rgyan; Madhyanta-vibhanga, dbus mtha' rnam'byed; Dharma-dharmata-vibhanga, chos dang chos nyid rnam'byed;* and *Uttara-tantra-shastra, rgyud bla ma.*

Five Topics on the True Meaning – *nges don skor lnga.*

Five Treatises on the Levels – *bstan bcos sa sde lnga,* by Asanga.

Four Exposition Tantras – *bshad rgyud bzhi,* of Ati Yoga.

Four Important Writings of the Vidyadharas – *rig 'dzin gyi gnyen yig bzhi.*

Four Sets of Scriptures on Vinaya – *'dul ba lung sde bzhi.*

Four Space Class Tantras – *klong sde bzhi rgyud.*

Fourfold Magical Net – *sgyu 'phrul sde bzhi.*

Four Hundred Sections on Madhyamaka – *Catushatakashastra-karika, dbu ma bzhi brgya pa,* by Aryadeva.

Four Sets of Scriptures on Vinaya – *Vinaya-gama, 'dul ba lung sde bzhi.*

Galpoche – *gal po che.* One of the Anu Yoga scriptures.

General Tantras – *spyi rgyud,* of the Anu Yoga tantras.

Great Mind Scripture – *sems lung chen mo.*

Great Space Tantra – *nam mkha' che.*

Great Treasury of Detailed Exposition – *bye brag bshad mdzod chen mo.*

Great Volume of the Buddha – *sangs rgyas bam po che.*

Hayagriva Tantra – *pad ma'i rgyud.*

Hearing Lineage – *snyan brgyud* [of the Instruction Class].

Highest Scripture – *Vinaya-uttaragrantha, 'dul ba gzhung bla ma.*

One Hundred Eight Treatises – rab byed brgya rtsa brgyad, by Dignaga.

Hundred Stories of Purna – Purna-pramukavadana sataka, gang pa'i rtogs brjod.

Indestructible Blissful Wrath Tantra – Vajrasukhakrodha, rdo rje bde khros.

Indestructible Confidence Tantra – rdo rje gdengs rgyud.

Infinite Bliss – bde 'jams, one of the Eighteen Major Scriptures of the Mind Class.

Inner Secret Seal Cycle – *nang gsang rgya'i skor,* of the Space Class.

Instruction of the Three Entrances – 'jug sgo gsum gyi man ngag.

Instructions of the Ten Miraculous Scriptures – man ngag 'phrul gyi lung bcu.

Instructions on Bodhichitta Written in Pure Gold on Stone – rdo la gser zhun, one of the Eighteen Major Scriptures of the Mind Class, which was written by Manjushrimitra as a confession to Prahevajra.

Instructions on the Great Bliss Sphere – bde chen thig le.

Jataka Tale Poetry – Buddhacarita-nama-makakavya, skyes rab snyan ngag, by Ashvaghosha.

Jewel Light Tantra – rinchen 'od kyi rgyud.

Jewel Mound Sutra – Ratnakuta-sutra, dkon mchog brtsegs pa.

Jewel-Studded Bliss – bde ba 'phra bkod, one of the Eighteen Major Scriptures of the Mind Class.

Kilaya Activity Tantra of Bidyotamala – phur pa phrin las kyi rgyud byi dyo ta ma la.

King of Assumption – yid spyod rgyal po, one of the Eighteen Major Scriptures of the Mind Class.

King of Mastery Tantra – dbang bskur rtog pa rgyal po'i rgyud.

King of Space – nam mkha'i rgyal po, one of the Eighteen Major Scriptures of the Mind Class.

Lamp of Meditative Experience – bsam gtan nyams kyi sgron ma, by Shri Singha.

Long Dhyana Dharani – gzungs ring bsam gtan.

Lotus Crown Tantra – pad ma cos pan rgyud.

Lotus Net – pad ma dra ba.

Lustrous Essence of the Sun – nyi ma'i snying po 'od dang ldan pa, by Kukkuraja.

Magical Net Tantra – Mayajala-tantra, sgyu 'phrul drwa ba.

Magical Vajra Activity Manual – sgyu 'phrul rdo rje'i las rim.

Majestic Blazing Tara Tantra – gzi ldan sgrol ma 'bar ba'i rgyud.

Mamo Bumtig Tantra – ma mo 'bum tig.

Mamo Tantra – ma mo'i rgyud.

Manjushri Body Tantra of Secret Black Moon– 'jam dpal sku yi rgyud zla gsang nag po.

Manjushri Root Tantra – 'jam dpal rtsa rgyud.

Manjushri Root Tantra of the Three Families – rigs gsum 'jam dpal rtsa rgyud.

Manjushri Six Realm Tantra – *'jam dpal rigs drug rgyud.*

Marvelous – *rmad du byung ba,* one of Eighteen Major Scriptures of the Mind Class.

Meditation on Avalokiteshvara – *'jig rten dbang phyug rtog pa.*

Melodious Speech Tantra of the Wrathful King, the Embodiment of Great Power – *gsung dbyangs khro rgyal dbang chen 'dus pa.*

Mind Tantra of Supreme Knowledge – *Vidyottama, rig pa mchog.*

Miscellaneous Cycle – *rde'u tshang gi skor.*

Nectar Quality Tantra of the Major and Minor Display – *bdud rtsi yon tan rol pa che chung.*

Never-Waning Banner – *mi nub pa'i rgyal mtshan,* one of the Eighteen Major Scriptures of the Mind Class.

Nonstraying Vajra – *rdo rje ma gol.*

Ocean Expanse Instructions – *man ngag rgya mthso'i klong,* one of the Major Scriptures of the Mind Class.

Ocean of Single Daka Practices – *rgya mtsho dpa' bo gcig sgrub.*

One Hundred Sixty Minor Dharanis – *gzungs phran brgya dang drug bcu.*

Ornament of the Middle Way – *Madhyamakalamkara, dbu ma rgyan,* by Shantarakshita.

Outer Spoked Seal Cycle, phyi rtsibs rgya'i skor, of the Space Class.

Padma Speech Tantra of Supreme Steed Display – *pad ma gsung gi rgyud rta mchog rol pa.*

Paramitas – *pha rol tu phyin pa.*

Parinirvana Sutra – *myang 'das.*

Perfection of Wisdom Tantra – *ye shes rdzogs pa'i rgyud.*

Play of the Cuckoo – *khu byug rol pa,* one of the main Anu Yoga scriptures.

Prajnaparamita in a Hundred Thousand Verses – *shes rab kyi pha rol tu phyin pa stong phrag brgya pa.*

Pratimoksha Sutra – *Pratimoksha-sutra, so thar mdo.*

Precious Chintamani – *Mahasannipata-ratnaketu, tsinda ma ni rin po che'i dus pa btog,* translated by Thonmi Sambhota.

Precious Discourse Tantra – *rin chen mdo rgyud.*

Precious Embodiment of Light Tantra – *kun 'dus rin po che 'od kyi rgyud.*

Presentation of Madhyamaka – *Madhyamakaloka, dbu ma snang ba,* by Kamalashila.

Rampant Elephant Tantra – *glang po rab 'bog,* one of the Eighteen Maha Yoga Tantras.

Rediscovered Treasures – *gter ma* [of the Instruction Class].

Resolving King's Cycle – *la zla rgyal po'i skor,* the second of the three categories of the Mind Class Instructions.

Root and Branches of the Stages – *sa'i rtsa lag*, by Pundarika.

Root, Scripture, and Commentary Sutras – *mdo rtsa, mdo lung,* and *mdo 'brel.*
These are thirteen sutras that belong to the Mind Class and are mostly called
the Thirteen Dolung, or Thirteen Sutras. The Five Earlier Translations and the
Thirteen Later Translations, along with *All-Creating Monarch, Marvelous,* and
the Thirteen Sutras, are the Twenty-One Major Mind Class Instructions
brought to Tibet by Vairotsana and Vimalamitra.

Root Tantra of the Ferocious One – *gtum po rtsa rgyud.*

Sacred Gold Light Sutra – *Suvarnaprabhasottama-sutra, gser 'od dam pa.*

Scripture of Display – *rol pa'i mdo,* an Anu Yoga scripture.

Scripture of the Embodiment of Realization – *mdo dgongs pa 'dus pa.*

Scripture on Discernment – *Vinaya-vibhanga, 'dul ba lung rnam par 'byed pa.*

Sealed Concentration of Mind Cycle – *dgongs pa gtad rgya'i skor.*

Secret Entrance Commentary – *gsang sgo 'grel ba.*

Secret General Tantra – *gsang ba spyi rgyud.*

Secret Small Seal Cycle – *gsang ba rgya'i chung gi skor.*

Secret Tantra of Manjushri – *'jam dpal gsang rgyud.*

Secret Vajrasattva Tantra – *gsang ba rdor sems.*

Seven Branch Tantras – *yan lag sde bdun,* of Ati Yoga.

Seven Shastras on Abhidharma – *mngon pa'i bstan bcos sde bdun.*

Seven Treatises on Logic – *sde bdun rnam 'grel,* by Dharmakirti.

Seventeen Paramitas of Mother and Son – *pha rol tu phyin pa yum sras bcu bdun.*

Shaking of Great Power – *brtsal chen sprug pa,* one of the Eighteen Major Scriptures
of the Mind Class.

Six Abhisheka Vidyadharas – *dbang bskur rig 'dzin drug,* an Anu Yoga scripture.

Six Tantra Sections – *rgyud sde drug.*

Six Topics of Enlightened Mind – *byang sems don drug.*

Six Vajra Lines – *rdo rje'i tshig drug.*

Six Vajra Words on Conviction – *thag chod rdo rje'i tshig drug.*

Sixfold Sphere – *thig le drug pa,* one of the Eighteen Major Scriptures of the Mind
Class.

Sixteen Maha Yoga Tantras – *ma ha yo ga'i rgyud sde bcu drug.*

Sixty Chapters of Instructions – *ti ka bam po drug bcu.*

Sixty Tantra Sections – *rgyud sde drug bcu.*

Skillful Lasso Tantra – *Amoghapasha-tantra, don yod zhags pa,* a Kriya Tantra text
on Avalokiteshvara.

Smashana, Mamo, Putra sadhanas – *dur khrod, ma mo, pu tra sgrub pa.*

Soaring Garuda – *khyung chen lding ba,* one of the Eighteen Major Scriptures of the Mind Class.

Spontaneous Summit – *rtse mo byung rgyal,* one of the Eighteen Major Scriptures of the Mind Class.

Spontaneously Perfect Quality Tantra of the Nonstraying Goddess – *yon tan lhun rdzogs lha mo ma gol.*

Stories of Sadaparudita – *rtag tu ngtu skor,* part of the *Prajnaparamita in Eight Thousand Verses, brgyad stong pa.*

Summit of the Indestructible Mount Meru Mansion – *Mahavajrameru-sikharakutagara, rdo rje ri rab khang bu brtsegs pa.*

Supramundane Scripture – *'jig rten 'das pa'i mdo,* one of the Anu Yoga scriptures.

Supreme Body Tantra Blazing Like Cosmic Fire – *sku mchog bskal pa me ltar 'bar ba'i rgyud.*

Supreme Knowledge Tantra – *Vidyottama, rig pa mchog.*

Supreme Lord – *rje btsun dam pa,* one of the Eighteen Major Scriptures of the Mind Class.

Supreme Pundarika Mind Tantra – *thugs mchog pun da ri ka.*

Supreme Samadhi – *ting 'dzin mchog,* an Anu Yoga scripture.

Sutikara Tantra – *su ti ka ra'i rgyud.*

Sutra Designed as a Jewel Chest – *Karandavyuha-sutra, mdo sde za ma tog bkod pa.*

Sutra of a Hundredfold Homage for Amendment of Breaches – *Sakshipuranasudraka-sutra, spang skong phyag brgya.*

Sutra of Discerning Imputations – *rnam 'byed rnam pa 'thag pa.*

Sutra of One Hundred Karmas – *Karmasataka-sutra, las brgya tham pa.*

Sutra of the Brahmin Master – *bram ze bla ma.*

Sutra of the Dense Array of Adornments – *Ghanavyuha-sutra, rgyan stugs.*

Sutra of the Descent to Lanka – *Lankavatara-sutra, lang kar gshegs pa.*

Sutra of the Great Multitude – *Avatamsaka-sutra, phal po che.*

Sutra of the Special Utterances – *Udanavarga-sutra, ched du brjod pa'i tshoms,* by Dharmatrata.

Sutra of the Ten Virtues – *dge ba bcu'i mdo,* translated by Thonmi Sambhota.

Sutra of the Ten Wheels of Kshitigarbha – *sa snying 'khor lo bcu pa yon tan mdo.*

Sutra of the Wise and the Foolish – *Damamuka-nama-sutra, mdzangs blun zhes bya ba'i mdo.*

Sutra on the Application of Mindfulness – *Smrityupasthana-sutra, mdo dran pa nyer bzhag.*

Sutra on the Description of Karma – *las rnam rjod.*

Sutra Refuting Bad Discipline – *tshul khrims ngan pa tshar gcod pa'i mdo.*

Sutra Repaid with Gratitude – *Pratyupakaraka-sutra, drin len bsab.*

Sutra Requested by Maitreya – *byams pas zhus pa.*

Sutra Showing Right and Wrong – *Arya-subhasubhakaryakaranabhava-nirdesa-nama-mahayana-sutra, 'phags pa legs nyes gyi rgyu dang 'bras bu bstan pa zhe bya ba theg pa chen po'i mdo.*

Tana Gana Amrita Torma Rakta Tantras – *ta na ga na sman gtor rak ta'i rgyud.*

Tantra Manifesting as the Inner Son Victorious in the Three Worlds – *khams gsum rnam rgyal sras khog snang ba'i rgyud.*

Tantra of Eminent Courage – *Subahupariprccha, dpung bzang.*

Tantra of Manjushri's Secret Teaching – *'jam dpal gsang ba bstan rgyud.*

Tantra of the Magical Net of Manjushri – *'jam dpal sgyu 'phrul dra ba.*

Tantra of Unexcelled Knowledge Vanquishing the Three Worlds – *rig pa mchog 'jig rten gsum rgyal.*

Tantra of Vajrapani's Empowerment Outlining the Three Precepts – *dam tshig gsum bkod lag na rdo rje dbang bskur ba'i rgyud.*

Tantra of Yamantaka's Words – *gshin rje'i gtam rgyud.*

Tantra Purifying the Lower Realms – *ngan song sbyong rgyud.*

Tarakuta Scripture – *sgrol ma brtsegs pa'i mdo.*

Ten Miraculous Transmissions. See *Instructions of the Ten Miraculous Transmissions.*

Ten Sutras – *mdo bcu.* An exposition tantra of the *All-Creating Monarch Tantra* in ten chapters. Along with the *mdo rtsa* and the *mdo 'brel* these are called the Thirteen Sutras of the Mind Class. They can be found in volume KA of the Nyingma Gyudbum.

Thirteen Later Translations – *phyi 'gyur bcu gsum.* The thirteen later translated scriptures of the Eighteen Major Scriptures of the Mind Class, a set of Dzogchen tantras taught by Shri Singha to Vairotsana and Tsang Lekdrub. Vairotsana translated five of them before his exile to Tsawarong while the remaining thirteen were later translated by Vimalamitra and Yudra Nyingpo.

Thirty Verses – *Trimsika-karika, sum cu pa'i rab byed*, by Vasubandhu.

Thousand-Armed Thousand-Eyed Lion's Roar – *phyag stong spyan stong gzungs seng ge gra.*

Three Baskets – *Tripitaka, sde snod gsum.*

Three Radiant Garlands – *rgyan 'phreng 'od gsum*, by Shri Singha.

Three Sections of Kriya Yoga – *kri yog sde gsum.*

Three-Legged Remati – *re ma ti rkang gsum sgrub pa.*

Treatise on the Five Aggregates – *Panchaskandha-prakarana, phung po'i rab byed* , by Vasubandhu.

Treatise on the Three Sets of Precepts – *sdom gsum bstan bcos*, by Asanga.

Tsatathasamgraha Tantra – *rsa ta tha sam gra ha.*

Tsundha Tantra – *tsun dha'i rgyud.*

Twenty Verses – *Vimshaka-karika, nyi shu pa'i rab byed,* by Vasubandhu.

Twenty-one Sutras and Tantras on Avalokiteshvara – *spyan ras gzigs la mdo rgyud nyer gcig.*

Twenty Thousand Sections of the Ninefold Expanse – *klong dgu bam po nyi khri.*

Two Unshakable Tantras – *mi gyo ba'i rgyud gnyis.*

Underground Vajra – *Vajrapatala, rdo rje sa 'og.*

Universal Bondage – *spyi 'chings,* one of the Eighteen Major Scriptures of the Mind Class.

Vajra Essence Ornament Tantras – *rdo rje snying po rgyan gyi rgyud.*

Vajra Essence Shower – *rdo rje snying po bab pa.*

Vajra Kilaya Tantra – *phur pa'i rgyud.*

Vajra Peak Tantra – *rdo rje rtse mo.*

Vajra Subduing the Three Worlds – *rdo rje sa gsum 'dul ba.*

Vajra Subjugator Root Tantra – *rdo rje rnam 'joms rtsa ba'i rgyud.*

Vajrasattva's Body Tantra – *rdo rje sems dpa'i sku'i rgyud.*

Vajrasattva's Magical Heart Sadhana – *sgyu 'phrul rdo rje sems dpa'i thugs kyi sgrub pa.*

Verses on Accomplishing Activity – *Karmasiddhi-prakarana, las grub rab tu byed pa,* by Vasubandhu.

Vishuddha Mind Tantra of Heruka Galpo – *yang dag thugs rgyud he ru ka gal po.*

Way of the Bodhisattva, The – *Bodhicharyavatara, spyod 'jug,* by Shantideva.

Wheel of Life – *srog gi 'khor lo,* one of the Eighteen Major Scriptures of the Mind Class.

White Lotus Sutra – *Pundarika-sutra, pad ma dkar po.*

White Sections, the Black Sections, and the Variegated Sections of the Mother and Son Cycle of the Space Class – *dkar nag khra gsum ma bu'i skor.*

Wisdom Mudra Root Tantra – *rtsa rgyud ye shes phyag rgya.*

Wish-Fulfilling Gem – *yid bzhin nor bu* one of the Eighteen Major Scriptures of the Mind Class.

Wish-Fulfilling Jewel – *Chintamani, tshin dha ma ni.*

Wish-Fulfilling Wheel – *yid bzhin 'khor lo.*

Wrathful Pundarika Tantra – *khro bo pun da ri ka'i rgyud.*

Yamantaka sadhanas – *gshin rje'i sgrub pa.*

Yamantaka Tantra – *gshin je'i rgyud.*

Sources for the Notes, Glossary, and Appendix

Dudjom Rinpoche, His Holiness. *The Nyingma School of Tibetan Buddhism: Its Fundamentals and History.* Translated by Gyurme Dorje and Matthew Kapstein. Boston: Wisdom, 1991.

Karmey, Samten G. *The Great Perfection: A Philosophical and Meditative Teaching in Tibetan Buddhism.* Leiden: Brill, 1988.

Namkhai Norbu, Chogyal, and Adriano Clemente, trans., *The Supreme Source.* Ithaca , N.Y.: Snow Lion, 1999.

Patrul Rinpoche. *The Words of My Perfect Teacher.* Translated by the Padmakara Translation Group. Boston: Shambhala, 1994.

Ricard, Matthieu, trans. *The Life of Shabkar.* Albany, N.Y.: State University of New York Press, 1994.

Tulku Thondup. *Buddha Mind, An Anthology of Longchen Rabjam's Writings on Dzogpa Chenpo.* Ithaca, N.Y.: Snow Lion, 1989.

Yeshe Tsogyal. *The Lotus-Born.* Translated by Erik Pema Kunzang. Boston: Shambhala, 1993.

Translator's Acknowledgments

I would like to thank my teachers, the late Kyabje Khamtrul Dongyu Nyima Rinpoche, Kyabje Dilgo Khyentse Rinpoche, and Apho Yeshe Rangdrol Rinpoche, whose inspiration and teachings formed the basis of my effort to understand this text. Sincere gratitude goes to all the masters who gave me advice during my translation of this biography. First, Taklung Tsetrul Pema Wangyal Rinpoche recommended that I translate this text and generously gave his time while I was working on the first draft in the early 1980s. During this time, the late Nyoshul Khen Rinpoche also answered many questions, as did Khenpo Palden Sherab. While working on the later drafts in the late eighties and late nineties, I was able to consult with Dugu Choegyal Rinpoche on many details, while Ala Zenkar Rinpoche, Jigme Khyentse Rinpoche, Khenpo Pema Sherab, and many others patiently gave their time to clarify doubts. Dugu Choegyal Rinpoche kindly provided his paintings for illustrations. I am most grateful to the translators Erik Pema Kunzang and Matthieu Ricard, who constantly encouraged me to finish this project; without their support I could not have completed the work. I am very grateful to my first editor, Michal Abrams, who went through the first drafts with great patience and accuracy. Many thanks go to my final editor, Michael Tweed, who carefully went through the later versions, meticulously preparing the text before you now. I also wish to thank the Association du Centre d'Etudes de Chanteloube in Dordogne, who helped support me while I was working on the first draft in the early 1980s, and to Klaus Hebben, who sponsored the final stages of the work. Warmest thanks also to Vivian Kurz, who provided valuable suggestions.

INDEX

Lightning Source UK Ltd.
Milton Keynes UK
UKHW042125021221
394903UK00001BA/16